Understanding Agency

Understanding Agency

Social Theory and
Responsible Action

Barry Barnes

SAGE Publications
London • Thousand Oaks • New Delhi

First published 2000

 SAGE Publications Ltd
6 Bonhill Street
London EC2A 4PU

SAGE Publications Inc
2455 Teller Road,
Thousand Oaks, California 91320

SAGE Publications India Pvt Ltd
32, M-Block Market
Greater Kailash - I
New Delhi 110 048

British Library Cataloguing in Publication data

A catalogue record for this book is available from the British Library
ISBN 0 7619 6367 7
ISBN 0 7619 6368 5 (pbk)

Library of Congress catalog card number available

Typeset by Anneset, Weston-super-Mare, Somerset
Printed in Great Britain by Athenaeum Press Ltd., Gateshead

O God, the author of peace
and lover of concord,
to know you is eternal life,
to serve you is perfect freedom
                        (Collect for Peace)

CONTENTS

ACKNOWLEDGEMENTS

I am above all indebted to Steve Loyal, both for turning my interest toward the writing of this book, and for all I gained from our conversations before he left for University College Dublin. To recall these conversations is to recall the enormous pleasure Steve always took in social theory, which made the conversations in themselves a source of pleasure. In addition, a significant part of Chapter 2 has evolved from some unpublished writing we did together, and I therefore owe Steve special thanks for his contribution to that part of the book. Since then a number of colleagues have helped the book along its way. John Bryant, Grave Davie, John DuPre, Regenia Gagnier, Chris Gill, Tony King, Nigel Pleasants and David Saunders have helped on specific points or with their general comments, so that the book is identifiably better as a result. But all my colleagues in the sociology department here at Exeter, and many in the larger school of which we are now part, have to be thanked for the suggestions and criticisms they have offered in talks and seminars over the last three years, and so similarly do several friends and colleagues elsewhere. I need especially to mention Bob Witkin and our sharing of thoughts on walks over windswept moors.

I need to acknowledge, as well, debts of another sort. Writing of this kind needs periods of solitude and isolation from distractions, and these are increasingly difficult to secure in the ever more frenetic environments of British universities. It has been good to work in a setting where this need is recognised, and so many of those in a position to do so put great thought and effort into meeting it. I am also very much aware of how many people in different kinds of role here deserve acknowledgement for their work to sustain an institutional environment appropriate for scholarly research. I should particularly like to record my thanks to Mary Guy for her continuing assistance as the manuscript evolved: it was help that went way beyond the call of duty.

Barry Barnes
Exeter University
June 1999

PREFACE

This book is an essay in social theory strongly inclined to empiricism and naturalism in its account of human beings and how they live. In particular, it holds that human beings are social creatures, that, to borrow a phrase from the literature of cultural studies, they are 'highly gregarious interdependent social primates' (Gagnier and Dupre, 1998), and it regards work in biology, psychology and sociology as offering ample evidence of their profound sociability. At the same time, it recognises that its standpoint is currently a little unusual, and that in many parts of social theory, and indeed of the social sciences generally, there is an aversion to it and a need for its merits to be reasserted. Having written the book from the perspective of a sociologist, I have occasionally thought of it as an attempt to revive a Durkheimian view of human beings in these contexts, but of course the claim that human beings may be understood naturalistically as social creatures can also be found in the Marxian and Aristotelian literatures, in Enlightenment thinkers like Adam Smith and David Hume, and in many other sources.

To suggest that this perspective needs to be reasserted is to imply that the social sciences are currently unduly individualistic, and I do indeed believe that this is so. It is evident not merely in economics and related fields wherein rational choice individualism is dominant, but even in sociology, where the neglect of the social in many parts of the literature is very striking. Zygmunt Bauman (1989) has put his finger on what is involved here:

> The existential modality of the social (unlike the structure of the societal) has been seldom held at the focus of sociological attention. It was gladly conceded to the field of philosophical anthropology and seen as constituting, at best, the distinct outer frontier of the area of sociology proper. There is no sociological consensus, therefore, as to the meaning, experiential content and behavioural consequences of the primary condition of 'being with others'. The ways in which that condition can be made sociologically relevant are yet to be fully explored in sociological practice.
>
> (p. 179)

There is, indeed, throughout the social sciences, a need for more systematic study of and reflection on 'being with others'. There has always been some active interest in the subject, and that interest is increasing as the social sciences focus more and more on language, culture and knowledge, and the communicative and interactive bases of these things, but there is no denying how many unfortunate consequences have flowed from its previous neglect. The relationship between 'the individual' and 'society', or 'social structure', has been addressed without proper regard for social interaction, with the result that 'society' itself has been conceived in unduly individualistic terms and the understanding of its components has been marked by attention to the 'subjective' and the 'objective' at the expense of the inter-subjective. Indeed, the relative neglect of inter-subjectivity has been little short of disastrous in macro-social theory and in related areas of the philosophy of the social sciences. Nor is that neglect becoming a thing of the past. Even in sociology, which has recognised a special responsibility to stress the sociability of human beings and to expose the limitations of individualism, many theorists now accept an individualistic perspective as a matter of course, and deploy concepts of individual agency or individual choice as the unquestioned frame for their accounts of human action. There is a need to keep in mind here, as this book constantly seeks to do, that the central problems of sociology are actually problems of collective agency.

The full implications of speaking of human beings naturalistically as 'creatures' are no more welcome in many parts of sociology and social theory than those of speaking of them as 'social'. Much is made in these fields of an allegedly irreducible distinction, between human beings and the natural order within which they are set. As sources of intentional actions, human beings are regarded as exempt from the normal run of naturalistic explanation and accounting applied everywhere around them. And this is often justified by an explicit dualism: a fundamental distinction is alleged to exist between natural objects and events, linked by relations of cause and effect, and human beings, whose independently inspired voluntary actions are set completely apart from the causal nexus. This particular form of dualism is completely rejected here.

Why the book focuses on 'agency', 'choice' and related concepts can now be made clear. Although there is no necessary connection here, these concepts are the recognised means by which individualism and dualism are expressed in modern social theory. They are used to refer to the independent powers of individual human beings, and in modern social theory they will be found deployed in discourses which both refer to such powers and rejoice in their existence. The intention here is to question the individualism that increasingly pervades theory, and still more the dualism of theorists and the extraordinary fear of the institution of causal connection that permeates and impairs so much of their current work. In opposition to individualism, the book will suggest that 'individuals' are not independent of each other in social interaction, and reflect on what this implies about our 'being with others'. In opposition to dualism, it will propose that voluntary actions should be understood naturalistically and monistically, and that references to agency and choice are not merely pro forma compatible with the discourse of cause and effect, but better understood if recourse is had to it.

'Agency', 'choice' and an array of closely related notions are used in everyday discourse, as we describe and account for our own voluntary actions. Theory, we might say, has borrowed these notions, and indeed, for simplicity and at the cost of a little imprecision, all those social theories wherein they have an important role will be referred to in what follows as voluntaristic theories. It might be thought a virtue of these social theories that they understand human action in much the same terms as those who produce it; and a problem for the account proposed here is that it tends to clash with ordinary understanding. It does indeed have to be shown, if the argument of this book is to stand, how the voluntarism of everyday life can be understood as the discourse of social creatures. Much of what follows is devoted to this task. Indeed, what is original in the book mainly resides in its description of voluntaristic discourse as the highly functional collective practice of sociable, communicative human beings. A sociological version of compatibilism is proposed, wherein this discourse is seen as the crucial medium through which collective agency is (causally) engendered and mobilised. On this account, it is the inherent sociability of human beings that makes voluntaristic notions applicable to them, and that same sociability that makes it possible for them profoundly to affect each other through the medium of their voluntaristic discourse.

Precedents for this point of view can, of course, be found in various literatures: there is nothing new under the sun. But it is not easy to find systematic reflection from such a perspective, or explicitly anti-individualist accounts of 'choice' and 'agency' such as follow here. It is tempting to account for the paucity of such reflection in terms of the dominance of the ideology of individualism, the rise of the cult of the individual as Durkheim called it; but it may be that there is a more general and profound explanation. One of the main things that sociable human beings do through the voluntaristic discourse with which they bind themselves together is to assign rights and responsibilities to each other as separate, independent units. Just as the institution of responsible action is a universal one, so too must be these entailed functions of voluntaristic discourse. But these are functions that require sociable interdependent human beings to treat each other as discrete points on their social maps, independent statuses toward which to direct the processes whereby responsibilities and rights are allocated. It may well be that the difficulty of understanding persons as social agents (in *state*) who discursively identify each other as autonomous agents (in *status*) is the fundamental source of most of the problems encountered in this area.

As itself a contribution to social theory, the aims of this book are to make a prima facie case for a very general way of conceptualising our social life, and then to provide some sense of its scope and significance. To meet these aims the range of topics it covers has had to be very wide, and the discussion of each correspondingly limited. It is a mere essay that looks to the literature for illustration but not proof of its claims, and that does not pretend to have done more than scratch the surface of what is available therein. In addition, since its concern is primarily to provide a simple positive picture for further reflection, it has often used widely known in preference to very recent material, and it has been a little less concerned than is customary with ongoing debates and controversies in the fields it draws upon. Even so, it contrives to clash with some central tenet or other in practically all of these fields; for its arguments cut extremely awkwardly across important academic boundaries. On the one hand, those theorists who are dualists or exceptionalists are likely to find the form of compatibilism defended here hard to reconcile with their traditional aversion to ordinary causal explanation in the human realm. On the other hand, those presently inclined to monism and compatibilism often have a strong inclination to individualism as well, and a consequent aversion to the kind of sociological explanation put forward here. It may be, however, that some benefit will emerge from this inadvertent double clash with accepted wisdom. For, whilst both the aversions described above are groundless and disabling, they stubbornly persist in the social sciences, and that persistence is actually reinforced by controversies between parties who cleave to one or other of them. It is probably easier to expose the inadequacies of both at once than to confront either separately.

Barry Barnes

PART 1

MATERIALS AND ARGUMENTS

This part of the book begins with a brief look at the use of voluntaristic concepts, both in the context of everyday life and as elements of social theory. The first chapter is particularly concerned with their role in everyday discourse. Here, actions characterised as voluntary, in contrast to those identified as caused, are often regarded as appropriate foci for praise or blame: their perpetrators are considered to be responsible for them and liable for their consequences. However, notoriously, the basis on which voluntary actions are identified is problematic. They are often related to invisible internal states in the human beings who enact them, but how the presence of these states is inferred remains obscure. Sometimes we impute them in purely expedient ways: for example, we may wish to hold a person liable for an action and, simply because of this, allege that she chose to perform it, and did it of her own volition as a free agent. But this move from responsible *status* to responsible *state* is recognised as illegitimate. We are supposed first to identify the state of free agency and only then assign the status of responsibility. A satisfactory account of how we act as we are supposed to here is, however, lacking.

The second chapter focuses on 'choice' and 'agency' as concepts used in social theory. It looks very briefly at rational choice, at Talcott Parsons' sociology, and at the now widely employed conception of individual agency particularly associated with the work of Roy Bhaskhar and Anthony Giddens. It is argued that whilst the notions do no essential work for any of these theorists, in the way that they do for ordinary users, the problems that arise in employing them are at least as serious for the latter as for the former. It is important to note that, in contrast to the preceding chapter, this one makes no mention of 'responsibility', since the concept has not been a central element in the building of any major form of social theory. Yet an understanding of the everyday employment of this concept, with its double significance – psychologically understood it implies internal capacities, sociologically understood it implies liability and answerability – is also the key to an understanding of the role of 'choice', 'agency' and related concepts in everyday contexts. And, as will eventually transpire, this makes the concept of responsibility of crucial theoretical importance as well.

The third chapter looks very briefly at some of the detailed work in the social sciences that has been guided by empirical curiosity about the actual use of voluntaristic notions. A little of the work of psychologists and micro-sociologists on the attribution of internal states and powers to individuals is reviewed – work that has mainly taken the form of experimental or empirical case study investigation – and some of the associated debates about the utility of theoretical entities are looked at. Studies of this kind are both empirically sophisticated and theoretically profound, and perhaps in the long term they will produce a basis for theoretical thinking in the social sciences that makes redundant the kind of discussion to be found in this book. At present, however, this is an extremely unsettled and controversial field of study. There are, in the social sciences, an unduly large number of competing conceptions (often now called ontologies) of human beings, but this area is truly replete with them. And until their number reduces somewhat, highly schematic accounts of chosen actions and responsible agents such as that to be offered here will continue to have some utility.

The final chapters of Part 1 consider two accounts of the basis and function of voluntaristic discourse and the nature of its relationship to the practical activity of everyday life. In Chapter 4, the widely accepted individualistic mode of understanding this discourse is addressed, and the argument against it given: voluntarism is not sustained in the communication between independent individuals, since it is clearly evident empirically that human beings are not such individuals. If they were, they would be incapable of creating and sustaining shared knowledge and unable to engender collective instrumental action, two things indispensable to any form of collective life and possible only for human beings who are non-independent social agents. To put the point in another idiom: the key characteristic of human beings for sociological theory – the characteristic that allows them to live, as invariably they do, in social units – is not their individual agency but their collective agency, and agency of this kind implies non-independent individuals who routinely, as a matter of course, affect each others' actions in their encounters.

Human beings are social agents, who affect each other as they interact. But human beings normally describe their ongoing activities by the use of voluntaristic notions. It would seem to follow that these notions are used to describe the actions of social agents. This simple point is central to the final crucial chapter of Part 1, which seeks to make voluntarism recognisable as the medium through which social agents identify each other, communicate their expectations of each other and thereby (causally) affect each others' actions. For all that it appears to refer to the internal states of individuals, voluntaristic discourse is actually the vehicle of human sociability, through which its users co-ordinate their actions and cognition, and thereby constitute every level of their amazingly elaborate social life.

1

EVERYDAY DISCOURSE

Choices and causes

If we look closely at how 'agency', 'choice', 'free will' and related notions are routinely used in the context of everyday life, we find so much complexity and variation that it is tempting to deny the possibility of giving any general account of it. Even if we confine our attention to the core of settled usage, and ignore, for example, the many individuals who use voluntaristic concepts to speak of their dogs or their computers, the problem remains. Generalisations about settled usage are idealisations which oversimplify what they purport to describe. Nonetheless, generalisation of just this kind is what will be engaged in here: an account will be given of characteristic features of usage, even whilst recognising the limitations of any such account.[1]

Perhaps the most characteristic feature of the everyday voluntaristic discourse wherein these notions belong is that paradigmatically it applies to people, and only to people. Only human beings are said to be free agents, able to make choices: in referring to humans in this way we give them a special status, distinct and separate from (other) natural objects. The separation is not total, of course: human beings are not referred to in this frame all the time. Sometimes the naturalistic, broadly causal[2] discourse employed elsewhere is properly applicable to humans as well. The voluntaristic frame appears to relate to some special dimension of humans and human behaviour, and sometimes this dimension is treated as its exclusive preserve. Choice is then said to exist only where causation does not, and a domain of voluntary action is created beyond the reach of ordinary causal explanation.

All this is broadly consistent with dictionary definitions. By recourse to the dictionary we find that to act voluntarily is to act: by choice; under the control of the will; as a free agent, an unconstrained, autonomous source of power. We are also told that free agency may involve acting spontaneously, in ways that cannot be predicted. Further recourse to the dictionary reveals how intimately connected these various notions are. The will is the power or faculty of choice; to choose is to will. Voluntary action involves free will; free will produces voluntary action. Again, that which is free, or voluntary, or willed, involves a lack of constraint. A free agent acts without restrictions upon her will: she acts without compulsion or coercion. In everyday discourse voluntary actions stand in contrast to actions which are compelled or coerced, which actions we ascribe to the operation of causes. It may be that externalities like social constraints or natural impediments prevent the exercise of will. But factors internal to the individual, yet distinct from her will, may also be operative, like drugs, or paralysing emotions, or uncontrollable urges, or excesses or deficiencies of hormones or enzymes. Both external and internal causes may be said to have predictable effects upon what people do, and to preclude free choice in what is done.

And yet the relationship of choice and causation is by no means so simple as this. Close to the dictionary though it may be, the account just given describes only a part of everyday usage. Thus, we may, as a matter of routine, ascribe behaviour to the effects of alcohol, regard it nonetheless as under voluntary control, and roundly blame the perpetrator for the effects of it. Or we may happily explain the different choices made by different people by reference to upbringing, or biological sex, or fixed characteristics of personality. Much of our everyday discourse manifests a robust compatibilism, in that it is content to regard actions as at once chosen and caused.[3] And whilst specific examples of such compatibilism may often merit dismissal as pure expediency – as when folk experts on social policy pronounce on the causal efficacy of things they do not like, like violent videos, in bringing about voluntary behaviour that nobody likes, like violence – in the last analysis compatibilism is a perfectly defensible orientation. Indeed, everyday discourse of this kind, which in the 1990s was memorably deployed in political debate by a subsequent British Prime Minister who promised to be 'tough on crime; tough on the causes of crime', may readily be legitimated by reference to systematic compatibilist philosophical theories.

It is worth noticing, too, that it is not merely that at times we are compatibilist and at other times not, in everyday discourse. Often, it may be that we do not know which view to take, or that compatibilist and incompatibilist accounts are set into competition with each other. Recall how in recent decades the existence of sex chromosomes has been recognised, and how the XX female and XY male patterns are now very widely known throughout our culture. Scarcely less well known is the existence of unusual or 'abnormal' complements, such as the XYY complement found in some males. Shortly after this complement was identified it was suggested that it might dispose its bearers in the direction of deviant and/or aggressive behaviour. It is immaterial here whether this is so – current opinion seems to have moved against the hypothesis – but it does represent an empirical possibility, however small, and the mere possibility has practical significance. On the first occasion that a known XYY male faced a murder charge, the defence pointed to the possibility of genetic causation of the violent act. If the act was indeed so caused, then, so they argued, it was not a voluntary or freely willed action; and since there was reasonable doubt on this matter a not-guilty verdict was appropriate. Formally considered, this argument has some plausibility. It is conceivable that the genetic information located on a second Y chromosome causes increased aggressiveness. Conceivably, then, it could have caused an act of murder: without the extra Y, the murderous blow would not have been struck. But if indeed the blow was caused, and if causation precludes choice, then choice and free will were not involved and the murder was no murder. And indeed it is arguable that in the case of a fellow human being possessed of a second Y chromosome, we should treat an action of this kind as possibly involuntary and hence excusable.[4]

The difficulty here, of course, arises when this incompatibilist form of reasoning is extended in a perfectly straightforward way to other chromosome complements. There is evidence that XY human beings are more prone to aggressive and deviant behaviour than are XX human beings. A possible hypothesis is that genetic information on the Y chromosome causes, by some route or other, the excess of aggression and/or deviance. But if this is so, then on the above argument genetic causation implies a lack of free choice in so far as the production of excessively aggressive behaviour is concerned, and may furnish grounds for withholding blame in any of the innumerable particular cases of such behaviour. Since men can't help it, or may possibly not be able to help it, how can we treat them with any confidence as if they could help it? Unfortunately, there are far more XY males than XYYs, and the prospect of treating half the population as victims of their Y chromosomes somehow lacks appeal. Normal male aggression is resolutely accounted a moral failing and the actions that embody it as chosen or under voluntary control, even though the possibility of a causal account of that aggression is also widely recognised. We may not wish to deny the possibility of genetic causation of male aggression, but at the same time we may be determined to hold males *responsible* for it, which seems to entail the existence of choice or free will. We may not wish to be tough on aggression and tough on its causes in this case; but we may incline to a related compatibilist view that is tough on aggression whilst recognising its causes. And the extent of the formal coherence of such a view will not necessarily be of decisive importance in the context of everyday discourse.

Note that another important concept has now entered the discussion. There is clearly a strong link between 'choice' and 'responsibility'. Agents who act voluntarily, of their own free will, are often said to be responsible for their actions. Agents acting under causal constraint are often said not to be so responsible, or the extent of their responsibility becomes questionable and difficult to establish. Indeed, a great deal of everyday discourse is bound up with the tasks of determining and assigning responsibility. And a great deal of the unease engendered by accounts which fail to make a strong distinction between what is chosen and what is caused arises from the consequent ambiguities in the attribution of responsibility and the practical problems to which it gives rise. A discussion of 'responsibility' is clearly essential to any attempt to understand ordinary voluntaristic discourse, and indeed ordinary causal discourse as well.

The institution of responsible action

Reference to responsibility intuitively evokes two different notions. It reminds us that we exist in a system of social institutions and social relationships wherein individual persons are accountable to others for what they do or what is done on their authority. But it also implies that a given individual is in a normal mental state, capable of reasoning and making independent judgements. Recourse to the dictionary serves to confirm intuition. In one sense, to be responsible for a decision or an action is to be answerable and accountable in relation to it, liable to praise and blame for it, obliged to respond to claims ensuing from it. It is indeed to occupy a *status* toward which expectations are directed. In another sense, however, responsibility is an internal *state*: an individual is responsible if she is capable of rational conduct, that is, if her cognitive and reasoning capabilities are in adequate working order, and permit her to operate as a recognisable moral agent.

Clearly, there is a need to consider further how the 'individual' and the 'social' dimension of our concept of responsibility relate to each other, and also, given the 'social' dimension, whether or not we can legitimately refer to responsibility as something that is recognised in all cultures. A useful discussion, tending toward the latter view, can be found in Bernard Williams' *Shame and Necessity* (1993), where four basic elements relevant to any construction of 'responsibility' are identified: *cause, intention, state* and *response*.

> We have four ideas: that in virtue of what he did, someone has brought about a bad state of affairs; that he did or did not intend that state of affairs; that he was or was not in a normal state of mind when he brought it about; and that it is his business, if anyone's, to make up for it. We might label these four elements cause, intention, state and response. These are the basic elements of any conception of responsibility.
>
> (Williams, 1993, p. 55)

Although Williams is a philosopher, his interests in this particular work are actually anthropological or sociological, and that makes it relevant here.[5] He identifies four fundamental elements of responsibility in the course of a discussion of classical Greek thought. His intention is to show how Greek thought and ours stand in very close analogy, and thereby to expose the inadequacy of facile evolutionary views of moral understanding which presume the superiority of what we presently accept. But in developing these points he offers the larger conjecture that the institution of responsible action is a cultural universal with four elementary components. It is an attractive conjecture, not lacking in supporting evidence. The four elements are indeed immediately recognisable components of our own current conceptions of responsibility. To identify their presence in classical Greek literature, as Williams does, is to imply that they had general recognition in the associated social contexts. And, more generally, there is no shortage of anthropological materials that indicate the presence of the four elements in the practice of many different cultures.

At the same time, however, Williams stresses that there can be no single correct notion of responsibility. The four elements are combined and elaborated in different ways in different contexts. We ourselves make different combinations, since we need different conceptions of responsibility in different circumstances. Sometimes, indeed, we employ combinations from which one or more of the four elements is omitted. Thus, for example, 'in modern law . . . people can be held criminally liable not only for outcomes they did not intend . . . but . . . for outcomes they did not even cause. . . . This introduces, in a sense, responsibility without causality' (Williams, 1993, p. 57). Instances of legal responsibility thus incurred include those wherein employers are held liable for the negligent actions of their employees. Moreover, there are other examples where cause is present but not intent, and responsibility must be taken for incompetence; and others again where state is absent, as in cases involving extreme drunkenness. And, of course, there are also innumerable cases where cause, intent and state all exist without legal responsibility being incurred, due to age perhaps, or statutes of limitations.

The case of responsibility without causality is a particularly interesting one in our own society, where it is sometimes called 'strict responsibility'. The existence of strict responsibility illustrates our willingness to allocate responsibility in terms of social convention without taking any interest in individual psychology at all: where strict responsibility applies, response must be made for the consequences of actions, without regard for whether they were chosen or caused, intended or unintended, by the agent responsible. At the same time, however, there is evidence of unease with the notion of strict responsibility, and of an increasing reluctance to enforce it. Ministerial responsibility has long been, in Britain, a paradigm example of strict responsibility. For example, ministers of the Crown were expected to resign, and thereby accept responsibility, for the errors of their officials. But whether or not this custom still exists is moot. Thus, during the period of Conservative Government in the 1990s, when a number of ministers resigned for relatively trivial personal reasons, no resignations signalled acceptance of ministerial responsibility, although there were many occasions when they might have. In one striking instance, when a minister was alleged to have systematically and repeatedly misled Parliament, the government successfully defended him by stressing his 'sincerity' and 'integrity' and disregarding the competence and appropriateness of the relevant actions altogether. It may be, indeed, that the Scott Report and the case of William Waldegrave MP mark the culmination of a process wherein ministerial responsibility has been reconstructed on the model of everyday notions of individual responsibility. The outcome of that would be, of course, that ministerial responsibility as strict responsibility no longer exists.[6]

Reflection on examples of responsibility attribution suggests a slight elaboration of Williams' basic account. Of his four elements, response, almost by definition, as it were, is implicit in all attributions, and since such attributions are made in all cultures it has the character of a cultural universal. The other three elements, whilst perhaps available in all cultures, are employed in just some accounts of what creates the need for response. These three elements tend to go together in the accounts that predominate in our particular culture. Their association constitutes our own familiar individualistic conception of responsibility, sometimes called 'moral responsibility', although that familiar conception is by no means our only basis for responsibility attribution. Attributions of strict responsibility are still important for us, and so too are attributions of collective responsibility, even though they both go against the tenor of our current individualism.[7]

All societies are systems of responsibilities, but references to individual responsibilities are never sufficient to describe them. What is less clear is whether or not they are always necessary. When things go wrong, there are always calls for them to be put right. Some societies call upon responsible individuals to put them right, either individuals directly (causally) implicated in events, or very distant ones (implicated as strictly responsible). In other societies, it may be collectives, or families, or institutions, or organisations, which are called upon to take responsibility in the first instance, and to make appropriate response. In these cases, it is important to ask whether any further imputation of responsibility is necessary, so that the current of responsibility attribution flows, in the end, right down to the individual level. If this is indeed essential, then Williams' account of the three elements of individual responsibility has a fundamental significance; if not, it remains important, nonetheless, particularly as a means of understanding ourselves.

Individual responsibility

In everyday life we assign responsibilities to individual persons unselfconsciously and without a great deal of explicit legitimation and justification. Systematic accounts of what is going on have to be sought elsewhere, in academic fields like psychology, or in professionalised fields like law and medicine. The accounts of individual responsibility developed in law and jurisprudence are particularly salient, because although

developed for use in esoteric contexts they are usually presented as cod-
ifications of everyday understanding, and they need to keep close to that
understanding if the law is to command respect. Accounts of this kind,
certainly in England and to a considerable extent in the USA, do make
reference to cause, intent and state, much as Williams describes, in developing a paradigmatic version of individual responsibility.[8]

It is part of this paradigm that to be responsible for something an agent
must have caused it, or as is sometimes said, been 'the cause' of it. There
must be a secure causal connection between some act of the agent and
the outcome at issue. Agent A points the gun and pulls the trigger; a
bullet is caused to speed off from the barrel; the bullet enters a body and
causes malfunction; the malfunction causes death. As far as cause is concerned this is a case for a murder trial. But the importance of free will in
the paradigm is evident when another person is involved in the sequence.
A gives the gun to B, who later pulls the trigger, etc. Here the intervening agent, B, complicates the issue since she is considered to have free
will. Although the gun would not have fired as it did without A's action,
causation is not normally imputed, because B is assumed to be an independent source of power and not a link in a causal chain: B, and not A,
may be to blame for the death, as its uncaused cause. This conception of
the agent as the uncaused cause of her (intended) actions is sometimes
expressed, as Kant expressed it, as belief in an unconditioned individual
reason:

> let us take a voluntary action, for example, a malicious lie . . . we trace the
> empirical character of the action to its sources, finding these in defective edu-
> cation, bad company, (etc.). . . . But . . . we nonetheless blame the agent. . . . Our
> blame is based on a law of reason whereby we regard reason as a cause that
> irrespective of all . . . empirical conditions could have determined the agent to
> act otherwise. Reason, irrespective of all empirical conditions of the act, is com-
> pletely free, and the lie is entirely due to its default.
>
> (Kant, 1781, p. 477)[9]

This vision of the agent as someone who by virtue of her reason may
always 'act otherwise' will be returned to several times in the course of
this book. For the moment, however, it will serve as an expression of a
widely recognised paradigm wherein the agent responsible for something
must be its cause and yet not be acting as the effect of some further cause.
To impute individual responsibility for something on this paradigm
involves working backwards along the chain of events that led to it,
seeking the nearest free action. To evade identification as 'cause', an agent
must either deny the validity of the causal chain, or that she was the
nearest agent to its end, or that she was acting freely. (Even this generalisation, however, has interesting exceptions. Consider the case of the
spy George Blake, held responsible for, and said by some to have caused,
the deaths of several sources working for British Intelligence through his

passing of secret information to the KGB. It is intriguing to notice here that the agents nearer to the end of the causal chain than Blake were *non-members*: there appears to be a contingent connection between the attribution of free will and recognition of membership.)

Let us move now from cause to intent. If the agent who has caused something to occur has done so unintentionally, she is not normally held responsible for it. But 'unintentional' here implies a lack of awareness not a lack of aim or desire. As far as our law is concerned, for example, if one shoots an enemy through the body of someone else, seeking no more than to kill the former, one is equally responsible for the fate of both. Indeed, perhaps it would be better to speak not of intent but of awareness, and to say that responsibility is entailed, not for what one intends to bring about, but for what one is aware one will bring about. Allowance is only made for effects beyond calculation by a 'reasonable' person, who knows 'what everyone knows' about bullets. (Note again the link between responsibility and membership.)

Finally, responsibilities may be avoided by claiming that one's 'state of mind' is in some relevant way abnormal. One relevant way is for the will to be overridden, or inoperative. In this state even intended actions are not responsible actions. Suppose B points a gun at A and threatens: 'kill Jones or else'. Then it might be that B carries responsibility for Jones' death and A escapes it. A, it might be said, is not 'the cause' because her will has been overridden; her act is itself caused and not chosen. Claims of coercion by other agents are one way of making out actions as caused in the appropriate sense. Physical necessity is another appropriate basis for such claims: damage caused by running from an avalanche or an escaped tiger is excusable since the agent had 'no choice'. Coercive people and physical dangers engender fear, and it can be said that fear suppresses will and results in caused rather than free action. And by analogy a great range of internal states may be cited: anger, passion, and the whole gamut of the emotions, as well as hormone levels, blood-sugar concentrations, enzyme imbalances and other bodily conditions, may all be identified as suppressants of will. There are, too, states where will is not externally overridden, but where the reason it normally serves is itself disordered or deranged. These states may be accounted the consequence of drugs or other 'internal' externalities, or they may be held to be conditions intrinsic to the mind itself. 'Mental illness' and 'insanity' are terms in routine use here, but they are constantly being supplemented by still more technical terms that originate in psychiatry and rapidly pass into the realm of everyday discourse. (Such terms tend to be resorted to when a person's actions are hard to make sense of as those of a member of the relevant culture.)

Our current paradigm of responsibility can be analysed into elements of cause, intent (awareness) and state, which suggests that the paradigm involves a specific view of the intrinsic characteristics of normal human beings. When we seek 'the cause' of an event and identify it as an act of the nearest free agent in a chain of antecedents, we clearly imply that the agent is the uncaused cause of the event and thus an agent in the fullest sense. We imply that she is a rational individual capable autonomously of activating internal powers or capacities. References to intent and state confirm that the connection between the agent and the antecedents of her actions is indeed through reason and proper awareness, rather than merely through accidental, causal links. Such an agent is the uncaused cause of her action and is responsible for its outcome accordingly. Had she been the caused cause, then she would not be responsible. To put the point in another way, if an agent's action can be made intelligible in terms of the institution of responsible action, then she is responsible for its consequences and may have to make response in relation to them; but if it is intelligible in terms of the institution of causal connection, then she is not responsible. Given the immense practical importance of this distinction, it is scarcely surprising that intense interest often focuses on which institution is relevant to the rendering of a given action, and that there is often a keen concern to keep the spheres of relevance of the two institutions distinct and separate. In terms of this paradigm, to speak of the causes of a chosen action is to come close to simultaneously asserting and denying the responsibility of the agent, and this amounts to far more than the abstract assertion of an intriguing paradox.

How much more is involved becomes clear if we reflect on the many institutionally crucial matters that are bound up with the state of responsibility. Responsible agents are not merely those who are liable to have to make response for their actions. They are also those who are entitled to demand response from others. Again, it is only they who are blamed for defective actions, and praised for exemplary ones. And it is to them that rights and entitlements are accorded, as well as duties and responsibilities. In everyday life, the responsible agent is a very basic social status that members are generally presumed to occupy and in terms of which they interact: when its attribution is rendered problematic, as it often may be in everyday discourse if choice and causation are conflated, then so is social interaction itself.

Responsibility as state

When a human being is in a normal mental state, with her reason in working order and her capacity for making choices unimpeded, she is treated as a responsible agent. The status she is thereby granted is of very great practical importance, and so too, therefore, is the state that entitles her to the status. It needs to be asked, accordingly, given that the state is internal and invisible, what external signs of its existence permit it to be attributed in what, for the most part, is a consistent and collectively agreed way. As before, a useful starting point for reflection is provided by work in law and jurisprudence. The treatment of individual respon-

sibility in the context of (English) law is very close to that in much everyday discourse. In particular, the law professes belief in free will: it insists
upon evidence that the state of mind of the criminal was one in which
her actions were voluntarily performed, and performed with evil intent
(*mens rea*), before it will convict. Since the legal system produces agreed
and acceptable verdicts about the guilt or innocence of accused persons,
this implies that it comes to agreed decisions about the internal mental
states of such persons. How then does it do so?

In practice, the law often walks around the problem by having recourse
to legal fictions. Thus, for example, knowledge is crucial to the formulation of intent, but the knowledge possessed by an accused is often
imputed rather than ascertained. As far as knowledge of the law itself is
concerned, the accused is normally presumed pro forma to know it and
its implications – a notably unrealistic presumption given that lawyers
themselves spend much of their time disagreeing on what the law
implies. With regard to other items of knowledge, an accused may be
reckoned to know what 'any reasonable person' should know, whether
about the consequences flowing from an action or about the rightness or
wrongfulness of the action. 'Any reasonable person' here is, tacitly, a
person familiar with particular conventions of what is reasonable, and
with a particular body of shared knowledge, by virtue of being a member
of a particular society. Thus, should one of the millions of followers of
the Prophet succeed in assassinating Salman Rushdie, her complete lack
of any sense of wrong-doing would furnish no defence; it would be taken
as evidence neither of ignorance nor of lack of *mens rea*. Nor would there
be much hope in a defence that relied upon the inner compulsion of religious obligation or the irrationality of religious conviction. Explicitly, the
entire edifice of our law is built upon belief in free will, and in crime as
intentional voluntary action, but in practice there is far less interest in
'states of mind' than such beliefs might be thought to imply. Conventions
exist, enforced by the power of the law, wherein formulaic attributions
serve as complete substitutes for what could as well be fictional inner
states. One reason for this, no doubt, is that a constant need to make con-
jectural, and hence contestable, attributions of 'states of mind' would be
liable to throw the application of law into confusion.

Needless to say, reference to internal states is not entirely replaced by
the devices of legal fiction. Ignorance, accident, reflex movement and
infancy are all possible defences in English law because they are thought
to preclude the existence of the inner state of *mens rea*. And hypnosis,
coercion, sleepwalking and insanity may all be cited in claiming that an
action was not the product of a free will. But whenever such references
are made, problems of establishing their validity arise. Many striking
illustrations of this have been associated with the identification of insanity. English law long proceeded here on the basis of McNaghten's rules,
which were taken to imply a narrow conception of insanity that min-
imised conjectures about inner states. Only where 'disease of the mind'

prevented knowledge of the nature or the quality of a criminal act did its perpetrator have the basis of an insanity defence. But in the USA the culture has been much more interested in states of mind and much more trusting of psychiatric expertise concerning these states. And US law has at times made moves to broaden legal tests of sanity, in order to make psychiatric testimony more relevant to the legal process. One example of such a move was the acceptance of the 'Durham rule' in several US states in the 1950s. The Durham rule recognised an absence of criminal responsibility where an action was 'the product of mental disease'.

The problems that arose with the use of this rule have been documented and illustrated by Jeffery (1967). 'Mental disease' is an invisible state imputed as a way of explaining visible actions or behaviours, but in many cases cited by Jeffery the actions 'explained' as products of the state are the sole evidence for attributing the state in the first place. Alcoholism and similar addictions are examples of states so attributed. The behavioural 'symptoms' of these 'diseases' were (then) the only evidence of their existence, and their standing as 'diseases' was entirely a matter of whether or not relevant bodies of expertise were willing to designate them as such. US psychiatrists often were so willing, and addictions came to count as defences for criminal actions under the Durham rule. So, by a similar route, did a number of other 'psychological' conditions, in particular those commonly diagnosed by the Freudians then dominant in psychiatry. The end point to which this development might have led is evident in the published opinions of some of the psychiatrists involved: for them crime itself was a 'symptom', 'the product of mental disease'; and every criminal was a suitable case for treatment. No more than anyone else, however, did these psychiatrists enjoy the kind of direct access to the invisible state of the criminal mind that might have made their assertions of its diseased condition into more than mere opinion.

The insanity defence is highly atypical. It represents a drastic solution to the problem of responsibility evasion, wherein what may be a lapse of a few moments is accounted for in terms of a chronic, continuing mental pathology. And since it is also a solution that in most cases merely replaces imprisonment with a form of hospitalisation that is scarcely distinguishable from it, and arguably worse, it is not extensively used.[10] It is far more common for illegal actions to be linked to transient mental states, which momentarily affect an accused who is presumed in the normal way of things to be a competent responsible agent, states of awareness and attentiveness, for example, or emotional states. Nonetheless, the insanity defence highlights the problem that plagues all of these cases alike. In mundane arguments about traffic collisions, for example, the resources of the institution of responsible action and of the institution of causal connection may be drawn upon to construct alternative viable versions of what really happened and why, and the invisible mental states of the drivers involved may be rendered in different ways.

The adversarial form of the legal process and the polished skills of the professional adversaries themselves serve to highlight the defeasibility of any account of responsibility involving internal states. Whether or not an accused was in a state of mind which rendered her responsible for what she did, whether what she did was caused or freely chosen, is endlessly debatable. This, however, is not the explicit view in the legal system itself. For example, in both the USA and the UK, whether or not an accused is insane, or mentally ill, is treated as a matter of empirical fact for a jury to determine. No doubt, there has been a perceived interest, in the legal system, in diverting attention away from *ad hoc* and improvisatory aspects of the way that responsibility is determined. Many consumers of law need something reliable and predictable in which to place their trust, and may be thought unlikely to warm to the view that legal profession-als make it up as they go along. On the other hand, the essential creative flexibility of law does seem to be becoming something that can be explic-itly acknowledged, and even proudly displayed. The recent treatment of stalking in English courts is just one of many examples here.[11]

What of general significance emerges from all this? Two important themes merit mention. First, attributions of invisible states are always problematic and contestable. This implies, of course, that diagnoses of actions as chosen or caused, of outcomes as intended or unintended, of agents as capable or incapable of rational conduct, cannot be read out of the actions themselves, or the visible features of their settings. Second, such diagnoses are nonetheless readily arrived at and accepted. Indeed, in the case of criminal trials a verdict almost invariably ensues, whatever the quality of the argument and evidence involved.

The task of the court, let us say, is to ascertain the *state* of an agent at a point of time, and on that basis to assign a *status* to her. Only two sta-tuses are available, guilty, say, and not guilty. Two speakers tell different stories of state, but the aim of each, quite explicitly and legitimately, is not to establish state at all: it is to secure status. These speakers address a jury whose decision processes are strictly a matter for them, but who must assign one status or the other if they wish to go home. The move that is supposed to be made is from state to status, but it is clear that strong back-pressure, to say the least, exists from status to state. Prior concerns with status can and at times clearly do shape and structure attri-butions of state, whereas the role of state in assigning status has yet to be elucidated, given that it exists at all. The most immediately obvious features of courtroom decisions actually raise the question of whether concepts like 'responsibility', 'choice', 'free will', 'agency' and so forth might not be secondary features of the institution of responsible action, mere rationalising accompaniments of procedures moved by pragmatic expediency.

In this respect, the courtroom offers an intriguing model with which to explore the everyday deployment of voluntaristic notions. We employ these notions as a part of the practical business of orienting ourselves to others and defining what we expect of them. We often have an interest in aligning ourselves to them as the occupants of one status rather than another. And we often impute internal states by way of legitimation and justification of the statuses we seek to assign. Conversely, we find it difficult to formulate what prior facts of the matter are relevant to our imputations of internal states, or to say what criteria should be recognised as the correct bases of such imputations. Overall, whilst we make extensive references to internal states, it is not at all clear what the grounds or even the cues for these references are, or what information they convey about the agents referred to. The point is a familiar one, of course. Just what it is to possess free will, to exercise agency, to be capable of rational conduct, or, for that matter, to be caused to act through coercion, or as a consequence of some mental pathology, are all notoriously problematic questions. The point has a special relevance here, however, in that the notions that give rise to these questions are notions very close to those routinely used in the context of much modern social theory.

Notes

1 It goes without saying that work engaged directly with actual discourse (Antaki, 1988, 1994), or actual text (McCloskey, 1986, 1994), merits great respect. But reference to usage demands abstraction from discourse, as its producers themselves routinely recognise. The significance of mathematical signs, for example, cannot be conveyed by treating all elements of an error-strewn mathematical discourse equally. Arguments in this area can only concern the appropriate and legitimate extent of abstraction.

2 It is arguable that natural scientific explanation, in the last analysis, is not causal, which issue is fudged here by calling it 'broadly causal'.

3 The doctrine of compatibilism will be discussed further in the next chapter, but for the moment the term may be taken to describe discourse wherein references to choice and to sufficient causation, even in relation to the very same action, are treated as compatible.

4 This topic will be discussed further in Chapter 7.

5 The approach here differs from that of the philosophers who have extensively discussed the issues of free will and responsibility. In fact it differs in a way that could invite confusion if detailed use were made of their work, because sociological and philosophical aims are importantly different, but not obviously so. This is why there is very little reference in this book to the enormous philosophical literature on free will and related topics. A quick way of conveying the different orientations involved is to note the enormous problems philosophers find with the notion of moral luck (Williams, 1981). That someone may be morally fortunate seems completely straightforward and unproblematic to me, and, more important, to be so just so long as a naturalistic perspective is taken on the relevant issues.

6 Government tactics in this case may have reflected its awareness that by the mid-1990s in Britain that great proportion of the general public engaged by the media was now the relevant audience for political theatre. In that audience responsibility was apparently conceived of, not in terms of the strict

requirements traditionally held appropriate to secure parliamentary accountability, but in terms of answering only for what had been willed and intended.
To such an audience, ministerial responsibility could be made out as a matter
of being answerable, not for actions, but only for personal fault: for state of
mind; for what had been willed. This was something sufficiently obscure to
allow a saving uncertainty into the situation. Subsequent cases under a
changed government tend to confirm that strict responsibility no longer exists
in this context. There seem also to be clear analogues of this kind of development in United States politics.

7 Twentieth-century armies have routinely held defeated populations collectively responsible for acts of resistance, and taken reprisals against them on
that basis. Schools have administered discipline in a fashion that took collective responsibility for granted. And practices of both these kinds continue as
a matter of routine in many settings today, even in the most 'advanced' societies, along with many other more subtle and complex expressions of the same
conception of responsibility. It is not only amongst the members of simple
societies in the habit of rustling each other's cattle or engaging in tit-for-tat
murders that the notion of collective responsibility has currency.

8 There is a relevant literature here going back to the celebrated work of Hart
and Honoré (1959). See also Hart (1968), Feinberg and Gross (1975), Feinberg
(1970).

9 That Kant thus links the power of reason to act otherwise so intimately to the
operation of the institution of blame is fascinating and important in the light
of the later arguments here. It would be interesting to know more of the social
context of this writing, but it is intriguing to note that this particular quote,
for which I am grateful to Nigel Pleasants, is from Kant's discussion of the
antinomies in the first Critique.

10 The insanity defence has been particularly associated with capital offences,
and has been energetically deployed to avoid the meting-out of condign punishment in such cases. And it is here that intriguing conceptual innovations,
like that of 'diminished responsibility', have emerged, to make the matter of
identifying the 'state of mind' of the accused still more problematic.

11 Thus, ingenious applications of notions of insanity and diminished responsibility seem now to be becoming acceptable precisely as ingenious applications.
And in some systems of civil law, similar ingenuity seems to have become
accepted as part of the business of 'finding money' with which to compen-
sate victims of accidents and misfortune (Lloyd-Bostock, 1983). Earlier it was
conjectured that in imputing responsibility for something we work 'backwards
along the chain of events that led to it, seeking the nearest free action' (p. 9).
But also increasingly sought after today is the richest or most heavily insured
actor, however far back in the chain. Somehow or other, she will be made out
as responsible, and a response from her required.

2

'CHOICE' AND 'AGENCY' IN SOCIAL THEORY

Rational choice theory

Social theory routinely imports concepts from the everyday discourse of the institution of responsible action, and adapts them to serve its own esoteric purposes. 'Choice' has long been employed as a theoretical notion in this way, and rational choice theory remains the most clear-cut and familiar example of such an appropriation. Rational choice is a theory very widely employed throughout the social sciences, in economics, in political theory and in sociology; and for many in these fields, particularly in the USA, it has the standing of a paradigm, with debate being conducted largely within it, rather than about it.[1] There are, however, different versions of rational choice theory and different understandings of what kind of theory it is. Some proponents present it as no more than an account of how people would behave if they were rational. Extraordinary though it may seem, others offer it as an account of how people ought to behave. But our interest need extend only to rational choice as an empirical theory, a theory of how human beings do in fact behave. Even in this guise, there are several versions of the theory, but all of them share a common core of basic assumptions.

Rational choice theory is a form of individualism, and as such its fundamental assumption is that every individual person is an *independent* centre of rational calculation. Each such individual has her own fixed goals, ranked in a fixed order of priorities or preferences. Each confronts an environment (which may in part be constituted by other individuals), and is able, by use of knowledge and reason, to calculate how different actions will affect it and thereby further her various preferences. Rational choice theory asserts simply that such an individual will act to optimal effect given her goals and preferences: she will choose that action which rational calculation marks out as best in those terms.

Rational choice theory allows patterns in the behaviour of large numbers of individuals to be predicted on the basis of very simple assumptions. Thus, for example, a pattern of traffic flow may be modelled as the product of so many rational choices by car drivers. Each driver may desire, say, to get home as quickly and safely as possible, and have no intention of producing a given flow pattern with delays and bottlenecks. But the pattern may nonetheless emerge from rational decisions by individual drivers, all pursuing individual desires, all rationally taking into account other drivers and their decisions, and all making use of their knowledge of the pattern of traffic flow itself, of where the delays are, where the quieter routes are, etc. Applied to human action at the macro-level in this way, rational choice has the character of what is now sometimes called a structuration theory. It is a theory which understands patterns, structures or systems of actions as the products of individual decisions, but which also relates the decisions to individuals' knowledge of the patterns, structures or systems which are being produced and reproduced. The patterns both help to account for individual decisions (in that they are known about and taken account of) and continue to exist as the products of individual decisions. Rational choice can thus supply a formally impeccable solution to the problem of relating micro- and macro-phenomena that has so long been an obsession of sociological theorists, and it merits their close attention for that reason alone.[2] If in addition its basic individualistic assumptions were correct, then it would be 'the solution' to the problem. (Sadly, they are not; and it is not.)

Because of its simplicity, and its assumption that individuals are independent, rational choice theory is easy to quantify, and that has allowed its use by economists, game-theorists and other social scientists as the basis of mathematical models of human action. Indeed, there is no other micro-theory in the social sciences which offers a developed basis for quantitative macro-modelling, and it has been suggested that this methodological advantage has had more to do with its wide use and acceptance than its empirical adequacy. For the moment, however, the extent of its empirical success may be set on one side. Our immediate concern is not with how far rational choice theory is correct, but with the use of the concepts of choice and causation within it.

A striking feature of rational choice theory is that it considers actions to be predictable precisely by virtue of being chosen. Know the situation and the actions feasible in it; know the wants of the individual and their respective priorities; the chosen action of the individual will now be predictable. Thus, in a situation where the individual has elicited two cash offers for her motor car, the predicted choice would normally be acceptance of the higher offer. This may legitimately be described as a voluntary rational action. It can also be described as a free action or as an action involving free will. In rational choice theory, however, such a description does not imply unpredictability. Nor does it imply freedom in the sense of lack of constraint. Consider a different kind of offer for the motor car. A gun is levelled at the owner who is invited to choose between handing over the keys and a bullet in the chest. Rational choice would (presumably) predict the handing over of the keys. The individual being robbed might speak of duress or constraint, or even of 'having no choice', but the handing over of the keys would still be intelligible as voluntary action to secure an optimal outcome in relation to wants or preferences. Indeed, formally speaking the choice in the second case would be of just the same kind as the choice in the first case, the optimal choice in the circumstances.

The notion of free choice is compatible with the notion of external constraint in the context of rational choice theory. It is also compatible with internal constraint. Suppose one develops a raging thirst and the desire for water becomes the top priority for rational action. Again, the predicted search for drink remains voluntary action and perfectly intelligible as chosen in preference to feasible alternatives. Nor is there any reason why what is true of action related to low water levels should not also be true of action related to high adrenaline levels or testosterone levels.

Considered as a fully general theory of human behaviour, rational choice theory can be held as a *compatibilist* theory.[3] It treats chosen actions as predictable and constrained, features normally considered characteristic of caused actions. And hence there is no need for its users to treat choice and causation as mutually exclusive alternatives. In so far as it speaks of the operation of free will, it is a free will that is perfectly compatible with determinism. But there is in any case no need for the theory to make mention of the will. It may simply state that individuals act optimally in relation to their preferences. To claim in addition that they do so through an exercise of will is to say nothing of empirical relevance in the context of a fully general rational choice theory.

On the other hand, references to will may do useful work in more modest versions of rational choice theory. Imagine that just a limited amount of will-power is available to the individual for the implementation of her choices. It will then make sense to speak of two kinds of actions: those whereby rational decisions are implemented by means of a will-power at the service of the intellect, and those where will-power has been overridden by some other factor, a source of pain, perhaps, or of emotional disturbance. Certainly, to distinguish between willed rational actions and actions of other kinds in this way is intuitively attractive, and to confine rational choice explanation to rationally willed action can only add to its plausibility, even if it also narrows its scope. A modest rational choice perspective of this kind has been put forward by Jon Elster (1984), who has written at length on weakness of will and the problems which arise when individuals have insufficient will-power to proceed with their rationally chosen actions. The major difficulty with this view is not that it transforms rational choice from a fully general theory into a partial one, but that in doing so it seriously undermines its credentials as a predictive theory. For now there are rational human actions powered by will, and non-rational human actions where will has been overpowered by some contingency or other, and it is no longer possible to predict how a person will act simply by working out what it is rational for her to do.

All versions of rational choice theory invite the thought that some kind of information-processing device underlies human actions, that the cognitive processes which precede them are like the operations of a reasoning machine equipped with inference procedures and a store of memories. Rationally chosen actions are actions produced via the machine, actions mediated by its memories and inferences rather than being directly stimulated, as it were, by external prompting. Such chosen actions are at the same time caused actions from this point of view, and the idea that choice processes may be mechanically modelled as caused processes is perfectly natural and straightforward. In a fully general rational choice theory, all actions are produced by the machine. In a partial theory chosen actions may count as a sub-set of caused actions, and other caused actions may be encountered wherein the normal operation of the machine is overridden, or disturbed, or absent. In a state of terror, for example, it may be that an individual acts irrationally and simply panics. And it is easy to imagine other emotions besides terror having similar consequences, and other factors besides emotions which might similarly disturb the machine's operation, tiredness perhaps, or blows to the head, or drugs or pathogens, or effects ultimately deriving from a Y chromosome.

Although it is not necessary for rational choice theory to adopt a machine model of rational calculation, many rational choice theorists do find a mechanical model of it attractive.[4] Many of them also adopt a manipulative attitude to human beings, one that seeks to control them, as it were, via their mechanical and predictable rationality. Thus, rational choice accounts of economic incentives treat them as means of affecting the rational calculations of others, so that they will act as desired. And legal sanctions and punishments may be treated in the same way, as devices for influencing rational calculation so that deviation from legal norms is lessened. Perhaps it is this concern with control that accounts for the attractions of a fully general rational choice theory, and its postulate of an individual who never runs out of will-power. Such an individual will always act rationally and always make free choices. What she does, therefore, will always be determined by rational considerations and always be predictable. Acknowledgement of the necessarily free will of such an individual is perfectly compatible with the complete determinism that is often the favoured metaphysic of those who regard knowledge simply as a means of maximising predictability. (It is true, of course, that complete determinism is the only metaphysic that can simply and rigorously be shown to be inconsistent with complete predictability.[5] But this point is rarely mentioned in current debates in social theory, wherein all contending parties associate predictability and determinism morally and tend because of this also to associate them metaphysically).

Voluntarism in Parsons' sociology

Rational choice theory is a version of utilitarianism, which whilst an important version of the individualistic style of thought, is by no means the only widespread form of it in the modern world. Another variant derives from Kant, whose moral philosophy turns on the relationship between the individual and universal moral imperatives. The individual is directly aware of these universal imperatives, and, as a rational being possessed of free will, it is her duty to act upon them. Morality for Kant is precisely duty conceived of in this way. Of course, the individual may not act morally, which represents a failure of her will. But the failure is never caused by constraint on the will. In Kant's philosophy, the will is always free, free not just from external causation but also from the internal pressure of desire. The will to moral action in Kant is as rational and unconditioned as the will to expedient action in a fully general rational choice theory.

Kantian preoccupations are evident in the work of sociological theorists from Durkheim through to Talcott Parsons. Parsons' position in *The Structure of Social Action* (1937) exemplifies them particularly well. Moreover, this first extended work of Parsons moves the discussion smoothly forward, since it represents an explicit reaction against utilitarianism, and theories of rational choice. In Parsons' account of utilitarianism, the individual has given 'need-dispositions' analogous to the wants referred to in rational choice theory. Again, as in rational choice theory, she can calculate the likely outcomes of her actions and hence can identify which action is optimal as far as satisfying her need-dispositions is concerned. But for Parsons, that 'optimal' action, which she would indeed perform if utilitarianism were correct, is neither genuinely optimal nor bound to be performed.

Parsons' primary criticism of utilitarianism is famous throughout the social sciences. The individuals of utilitarian theory, separately pursuing the satisfaction of their wants and needs, will inevitably come into conflict. The outcome will be a state of war, Hobbesian war, the war of everyone against everyone else. But human beings manifestly do not exist in such a state. Therefore utilitarianism must be false, and an alternative social theory must be found. There is, however, another criticism of utilitarianism in Parsons. Need-dispositions, he says, are biological givens, experienced as 'external' causes as far as the individual is concerned. The acting individual is actually an active principle in the mind of the individual – her *ego* in Freud's terms – and need-dispositions are externalities as far as the ego is concerned. Need-dispositions operate causally, as external constraints on the ego that prevent it from exercising choice. Reference to them produces a 'reductionist', 'biological' account of human activity which social scientists should reject. For if it is accepted, human action becomes nothing more than a passive response to externalities, the predictable effect of need-dispositions, something devoid of free will, which is not to be contemplated.

Thus, Parsons announces himself in this early work as in search of a theory which will (a) account for the existence of social order, and (b) be voluntaristic, non-causal and non-reductive. His search is for an *incompatibilist* version of voluntarism. The Kantian notion of a free will with direct internal access to universal moral imperatives has an obvious attractiveness given this, and doubtless appealed to Parsons; but the Kantian theme appears in his work in a very heavily naturalised form. In Parsons, we find not universal moral imperatives of which we are transcendentally aware, but socially functional values and norms which inhabit our consciences (or superegos as Freud would say) and make their presence felt as guilt when we deviate from them. These values and norms get into our conscience during socialisation. They are introjected and internalised, and once in place they incite appropriately functional, order-sustaining action. Socialised individuals, liable to feel guilt when breaking norms as much as pain when ignoring desire, now have incentives to moral, order-sustaining action, *as well as* to egoistic order-threatening action. Given that in consequence they act sufficiently often in an order-sustaining way, order will persist.

How precisely, though, do values and norms affect ego? Norms could be described as acting causally just like 'need-dispositions', given that both are internal to the individual's body but external to the acting ego within the individual. Thus, just as need for water causes thirst, which causes a search for water, so planning a theft might be said to cause guilt, which in turn causes reversion to honesty. And one can imagine scenarios where causation from need clashes with causation from guilt and the stronger causal power wins (Figure 2.1).

This, however, was the very opposite of what Parsons himself wanted to say. He insisted that it was a matter of *choice* for the individual,

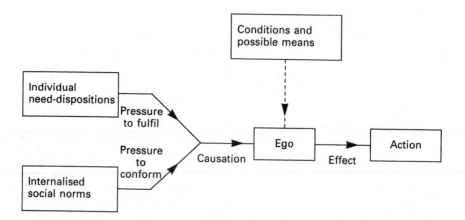

Figure 2.1. The connection between norms and actions understood causally

whether to avoid the pain of unfulfilled needs or the guilt of broken norms. Indeed, Parsons seems not just to have insisted on a voluntary link between norms and actions, but to have taken the opportunity to redescribe the link between needs and actions as voluntary and non-causal as well, so that needs and norms influence action, as in Figure 2.2.

Parsons' actor cannot choose the pains and pleasures associated with actions, but *can* choose how far to take account of them in acting. Naturally, as the pain of deviating from norms increases, the actor will choose conformity more frequently, but it is choice nonetheless which results in action. Parsons was determined to reject any wholly causal and hence 'reductive' account of human action, whether it made action a consequence of needs, or of needs and norms operating together. He could have avoided such a 'reduction' by asserting the unpredictability of freely willed action, its essential mystery, its transcendental character and inaccessibility to empirical enquiry. But Parsons wanted predictability and genuine choice as well. Hence he spoke of patterns of voluntary action systematically varying with the intensity of need, the thoroughness of socialisation, the amount of effort needed to conform to norms in different situations, and so on. All these things influenced patterns of choice, and by studying them the patterns could be made intelligible and predictable.

In speaking of influences on patterns of choice, however, Parsons produced a theory that, whilst formally voluntaristic, could as well have been causal. The scheme in Figure 2.1 serves equally well for all practical (sociological) purposes as the scheme in Figure 2.2. The trends and tendencies in patterns of social action will vary in relation to need and to situation in ways equally well understood as the outcome of predictable influences or of causes. And Parsons provided no additional 'facts of the matter' with which to discriminate between his voluntaristic account and a causal, or even a deterministic one. What his account in no way implied, however, was *sociological* determinism. Action was insistently related to

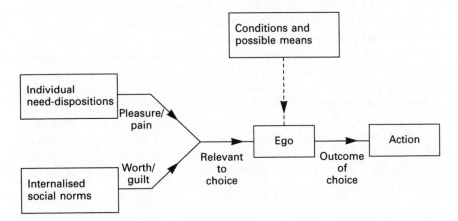

Figure 2.2. The connection between norms and actions in Parsons

the opposed pressures of (social) norms and (individual) needs: pressure from social norms accounted for the generation of an essential supply of conforming, order-sustaining action, as a proportion of total output, as it were, not as the entire output of action. Parsons did not seek to make out persons as 'cultural dopes' or 'sociological dopes'.[6] Indeed he made strenuous efforts to avoid doing so in this early work.

Such efforts are less apparent in his later writings. Indeed, in the period following the Second World War, he increasingly ignored the issue of voluntarism. We find him suggesting that whilst many kinds of action may be produced in social contexts, only the order-sustaining, conforming ones need be considered by sociologists. And then we find him not merely ignoring 'egoistic' actions but forgetting that they are there to be ignored. Or, if this is not strictly true, then at least it is how audiences at the time tended more and more to read him. Parsons achieved fame for his insights, not into the individual enactment of norms, but rather into the systems or structures they constituted, and how those structures remained stable. In his later functionalist theory, interest concentrates on the relationship of norms with social statuses. Any given status is one of a set of statuses constituting a social institution. The institution itself is part of a system of institutions, the social system. It is the macro properties of the system that are important, and those of its features that account for its equilibrium and persistence. Individuals are of little interest from this perspective: it may even suffice to regard them as mere carriers of the system and to ignore the springs of individual action altogether.

Parsons' later macro-sociology evolved in a period during which curiosity about individuals declined. For some theorists in this period, the metaphor of society as structure became literal description, and structures became real objects with intrinsic powers. External causal determination by structures was assumed to engender action, and not individual choice, will or agency. Now individual persons did indeed often become 'dopes', acting in conformity to whatever external determinant a theory favoured, and in the period of the dominance of structuralism such individuals could be found in many fields, including sociology, anthropology, linguistics and Marxism. That period was, however, very short, so that, for example, the van of sociological theory had left it well behind by the end of the 1960s. From that time to the present the social sciences have been moving with all the awesome power and inevitability of a change in fashion toward a reassertion of the individual human being as the centre of their concern. And the literature of social theory has realigned itself around the assumption that individual human beings are possessed of agency.

'Agency'

For an individual to possess agency is for her to possess internal powers and capacities, which, through their exercise, make her an *active* entity constantly intervening in the course of events ongoing around her. This, at least, seems to be the most widely recognised definition, and it is surely uncontentious to acknowledge that on that definition human beings are indeed agents. All that seems to be entailed here is that human beings are internally complex, that there is a lot going on inside them, and that what goes on inside them is material to understanding how they act upon what exists outside them. In practice, however, citations of human agency involve more than this. They tend to be made by theorists keen to sustain a very strong separation between the human and the physical, and to insist that what goes on inside human beings is different from and irreducible to what goes on outside.[7] This is what is implied by references to agency in ordinary discourse. When blame is being attributed there is nothing unsurprising in hearing: 'you were a free agent; you didn't have to do it; you could have acted otherwise'. To remind someone of their agency in this way is little different from reminding them of their free will or power of choice. And both kinds of reminder imply a crucial distinction between people, who are able to 'act otherwise', and things, which are not, even if the precise nature of this distinction remains obscure.

When social theorists borrowed the notion of choice they cared little for this distinction: rational choice theorists emphasised the predictability of choices and were in no way averse to mechanistic, deterministic or physicalist models of the choice process. It may be for this very reason that theorists who do insistently separate the human and the non-human have now taken up instead the related notion of agency. Roy Bhaskar (1979), for example, who has discussed the notion at length, relates 'agency' specifically to independent powers of the human mind. Although the existence of such powers is not inconsistent, so Bhaskar claims, with a naturalistic, or even a scientific/causal, approach to the study of human activity, his account nonetheless does violence to naturalism, as commonly understood, in that it makes a fundamental distinction between the human and the physical. Bhaskar argues for the necessity of an *autonomous psychology*, capable of explaining actions (although not predicting them) by relating them to individual agency and treating them as caused by reasons. To this end, he identifies the powers of the mind as emergent phenomena, irreducible to anything simpler or more fundamental, references to which are irreplaceable in principle by references to anything physical or material.[8] Indeed, Bhaskar's account not only defends the autonomy of psychology; in effect, if not in intention, it defends the dualism of everyday voluntarism as well, just where its basis might seem to be most problematic. 'It is analytic to the concept of an action that the agent could have acted otherwise,' he says (1979,

p. 146). In ordinary discourse the ability to act otherwise is routinely understood to be something that human beings possess but not natural objects. It is not customary to say of compasses that they could have aligned themselves otherwise, or of earthquakes, hard to predict though they are, that they could have quaked otherwise. Causal accounts of such physical phenomena help us to understand why they occurred as they did and not otherwise, but in truth all phenomena without exception, including human actions, occur in this fashion. What inclines us to refer to the 'could have been otherwise' quality of human actions, other than a desire to separate ourselves from the natural order, will need further consideration later.

Most theorists who make reference to agency agree with Bhaskar that it consists in internal powers possessed by individual human beings, powers that make human actions unpredictable by reference to external causes, or by the application to humans of knowledge valid for external physical or natural phenomena. They thereby, in effect, accept the existence of a fundamental difference between the human and the physical as objects of knowledge. And they generally present this view as a matter of dogma or prior commitment, rather than as something justifiable as the outcome of empirical enquiry. Certainly, in these respects, Bhaskar's view agrees with that of Anthony Giddens, who, whilst he has not addressed the concept of agency in the same detail, has been even more influential in encouraging its use and dissemination.

Giddens' work has been especially important in guiding sociological theorists toward a perspective wherein human agency is central. This is because, whilst his now very well-known 'structuration theory' rejects the view that human action can be externally determined by system or structure, it nonetheless acknowledges the existence of these macro entities as possible objects of sociological enquiry. Active agents are said to draw upon the elements of social structure and put them to use, thereby constituting the specific social system in which they live and reconstituting the social structure itself as a set of rules and resources available to be drawn upon and used.[9] For an audience many of whom had made the long march through the Marxisms, such a theory offered a way of quietly walking away from structural determinism whilst remaining in continuity with tradition and ancestry.

It is not Giddens' understanding of social structure that is germane to the present discussion, however, but his notion of agency. This is the basis of an understanding of individuals that has interesting similarities with Parsons', although it is distinctive in two important ways. First, whereas Parsons located active power in a part of the psyche, the Freudian ego, Giddens initially located it in the entire embodied human being. Secondly, whereas Parsons identified the active power of human beings simply as the power to choose (will), Giddens identified it as the power to make a difference, to act against external constraints and to transform the structures and systems from which they derived. Giddens' definition was that of a theorist for whom the possibility of change was all-important.[10] In other respects, Parsons' actor, with her power to choose, and Giddens' agent, with her power to intervene, are closely analogous. Just as freedom is necessary to the making of genuine choices, so also is it essential to agency. If internal powers could be activated only by external determination, then there would be no agency; if the agent could not exercise them as she chose, then there would be no agency. 'It is analytical to the concept of agency that a person (i.e. an agent) "could have acted otherwise"' (Giddens, 1976, p. 75). In so far as a human being lacks the ability to act otherwise, she is not an agent, and her behaviour is not action. But human beings do always have the ability to act otherwise, and the social systems they live in are reproduced, not merely by what individuals do, but by what they do as possessors of individual agency. Or so Giddens assumed; for, like Bhaskhar's, his conviction of the existence of an individual agency involving the capacity to 'act otherwise' was a prior conviction, and not an inference from anything empirical.

What practical difference does it make that individuals have agency? Clearly, assertions of agency have the negative function of denying structural determination. In Giddens' well-known formulation, structure may both constrain and facilitate action, but not determine it, just because individuals have agency. But what else follows is unclear, unless it is that an individual might do anything at all as a possessor of agency – using or not using the resources of structure, sustaining or transforming or ignoring the status quo. This does indeed seem to be the positive implication of Giddens' assertion of agency; but in truth he has taken little interest in this plethora of possibilities, and given remarkably little attention to agency as a power to transform, to resist, or even to act unpredictably. What has interested him is why individuals with agency nonetheless act routinely, in ways that reconstitute system and structure, nearly all the time. He has called attention to how agents draw on the resources of social structure in order routinely to reproduce the particular social system they inhabit, and has insisted that an account of why they do so is necessary. Having proclaimed the transformative power inherent in the individual agent, his aim has been to explain why so little use is made of that power. For Giddens, the practical problem arising from the existence of individual agency has been that of reconciling it with the ubiquity of routine.

A brief aside is necessary here on the importance of routine in the larger context of Giddens' social theory. Giddens treats routine as a specific kind of action and associates it with the reproduction of the status quo.[11] Similarly, non-routine, creative action is specifically associated with the transformation of systems or structures. This association of a valued form of action with a valued macro phenomenon, and of their less well-regarded opposites with each other, seems to be taken for granted as an obvious one, and is not explicitly justified. Yet in truth it is by no means obvious, and indeed it is very important that it is not taken for granted here; for important elements in the argument of this book point to the conclusion that no such association exists, as will become clear in due course. Let us return, however, to the immediate problem of understanding routine, which Giddens has rightly identified as one of great theoretical importance.

One of the strangest features of social theory is that mundane routine social action has long presented it with one of its most serious challenges. Indeed, all those theoretical schemes that stress the activity and the reasoning powers of individuals have had to cite exogenous factors, and alien or *ad hoc* theoretical devices, in order to make sense of it. Thus, Herbert Simon (1957, 1982) long ago recognised the problem that routinised activity represented for rational choice theory. For Simon, people are not in the normal way of things rational utility maximisers; they are satisficers who follow routine. Only in exceptional circumstances do they actively and rationally appraise situations, gather all possible information, and seek to implement the best modes of action rather than the routinely accepted modes. Simon's way of accounting for routine was exogenous to rational choice theory: he had to go beyond the confines of the theory in order to solve the problem with which routine action presented it. Indeed, it is perhaps a pity that the truly radical character of the innovation here, and the profound sociological interest of the resulting theory, have been slightly obscured by the associated vocabulary, and especially by its characterisation of satisficers as possessed of 'bounded rationality'. Simon displays routine as a fundamental problem for a rigorous rational choice theory.

Another theorist who saw that rational choice (utilitarianism) was an insufficient basis for an understanding of routine social action was Talcott Parsons. As we have seen, his response was to supplement it with a very different view of the individual psyche inspired by Freud. For Parsons, much, although not all, routine action could be understood by referring to internalised norms.[12] But whether one regards Parsons as a voluntarist who used an exogenous causal theory to help to account for routine, or as a Freudian who used an exogenous voluntarism, what is clear is how very problematic routines are in this context. The main body of routine action is neither entirely individually rational nor normatively oriented, nor easy to understand as a combination of the two.

Since the possession of agency does not account for the manner or extent of its exercise, Giddens too was obliged to cite exogenous factors to make sense of routine. He was, of course, aware of the proposals of his predecessors in social theory but he explicitly rejected them. He declined to give an essential role to 'economic' needs, wants or interests, or indeed to external sources of motivation of any kind, in solving the problem of the persistence of routine. And he explicitly rejected as well the internal sources cited by Parsons. To cite the power of internalised norms implanted in the superego was, according to Giddens, to offer a deterministic account of action which denied 'the freedom of the acting subject' and her ability to 'act otherwise' (1976, p. 95).[13] Nonetheless, the form of his account was very close to that of Parsons. He dismissed Parsons' vision of an internally differentiated actor and his vaguely Freudian view of the psyche, but only to offer an account of his own of just the same kind. Although he did indeed set aside the guilt-engendering norms and values postulated by Parsons, they were replaced with a functional equivalent in the shape of an anxiety-engendering individual need for 'ontological security':

> Actors' wants remain rooted in a basic security system, largely unconscious and established in the first years of life. The initial formation of the basic security system may be regarded as involving modes of tension management, in the course of which the child becomes 'projected outwards' into the social world, and the foundations of ego-identity created. It seems plausible to suggest that these deep-lying modes of tension management (principally reduction and control of anxiety) are most effective when an individual experiences what Laing calls ontological security.... Ontological security can be taken to depend upon the implicit faith actors have in the conventions (codes of signification and forms of normative regulation) via which, in the duality of structure, the reproduction of social life is effected. In most circumstances in social life, the sense of ontological security is routinely grounded in mutual knowledge employed such that interaction is 'unproblematic', or can be largely 'taken for granted'.
>
> (1979, pp. 218–19)

Faced with the need to account for the patterned and orderly character of social action, Giddens abandoned his original emphasis on the undifferentiated and embodied character of the individual agent and looked to the internal states of a differentiated psyche. And like Parsons he turned for inspiration to Freudian, and hence causal, accounts of the relations between its components. As a consequence, the analogies between Giddens' and Parsons' solutions are extremely strong.[14] Just as norms press on decisions in Parsons, so ontological security presses on decisions in Giddens. Just as an action may be selected to avoid the pain of guilt in Parsons, so it may be selected to avoid the anxiety of ontological insecurity in Giddens. And just as an assertion of the direct causal impact of norms is an alternative formulation to Parsons' own, so an assertion of the direct causal impact of the need for ontological security affords a viable alternative to Giddens'.

Like Parsons, Giddens has sought to account for the acknowledged orderliness and predictability of social life, whilst insisting on the insufficiency of causal accounts of it and emphatically rejecting determinism. But both authors have drawn upon a causal psychology in order to meet their aims here, and both have failed to show why their resulting theories should not be read as causal, or even as deterministic ones. These are theorists who would have their cake and eat it as well. Giddens himself (1976, p. 95) has indicated how difficult it is to do this in his crit-

icisms of Parsons. Parsons' formally voluntarist and incompatibilist sociology is alleged, because of its citation of norms, to leave no room for
individual agency, and hence, in practice, to be deterministic. But the
same criticism could be directed against Giddens' own sociology, because
of its citation of 'ontological security' to account for actions that 'could
have been otherwise'. No more than Parsons has Giddens adequately
rationalised his insistence on according a special status to human actions.
Nowhere has he provided intelligible grounds for asserting of an action
that it 'could have been otherwise'. And nowhere has he shown why the
power 'to act otherwise' should be listed amongst the various individual
powers that human beings possess.

Conclusions

All the many varieties of social theory are concerned with voluntary
actions. There are theories, systems theory for example, which study
macro-patterns in vast arrays of actions without taking any account of
that.[15] But most social theory acknowledges the problems involved in
identifying just what the distinctive characteristics of voluntary actions
are. The approach that takes the least interest in these problems is rational choice theory, where practitioners tend to compatibilism and determinism, but also tend to treat these issues as of little importance. Rational
choice theorists politely refer to a rationally choosing individual as they
make ambitious efforts to predict and control her behaviour. The human
being as choosing-machine seems to be an acceptable model for them,
but not the focus for much reflection.

The contrast between the approach of these theorists and that of sociologists is very striking. Sociologists have been intensely concerned with
the nature of voluntary action, and the relationship between causation
and choice has been of great importance for them. Unfortunately,
however, a great deal of this concern seems to have been inspired by
extrinsic considerations. Talcott Parsons insisted on a strong distinction
between the human and the animal or biological as a moral necessity: it
was an unrationalised aversion to a 'reductive' determinism, indeed to
the use of any of the resources of the institution of causal connection in
accounting for individual human actions, that informed the initial voluntarism of his social theory. Anthony Giddens seems to have had the
same aversion, along with a prior political commitment to a view of the
individual as a source of independent power, and hence as someone who,
in theory, can make a difference to the prevailing order. And many other
theorists seem, like Parsons and Giddens, to be averse to determinism on
what they take to be moral or political grounds.

The prior adoption of morally or politically expedient theoretical
notions seems to be wholly acceptable in the current context of social
theory, where they may be presented as legitimate ontological commit-

ments.[16] But as well as the obvious objections to this too easily rationalised partiality, it can also be asked what is supposed to give theoretical ideas moral or political salience. It is true that at the present time, references to individual agency are part of an optimistic vision of human beings actively involved in richly rewarding lives based on a free choice of lifestyles and a new 'identity politics'. And it may seem natural in the light of this to contrast a theoretical stance 'implying' an optimistic politics of empowerment and emancipation, with a determinism that is inherently fatalistic and reactionary. But it is clear as a matter of history that the kind of political work that, at one time in one context, was done using notions of free agency or free will has, elsewhere and at other times, been done by a determinism that denied their existence. Indeed, determinism has often been deployed as a radically optimistic ideology and could easily be again, whilst voluntarism has often been the language of those seeking to enforce deference to established institutions.[17] At present, the association seems set the other way round, but what accounts for this state of affairs, and how long it is likely to last, it is difficult to say.

For present purposes, however, there is no need to say. The only essential point here is that social theorists have no adequate technical rationale for their references to choice and agency, and no account of how to distinguish actions involving choice or agency from other actions or behaviours. All too often their theories are an eclectic concoction of causal and voluntaristic notions, notions immiscible with each other, but mixed nonetheless, as it were, by shaking hard. And whilst the causal components of the resulting potion may have a useful role, it remains obscure what positive work the voluntaristic notions are supposed to do.[18] An incompatibilist social theory could do work if it were based on a conception of free choice as wholly uncaused and unpredictable. Then the distinction of the caused and the chosen could be used to mark the bounds of predictive explanatory science in the human realm. But this is a position rarely taken in the social sciences for the obvious reason that it implies the redundancy of that project. Theorists in the social sciences are bound to become involved, however reluctantly, in predictive and/or explanatory projects. Even to suggest that today's routines are likely, for the most part, to be tomorrow's routines, and to suggest why, is to be (modestly) predictive and explanatory. But once theories become predictive or explanatory it is going to be asked whether they are not 'really' causal theories, adorned in a wholly superfluous metaphysics of agency; for our familiar discourse of prediction and explanation is a broadly causal one. And if reply is made that human actions, in the last analysis, 'could have been otherwise', that, as it stands, will count merely as another assertion of the metaphysics in question.

Notes

1 Amongst the innumerable expositions of rational choice, Abell (1991), Coleman (1990), Coleman and Fararo (1992) and Elster (1986) are recognised as of special interest to sociologists and social theorists. For my own reflections on the theory see Barnes (1995). Critical materials are cited in the notes to Chapter 4.

2 Thomas Schelling (1960) was long the acknowledged genius in the production of work of this kind, and the work remains a wonderful theoretical resource.

3 Compatibilism in this book will be understood as the view that the existence of voluntary actions sensibly described as involving will or agency is not inconsistent with determinism. It is often understood as the specific perspective of complete determinists and reductionists, but no position is taken on either of these philosophical doctrines in this book.

4 The machine is used as a *symbol* of complete reliability and predictability here. This very specialised usage of 'machine' and 'mechanism' is ubiquitous in the social sciences.

5 For those who like this kind of thing, a very simple presentation of the point is given in Mackay (1967).

6 The term was coined by Harold Garfinkel (1967).

7 Just as this book does not oppose voluntarism *per se*, so it does not oppose references to agency *per se*. It is dualist accounts of human agency that will be opposed. 'Agency' and similar notions can be, and, as a matter of history, have been, made the basis of rigorously monistic theories. And they can be applied to things as well as people, as in Harré and Madden (1975). It is worth noticing, too, that in recent times those moves from dualism to monism that have insisted on ubiquitous agency have been widely preferred to those that insist on ubiquitous causation. Conceivably, 'agency' wins out over 'cause' because imperialistic scientists and technical experts are now found more threatening to human integrity than priests and bishops.

8 This position of Bhaskar's is a dualist one that separates the human and the natural and is best understood therefore as anti-naturalistic despite Bhaskar's own gloss on it. It is hard to see what sensible distinction is worth making between natural phenomena immune to the ordinary naturalistic forms of understanding used everywhere else, and non-natural phenomena.

9 Giddens (1976, p. 127) idiosyncratically defines 'social structures' as sets of 'rules and resources' that active agents draw upon and use in their practical activity, thereby reconstituting (and/or transforming) the particular 'social systems' they inhabit. The resulting account of the 'duality' of structure and agency seems formally to be a monistic one, wherein all actions without exception are those of individuals possessed of agency, and all involve the use of elements of structure; but the account is nonetheless often understood as a dualist one, and sometimes criticised as dualist despite itself, as it were (Loyal, 1997).

10 This is where there is an evident moral dualism in Giddens. 'Good' actions make a difference; 'bad' ones continue routine, and reconstitute system as it is. Giddens' 'critical' social theory needs an evaluative dualism of some kind, and if that involving agency and structure is indeed to be discarded then something must replace it.

11 Curiously, the ethnomethodologists, whose work inspired Giddens' thinking about 'agency', never treated routine in this way and actually insisted on treat-

ing all expressions of social order alike as artful accomplishments. There are places in Giddens where he seems to take the same view, but elsewhere he manifestly does not and instead gives emphasis to the dead repetitive character of routine. Perhaps his work is simply confused on the issue.

12 Parsons (1937, p. 253) recognised that to conform to norms could involve departing from routine and required 'effort'. If his theory was a norm-based one, then we could say that routine action is sometimes linked to an exogenous laziness. This would link him to Simon, and to Schelling, who might have wanted to add that the laziest way of acting can often be a prominent solution to a co-ordination problem.

13 It has already been argued that this would be an unjust criticism of Parsons (1937), and of course he never explicitly renounced his voluntarism.

14 The analogy between Parsons and Giddens in their use of Freud is explored in Loyal (1997).

15 It is of no relevance here, but for the record, I regard systems theory positively as an approach that merits development alongside the kind of theory proposed in this book. That is not to deny that many actual instances of systems theory applied in sociology have been unsatisfactory.

16 A defence of prior extrinsic commitments of this kind can be based on the claim that theoretical concepts must always be selected prior to addressing empirical states of affairs, in order to make the description of those states of affairs possible. This makes it legitimate to select concepts that favour political or moral objectives, so it is said, since some kind of prior selection must in any case be made. Perhaps the most important objection to this, from a naturalistic perspective, is that nothing should compromise the interaction of theoretical notions with experience, if they are to play their proper part in a field respectful of the results of empirical enquiry. What the role of metaphysical and deeply theoretical notions should be in the social sciences is an open question; but to give them priority over (in practice, immunity to) the results of empirical enquiry suggests that other projects are regarded as more important than the enquiry itself.

17 In 1689 John Seldon wrote of: 'The Puritans who will allow no freewill at all, but God does all, yet will allow the subject his liberty to do, or not to do, notwithstanding the King, the God upon earth. The Arminians, who hold we have freewill, yet say, when we come to the King, there must be all obedience, and no liberty to be stood for' (1689, p. 20). Determinism may indeed 'imply' freedom, and voluntarism constraint, in the appropriate context.

18 Perhaps these notions are taken up because they carry such positive connotations within the common culture where theorists increasingly seek a role. Certainly, theorists do elaborate on widely accepted stereotypes and evaluations, and the resulting designer-sociologies help ordinary members of society to give expression to what they already believe. This is a crucial part of the role of the modern intellectual. Nonetheless, in undertaking it, social theory may be buying relevance too dearly. Pleasants (1999) argues that many social theorists, for all their self-descriptions as critical theorists, are now become utterly anodyne and uncritical. If correct, he raises an interesting historical question. Are they recently become so, or was it always thus? Was Habermas always against 'technocracy' in the precise way he is now, and did Giddens always conceive of 'radical politics' as he now does, or has there been the familiar drift with age?

3

A BRIEF DIGRESSION ON ATTRIBUTION

Attribution theory

This chapter looks at psychological and sociological work on the use of voluntaristic notions, and in particular at their use in attributing powers and states of mind to persons and thereby making sense of their actions. Even the superficial and selective approach to this material in what follows will indicate how difficult and complicated much of it is, and how vexatious some of the controversy to which it gives rise. This work is concerned with the attribution of invisible internal states to human beings, and is perhaps the most contentious part of a larger debate about the use and standing of theoretical entities.[1] Given this, it may be worth mentioning at the outset that the most difficult issues in the chapter are not crucial to what follows, and that its purpose is mainly to confirm that the problems of attribution identified informally earlier also arise, and resist solution, in this different and more technical context.

As we impute responsibility for actions in the context of everyday life, we frequently disagree about the states of mind of their initiators and the extent of their independent powers and capacities. In particular, we frequently disagree about whether to attribute a given action to choice or causation. Attributions of this kind are hard to evaluate because they cite invisible states or powers, but instead of seeking to evaluate them, it is possible to treat them as empirical phenomena and to make them the subject of scientific curiosity. Thus, in psychology, attribution theorists have studied how far actions are attributed to inner states and how far to external causes. They have treated this as an empirical problem to be investigated by experiment and observation.[2]

Although attribution theorists have stressed the impressively competent, even the scientific character, of the behaviour of their experimental subjects, they also claim to have identified many systematic forms of bias in it. Let us look at this attribution bias first. In one experiment, on male subjects, Thibaut and Riecken (1955) created a situation wherein an individual (the subject of the experiment, X) requested another individual (Y) to perform a simple task. Y, an actor complicit with the experimenter, invariably performed the task as requested. The only variable in the experiment, as it was repeated with a series of subjects, was the apparent social status of Y. Sometimes Y was introduced to X as a powerful individual of high social status; at other times Y was introduced as of low status. Later, X was asked if the compliance of Y was the result of external pressure or of the fact that Y was a 'nice guy' who just wanted to be helpful. The finding was that when Y was perceived as of high social status his compliance was overwhelmingly attributed to helpfulness and 'just wanting to'; whereas, when Y was perceived as of low status, attribution of compliance to external pressure was much more common. (It is tempting to say that compliance was attributed to free will when Y was perceived as high status and powerful, and to external causation when Y was perceived as low status.)

Like many other forms of experiment in social psychology, this one involved artificially created situations and systematic deception of the subject. Three other features are also characteristic of most attribution experiments. First, subjects were offered alternative ways of accounting for an action or event; they were encouraged to attribute the action to one of two possible antecedents. Secondly, the antecedents were, on the one hand, an internal, invisible, entity and, on the other, an external cause. Finally, variation in the balance of attributions was monitored as a specific feature of the situation was systematically varied. Thus, in the Thibaut and Riecken experiment, subjects were encouraged to attribute compliant action either to 'wanting to' or to 'pressure'. The 'wanting to' was an internal, invisible state and the 'pressure' was an externality. As the social status of the performer of the action was varied from high to low, so the balance of attributions moved from the internal antecedent to the external one.

It may be useful to cite a second example with much the same form. Deaux and Emswiller (1974) showed subjects a task being successfully performed and encouraged them to account for that success either by reference to skill (internal/invisible) or luck (external). This time it was the gender status of the performer of the action that was varied: when it was switched from male to female the balance of attributions moved from skill to luck. Deaux and Emswiller also varied the type of task involved: they found that whilst 'characteristically male' tasks elicited strong male/skill, female/luck correlations in attributions, 'characteristically female' tasks did not elicit the opposite correlation. Overall, as in Thibaut and Riecken's experiment, internal attributions were more likely to be elicited by the higher of the two statuses being compared.

The variability in the attributions elicited in these experiments may serve to highlight the difficulty of correctly identifying the presence of internal, invisible states. But of course the experiments were designed to produce variability, and were bound to throw more light on attribution biases than on the basis of correct attribution, if there is such a thing. Thus, the results of this type of experiment confirm the existence of the back-pressure from status to state discussed in earlier chapters.

Sometimes attributors accept that an agent should be treated in a specific way, or counted as of a specific status, and this bears upon their attributions of state. Alternatively, they may seek to bring it about that an agent is treated in a given way and accorded a given status. Their attributions may be designed to secure favourable evaluations from others, for example, and correspondingly favourable treatment. In fact, biased self-attributions engendered by concern with self-justification are very frequently observed. Attributors claim credit for their own good actions by stressing that they were chosen, and seek to avoid blame for their more questionable ones by presenting them as caused actions that could not have been helped. There is also evidence to show that individuals change their attributions as they address different groups, so that what they say counts as self-justification for whatever group is being addressed. Moreover, the concern with justification evident in self-attributions is also apparent in group-related attributions. Individuals tend to make favourable contrasts between groups in which they have membership and other groups. Sometimes they possess strongly evaluative stereotypes of in-groups and out-groups that structure their attributions. In-groups normally act correctly out of choice: when they act incorrectly, accident or causation is likely to be involved. Out-groups normally act questionably out of choice: when they act correctly, it may well be through causation or accident. Patterns of this kind have been reported in the attributions of those who deploy strongly evaluative racial or ethnic stereotypes. Needless to say, these may exist as strongly conflicting attributions sustained by distinct sub-groups in a larger social order, and give rise to serious practical difficulties (Hewstone, 1989).

Important though it is, the concern to justify and vindicate is not the only one to bear back upon the attribution of inner states. There is evidence, too, that attributors seek to produce and sustain shared coherent pictures of the overall character of agents and their actions, generally pictures which offer a reassuring and optimistic conception of the human condition. Thus, studies suggest that attributors are systematically biased in favour of persons and their internal powers, and against situations and external causes, when they account for actions. Even in the teeth of what appears to be evidence pointing strongly in the other direction, they seek to sustain an overall picture of life wherein events are under human control and more the outcome of choice than of circumstances. Indeed, the tendency to attribute change to human agency and to play down the importance of other relevant facts has long been called 'the fundamental error of attribution' (Heider, 1958).[3]

Also indicative of anthropocentrism are studies that claim to identify a bias toward providentialism in attributions. There is a 'belief in a just world', in which people get their deserts, where they must be to blame for their own misfortunes and somehow have chosen to bring them upon themselves, where they are entitled to claim the credit for their own success and to point to it as a sign of their effort and agency (Lerner,

1980). Believers in this kind of a world bias their attributions so that there is no such thing as an innocent victim, a miscarriage of justice, a crime that pays, a truth driven out by lies. They tend to deny incongruities between moral and natural orders, between the ideal and the actual, and to construct inner states accordingly. ' "The Just World Theory" implies that, in effect, people work backwards in their reaction to victims. They assess what is happening, and then calculate what it would take for someone to deserve that fate . . . they may have to resort to finding his character personally deficient' (Lerner, 1980, p. 55).

Many other kinds of *ex post facto* considerations have been identified by attribution theorists, and no doubt more again await identification. Indeed it is a plausible conjecture that practically any of the innumerable pragmatic concerns of human beings are capable of having a feedback effect upon attribution practices. For present purposes, however, there is no need for a list of such concerns. It is enough to note how the empirical studies in the literature of attribution theory largely confirm what was proposed earlier: attributions of state give accounts of actions as having invisible antecedents; such attributions vary, and vary systematically; a part, at very least, of that variation may plausibly be related to *ex post facto* considerations feeding back into the attribution process.

Attribution as contingent action

Whilst attribution studies serve to confirm that the relationship of attributions to invisible inner states is problematic to say the least, other work has looked away from the alleged states altogether, and sought to understand references to their existence in other ways. This has been the dominant approach to attribution in sociology, ethnomethodology and a number of related fields, some of very recent provenance. In these contexts the approach has been to treat attributions as contingent social actions and to understand them by reference to attributors themselves and the specific situations in which they are located. In sociology, this kind of approach can be traced to an influential but remarkably succinct paper by C. Wright Mills on motives. Here Mills recommends that motive-attributing actions should not be related to 'private states in individuals' (1940, p. 904), but should instead be studied as social phenomena. And he notes how motive imputation depends upon the existence of socially accepted vocabularies of motives, and how these accepted vocabularies vary across cultures and also across situations within a given culture. Thus, present-day society routinely understands economic utilitarian motives as accounts of the bases of action but has a little more difficulty with vocabularies of love or of duty; as for vocabularies of religious motivation, whether they attribute actions to God's intervention or to the desire to serve Him, they are no longer routinely acceptable and may even elicit suspicion and distrust. For us, today, it is a simple matter to give an action the status of an economically motivated action and to orient ourselves toward it on that basis; but we have lost the ancestral ability to make out actions as religiously motivated.

This simple account has some interesting implications, as Mills makes clear. There would appear to be no limit on the invisible states that might be said to inhere in human beings, and different kinds can be expected to exist in different cultures. Since the states themselves are forever inaccessible, it will not be possible by direct inspection to show that one kind of invisible is closer to what really appertains than another – that 'our' motives are superior in this sense to 'theirs', or 'our' scheme of motives is superior to 'their' scheme, say of possessing spirits. It must be accepted, as well, that whatever visible phenomenon inspires us to refer to one sort of invisible entity may inspire another culture to refer to another sort altogether. A fit may betoken a neurological disorder for some of us, but spirit possession elsewhere. What we put down to economic motivation may be put down to religious motivation elsewhere. Moreover, the two cultures cited here could well be 'our' culture now, and 'our' culture, say a decade ago. It has to be recognised that the basis of the attribution of internal states changes over time, and indeed from moment to moment. All these are points relevant to the practice of historical sociology, and their neglect can undermine the credibility of sociological research on topics as diverse as poverty, social class, political orientation, religious affiliation, suicide and sexual orientation.

What Mills has to say about motives may be expanded, and applied to theoretical states or entities generally. As these states are inaccessible, it is hard to see in what way their actual nature can constrain what is said about them. An individual might believe in the existence of any or all of innumerable such entities – motives, drives, fairies, possessing spirits, or whatever – and assert their presence or absence in any specific case, without contradictory indications from the entities themselves. Presumably, when there is agreement on the presence of some invisible state, it must be, first, because it is the kind of invisible that a specific culture recognises as existing, and, second, because there is something other than the state itself that sustains the members of the culture in the opinion that it exists in that particular case: the term for the invisible must feature in the vocabulary of the culture, and something must prompt the membership to apply it in specific situations.

All this is, indeed, recognised, practically everywhere, both as of great significance and as correct. However, it leaves open the question of what disposes a membership to agree on the involvement of some invisible entity in a given situation. A common response to this problem is to claim that a visible sign or criterion must exist that all recognise as a legitimate basis for making reference to the invisible theoretical entity. This too is prefigured in Mills, who insists that any answer to the problem must lie, not in the private realm, but in the public sphere where states of affairs are accessible to all. Nonetheless, there are also elements of Mills' account which suggest that explanation by reference to visible signs or criteria is insufficient. Thus, Mills stresses how an accepted vocabulary of motives can *always* be drawn upon to make actions intelligible and to justify them. The motives constitute, as it were, a sense-making system present in the culture that members may use as they will in accounting for actions and co-ordinating further actions as responses to them.

This point has been extensively elaborated upon by ethnomethodologists, following the seminal work of Harold Garfinkel (1967) and his well-exemplified discussions of 'the documentary method of interpretation'. Documentary method takes an appearance as something which points to the existence of a hidden underlying pattern. But 'not only is the underlying pattern derived from its individual documentary evidences, (they) in their turn are interpreted on the basis of "what is known" about the underlying pattern. Each is used to elaborate the other' (Garfinkel, 1967, p. 78). Thus, a given kind of action may be taken as a sign that a motive has been operative, but motives and what is known of them are employed to interpret what people do as actions of this or that kind. The sign, as it were, does not remain independent of what it is supposed to signify, and the two things change together as the discourse of action and motivation is used. Consequently, no shared sign (or criterion) can be used to account for an attribution referring to a theoretical entity, since the standing of the sign as a shared sign is dependent on a changing understanding of the theoretical entity and what might be counted a sign of its presence. Ethnomethodological case studies of the use of documentary method show how signs or criteria change in the course of time, by virtue of being used. And this calls their role in accounting for attributions into question; since what signs or criteria themselves amount to in any given case has to be understood as a product of attribution. Perhaps we should say that the studies display attributions as the products, not of criteria, but of people who may take account of criteria. Like the orderliness of any other kind of human action, that evident even in the routine attribution of motives, drives, intentions (and hence, presumably, of agency or free will) is, in ethnomethodological parlance, the contingent accomplishment of persons.[4]

It is all too easy to imagine that our accounts of things may be justified simply by our making reference to those things, or, with invisible things, to visible signs of their existence, or publicly available criteria that specify when they may be cited. Ethnomethodological studies are invaluable in exposing the insufficiency of this mode of thinking, but in doing this they once more make the orderliness of our accounts and attributions into a major problem. It is all very well to speak of such order as a contingent artful accomplishment of persons, but it needs to be asked why it is order that persons accomplish rather than chaos, or one order rather than another. Unfortunately, in this context the question is often sidestepped, and when it is addressed it invariably proves to be highly controversial. The issues involved can only be hinted at here, but broadly speaking they derive from conflicting evaluations of the practice of making reference to invisible states, and particularly mental or psychological states. If what is done with them is perceived as having pragmatic utility and reckoned worthy of respect on that account, then the tendency will be to enquire into this kind of attribution activity and to try to relate what it consists in to what it accomplishes. But if the attribution of inaccessible states is negatively evaluated, as a kind of error or failing, then efforts to understand it further are likely to be dismissed as compounding the error.

There is an inescapable tension between these two perspectives. In order to give an account of the pragmatic value of some practice or form of activity it is normal to relate it to the purposes, or the interests, or the goals and objectives of human beings. But this is to solve the problem of the attribution of one inner state by making reference to the existence of another, or so it would seem. Earlier in this book, for example, it was implied that the attribution of the invisible state of free will to a defendant might be accounted for by the attribution of an (invisible) purpose or pragmatic concern to a prosecuting counsel. Needless to say, if no objection is taken to the citation of invisible states, there is no problem here, but for those with a principled opposition to their use it is a different matter. Very many sociologists and psychologists do currently adopt a principled position of this sort, especially where the alleged invisible states are those of human beings. And amongst them the problem just outlined is widely perceived both as insurmountable and of crucial importance. It is held to preclude any reference to purposes or goals or interests, whether conscious or unconscious, as a way of accounting for attributions, or for that matter any other kind of human activity.[5] Indeed, so strong is the commitment to this position in some fields that their members criticise attempts to refer not just to invisible states, but to visible actions, events and objects as well. Conceptualised objects are regarded as theoretical entities in just the way that invisible states are, and objection is taken to any account that presumes that they are 'really there'. The initial ethnomethodological presentation of accounts and attributions as accomplishments has in this way been the prelude to the denial that our discourse has any kind of referential function at all.

The outcome has been the exclusive concern with speech and visible human activity, and the refusal to acknowledge any external referents of speech or substrates to activity, characteristic of research in fields of study like discourse analysis, radical social constructivism, praxiology and discursive psychology.[6] This work is sometimes legitimated by pronouncements to the effect that only speech, or talk, or discourse, or practice, really exists, and that only that kind of entity merits any kind of systematic study. Needless to say, work done under the auspices of one of these competing ontological self-denying ordinances is bound to be critical of the form of social theory addressed in this book. From that perspective, concepts like Parsons' actor or Giddens' agent or the independent individual of rational choice theory are intelligible only as used in an enclosed realm of theoretical discourse, and have no additional significance at all. And this is merely the best gloss that can be put upon them. Less charitably, all theorising of this kind may be made out as a gratuitous and perverse form of activity, only spared denunciation as a gross misrepresentation of what it purports to describe because the notion of representation is itself rejected.[7]

The work of discourse analysts, radical social constructivists and those with similar leanings has earned them a notoriety extending well beyond the ambit of the social sciences. Being at once disturbing and difficult to address, their claims are often made the targets of shallow invective.[8] However, unjust criticism does not make what is criticised correct, and the claims at issue here are not correct. The empirical monitoring of human speech and activity is not importantly different from the monitoring of all manner of other things; if discursive activity can be referred to as real then there is no evident reason why all the many other phenomena we address through our senses, just as we address speech and action, should not be as well. Again, to render the noises made by people as speech, and the movements they make as action, is a profoundly theoretical project; the idealisation, abstraction, reification, resort to conjecture and general 'artfulness' involved in transcribing the output of a cassette recorder, say, as 'speech' or 'discourse' is not notably different from activities that make phenomena visible or credible in other fields of study. The notion that any intellectual enterprise can proceed without resort to 'theorising' is untenable, and the idea that there is anything remarkable about the theorising implicated in the study of speech or discourse has no foundation. Assertions that only discourse is real may have ideological utility in fields equipped solely for the study of discourse, but assertions of this kind are familiar accompaniments of all kinds of specialised intellectual activity, and from the outside it may reasonably be thought that there is not a great deal to choose between one example and another.

Sensible attribution

The enduring value in the present context of the work just discussed lies very much in its early general insights. Different repertoires or 'vocabularies' of internal states exist in different cultures. Their application occurs through the contingent social actions of those who use the vocabularies to attribute states to agents. Attributions are themselves contingent actions, and how they came about must be regarded as entirely an empirical problem. However, efforts to move on from here to solve the empirical problem posed by attributions of free will, agency and responsibility lead to an impasse. It is clear that these attributions are not inspired by inner states themselves, and it is also evident that they are sometimes assigned *ex post facto*, by agents who consider only the expedient consequences of their attributions. But there can be no doubt that visibly *ex post facto* attributions are generally regarded as illicit and improper. And more generally, for all that an improvisatory and unpredictable element is a necessary part of attribution here, attributors do not doubt that more than their fancy is invoved in how they proceed, and that there are right and wrong ways of inferring to invisible states from features of agents or actions themselves. What remains still obscure, however, is what the features are that attributors reckon they should properly take account of when they identify an action as chosen rather than caused, or an agent as in a responsible state of mind.

At this point it is interesting to return to attribution theory, which has been concerned with just this problem. That this involves a fundamental shift of theoretical framework goes without saying. Instead of recognising different 'vocabularies' of inner states in terms of which attributors may legitimately make sense of actions, most attribution theorists have treated variations in attributions in terms of biases which produce deviations from what is rational and correct. Indeed many attribution theorists, for all the remarkable variability in 'attribution behaviour' that their studies have exposed, have tended to take for granted that there is a single true account to be discovered of the nature of invisible psychological states. They have cited the analogy with the physical sciences, where attribution to invisible theoretical entities is also necessary. As scientists have learned more about the world, so they have improved their attributions, eliminated incorrect theories and postulated better ones. Through this progressive development, so it is said, they have arrived at their current correct theoretical account of the natural world. Obviously then, attributions may be correct, even when invisible entities are involved.

The analogy relied on here is, however, very much a double-edged one, which may serve at once to indicate the value of theorising about invisible states and to re-emphasise how problematic and contestable it is.[9] Physical scientists do indeed describe the world by drawing upon a vast array of invisible theoretical entities: forces and fields, atoms and molecules, and so forth. But the mundane fact that the real existence of these theoretical entities is accepted routinely, on the authority of science as it were, must not distract us from the deeper point that the grounds for that acceptance remain unclear. The epistemological and ontological status of its current theoretical entities remains an unsettled matter in the philosophy of science, and there is nothing to suggest that these entities, unlike the long sequence of their since modified or discarded predecessors in the history of science, are in any sense final. Indeed the status of its invisible entities remains unsettled in the practical context of scientific research. Scientific controversy and conflict remain far more common than is often believed, and different fields or groupings within science may attribute the same phenomena to the different theoretical entities incarnate in activities based on competing paradigms. Moreover, even in the absence of controversy, the actively managed relationship between document and pattern described by Garfinkel is very much apparent in the context of the natural sciences, both in the way that accepted knowledge is 'routinely' sustained and applied and in the way that it is adapted and modified in the light of new information.[10]

Even on the basis of the analogy with the physical sciences, it is hard to imagine that attributions could come to embody 'the truth' about our inner states. Here, as elsewhere, it is better to accept the conceptual relativism implicit in sociological and ethnomethodological work, and to acknowledge that different vocabularies of states may be deployed in different ways, all of which stand as viable means of making sense of action. But if the ideology of attribution theory is in that respect inadequate, its experiments remain of great interest. It is rightly claimed that subjects in these experiments, for all that their attributions are so very frequently 'biased', generally proceed in a recognisably 'scientific', inductively sensible way, and that this way of proceeding may be assumed to have a normative force for them in everyday life.[11]

What might be meant by 'inductively sensible' here? Recall Deaux and Emswiller's study of the attribution of 'skill' and 'luck', but imagine that kind of attribution informed not by one event but by many, occurring over time in a larger context. Suppose the relevant actions are those of a woman snooker player who keeps winning. This is attributable to luck or to skill, both initially and, pro forma, at any later point in the winning sequence. Sense can always be made of her victories as revelations of skill, or as products of (increasingly extreme) good fortune. Nonetheless, the 'scientifically' inclined attributor, even if at the outset she had cited 'luck', would be expected to shift to 'skill' over time. The shift to 'skill', after three or four lost frames, say, would be a sound practical inference, especially for an opponent playing for substantial stakes. A sensible attributor would make this inference; she would learn inductively from experience and correct her initial attribution. And this is no doubt what an attribution theorist would regard as the most likely thing to happen in actual situations of this kind.

In contrast, for those uncompromisingly committed to the view that only speech exists, there is, presumably, no experience here from which to learn. And it is also fair to say, by way of criticism, that learning from experience is not acknowledged as it should be, as a relevant consideration in the giving of accounts, even by the most ecumenical of ethnomethodologists. However, it needs to be added here that a properly thorough discussion of the issue would rapidly reveal it to be far less clear-cut than it seems. Learning always occurs in a cultural context in context-dependent ways. We might be happy to regard the work of Deaux and Emswiller as a revelation of attribution bias, and to condemn a failure to acknowledge the skills of women after a prolonged display of them as perverse and irrational, but that, it could be said, is merely a contingent fact about us. Perhaps it is only because the accepted knowl-edge of our culture stresses the equality of men and women, and their similar abilities to acquire skills, that we see things in this way. Perhaps, in a culture with prejudices aligned in the opposite direction, 'learning from experience' would not proceed as just described, and neither would it be thought rational or inductively sensible for it to proceed in that way. These, however, are points that cannot be taken further here.[12] It must suffice to offer the suggestion, in broad if not full agreement with the work of attribution theorists, that in given cultural settings human beings learn inductively from experience in ways relevant to their practical con-cerns, and that attributions to invisible states may change coherently and systematically as they do so. Where such a state is believed to be present, we expect its effects to manifest themselves at the level of action, and if they never do we may become sceptical of the presence of the state. Where such a state is believed to be absent, the repeated appearance of its familiar effects may be found puzzling and eventually prompt the idea that the state is present after all. The consequent modifications to our received knowledge may serve to increase its utility in relation to our pragmatic concerns.

For all that it raises formidable formal problems, the attribution of invisible states and powers is frequently straightforward and pragmati-cally sensible. The pragmatic good sense of many actual attributions is particularly evident in the case we have just considered, of the attribu-tion of skill. Skills are ubiquitously attributed as a matter of course, on the basis of (formally contestable) inferences from observed perfor-mances. They are often thought of as in some sense residing inside the person, as being internal states, but the value of the attribution of a skill to a person lies in its serving as a marker of the (inductively inferred) possibility of further skilled performances by the person. Whether and how the skill exists as an internal state may be debatable, but the value of attributing it is much less so. Of skills, it is reasonable to say that, whatever the formal problems, they are attributed sensibly.

Might the same be said of rationality and will? Independent of the vexed question of whether such inner states 'really exist', might we nonetheless claim that they are attributed sensibly, in the way that skills are? Presumably, if it is legitimate to make inductive inferences from per-formances to skills, then it is equally legitimate to make such inferences from rational actions to rationality, and from chosen actions to will or agency. With this argument anyone happy that skills exist may dodge the issues associated with invisible states and hold that rationality and will can exist in the same way – whatever that way may be. The sensible attri-bution of responsible agency may then proceed from the observation of rational actions and chosen actions, and the sole problem will be the empirical one of specifying what makes actions rational and/or chosen. If this is indeed specified, and the relevant actions are actually identified, then attributions of rationality and free will inferred from them will create the expectation of further rational and/or chosen actions from the same agents, just as an attribution of skill inferred from performances creates the expectation of further skilled performances. Unfortunately, however, whilst it is easy to characterise actions that embody recognised skills, it is a far more difficult matter to identify rational actions or chosen actions, and to specify what distinguishes them from actions or behaviours of other kinds. Nor are attribution studies helpful here. In particular, they throw no light on the so far intractable problem of discriminating between chosen and caused actions (save by revealing the 'biases' that generate relative preferences for the one attribution or the other *ex post facto*). There are two sense-making schemes, the institution of responsible action and the institution of causal connection. But what inspires and justifies the use of the one rather than the other – what corresponds to the pragmatic considerations that inform references to skill or else luck – has not so far been identified, if indeed it exists. It appears to be perfectly feasible to render any supposedly chosen action equally well as caused and not chosen. And although we tend to identify chosen actions as 'actions that could have been otherwise', what makes them so, if anything, remains moot.

Notes

1 The discussion will mainly be confined to empirically based work. A substantial philosophical literature also bears upon the problem, and indeed is extensively cited in the controversies in psychology and sociology, but it is largely passed over here.

2 An impressive review of work in attribution theory wherein sociological issues are given recognition is Hewstone (1989). Also of relevance to the specific context of discussion here is Shaver (1985).

3 No doubt it is an anachronism to refer to agency in describing the alleged error, but what is suggested thereby is worth reflecting on.

4 This coupling of what is routine and what is actively accomplished is important. The case studies of Garfinkel and other ethnomethodologists are particularly interesting as revelations of the ingenuity and artfulness involved in routine action, in 'going on in the same way'. Indeed, there is a very close analogy between the themes discussed under the rubric of documentary method here and those to be discussed in Chapter 8 under the rubric of the intransitivity of sameness. Heritage (1984) links work in ethnomethodology with work in the sociology of knowledge via this analogy.

5 In the work of Harold Garfinkel (1967), there are frequent suggestions that the orderliness of accounts may be understood in terms of the practical purposes or interests of those who construct them, and that discourse may to this extent be understood as performative – something intelligible in terms of what it is used to do, or how it is made to function. But this work appears to have inspired no further curiosity about the purposes or interests of human beings, possibly for the reasons outlined in the main text.

6 It is perhaps misleading to bundle all these fields together, when practition-

ers mark fundamental distinctions between them. See, however, Coulter (1989), Parker (1992), Edwards and Potter (1992), Gergen (1994), Harré (1986), Harré and Gillett (1994), Smith *et al.* (1995).

7 This position requires that the investigator, of discourse for example, may only look within discourse itself for the means of understanding its orderliness and regularity. The resulting search has resulted, as might be expected, in the identification of new kinds of theoretical entity internal to discourse itself. Discourse is discussed in terms of its 'logic' or 'grammar', or its 'rule-governed' character, something not altogether consistent it might be thought. Indeed, just this has been thought by practitioners themselves in these extraordinarily reflexive fields, with the result that many of them see value in their discourse only in that it negates what is claimed in discourse of other kinds.

8 The so-called 'science wars', wherein natural scientists have been flailing somewhat indiscriminately at their supposed enemies, are a striking illustration of this. The claim that concepts refer to nothing, that human knowledge is accordingly not 'about' anything, and indeed that nothing really exists for it to be about, seems to irritate some natural scientists in just the way that claims on behalf of a reductionist physicalism irritate some social scientists, and no doubt for the same reason.

9 The edge not discussed in the main text is a corresponding source of difficulties for those of an anti-theoretical turn of mind; it makes it incumbent on them to clarify just why they insist on their position given the immense success of theorising as part and parcel of the activities of the natural sciences.

10 Any recent contribution to the sociology of science would probably make the point, but see Kuhn (1970), Barnes (1982a, 1982b) and Barnes *et al.* (1996).

11 Kelley (1967, 1973) is generally cited as the original proponent of this view.

12 Bayesian theories of inductive inference, with their recognition of the relevance of given prior probabilities, would make a good starting point for taking this discussion further.

4

ON INDIVIDUALISM IN SOCIAL THEORY

More on 'agency'

Almost all forms of individualism seek to account for action in terms of internal states or powers, and are willing to face the problems that arise from thereby making reference to invisible theoretical entities. Certainly, this is so in modern social theory. In this context, it is now common to refer to human beings as possessed of *agency*, and to make sense of their actions as those of individuals so endowed. Some valuable work, albeit of a wholly negative kind, has been inspired by the notion of agency. It came into use as sociologists became dissatisfied with accounts of action as the products of externalities, and alienated by the suggestion that human beings in themselves were purely responsive entities. In particular, it was used to deny the power of norms and rules to determine actions: human beings, it was said, had agency in relation to rules. But references to agency have come to be used to proclaim the autonomy of the individual over all kinds of other allegedly causal factors, both 'structural' and 'cultural', and they are being used ever more widely in this way.

References to agency of this kind invite us to re-orient our understanding of the aetiology of social situations. Let there be some entity, X, which is routinely pointed to as causing or explaining action: X may be a rule, for example, or a social norm. Then to say that individuals have agency in relation to X both calls into question X's causal role and invites a different account of its salience: perhaps we should say that X is taken account of in the way individuals act, or that X is put to use in action. This kind of account, wherein individuals are active in relation to X, may still serve to account for why X persists in the social order, and even to account for the superficial appearance of individual passivity in relation to X. Most of the time, the best way for the active individual to take account of X may be precisely for her to act routinely, in the way that X 'implies'. Needless to say, the mere fact that actions are in conformity with some external requirement does not imply that those actions are a passive expression of it: to act consistently with a rule, for example, is not remotely the same thing as to act guided by a rule, still less to act as a rule compels one to act.[1]

Specific examples of human beings allegedly manifesting agency – for example, in their following of rules or norms – are generally straightforward to understand and perfectly credible. Norms may be followed in many different ways, and the specific actions by virtue of which agents are reckoned to be following norms can readily be shown to be unpredictable from the norms themselves. Ethnomethodological studies have specialised in doing just this. But whilst this kind of study may offer valuable insight into the insufficiency of a norm, or an item of culture, or whatever else, as a determinant of the action associated with it, the current custom of highlighting that insufficiency by reference to individual agency creates problems. 'Agency' is said to refer to the independent power the agent exercises over what is external to her. But what is supposed to demonstrate the independence of that power remains obscure. What justifies the treatment of rules, or indeed 'structural' and 'cultural' elements of whatever kind, as external is no clearer. And even if such elements could be treated as externalities over which individuals in some sense 'had agency', it would remain to be asked whether those individuals were not the puppets of internal drives or hormone levels, or if not puppets of the bodily internal then puppets of the psychic internal.

Anthony Giddens and Roy Bhaskar both try to solve these problems at a stroke by recourse to a metaphysical individualism. 'Agency' is said to denote the independent power of the individual, not in relation to rules, or culture, or indeed anything specific at all, but in relation to whatever might be cited as a possible constraint upon her. Because of the (alleged) existence of human agency in this unqualified sense, it is always possible to say of an action that it 'could have been otherwise'. This they adopt as their ontology. And thereby they give the postulate of the existence of agency a priority over what might be learned empirically that in practice goes well beyond what is appropriate in any properly naturalistic social theory.[2] Rather than documenting the insufficiency of some supposed cause in understanding an aspect of human action, they imply that no cause or set of causes will ever be sufficient. Rather than reminding us that human beings are complex creatures, within whom all kinds of weird and wonderful things occur that we are unlikely ever fully to understand, they effectively set human beings outside the frame of naturalistic understanding altogether.

If one prefers to maintain a genuine continuity between social theory and scientific understanding, then this metaphysic has to be abandoned. There is no need to deny, however, that the notion of agency can do valuable work. To say that human beings have agency in relation to some specific class of things may be empirically plausible and pragmatically valuable, as when the status of norms as causes of action is challenged. It may also be legitimate to claim that we possess agency in a more general sense, where what is meant is that our existing knowledge as a whole does not permit an adequate causal explanation of how we act. But the function of the term here is still a wholly negative one, and still offers no justification for acknowledging the existence of agency as an independent individual power. The term is being deployed here merely as a device to mark the insufficiency of a given body of knowledge – typically knowledge structured according to the institution of causal connection. Use of the concept of agency in this restrained way implies no incompatibility with a wholly causal or deterministic conception of human behaviour. It merely gives expression to the uncontroversial view that existing patterns of causal understanding are incomplete, and currently insufficient, a view that biologists, for example, could easily reconcile with the presence of yet-to-be-elucidated causal systems within the human body. 'Agency' will sometimes be used in this purely naturalistic sense in this book, and particularly to denote the active orientation (the necessarily active orientation) that agents have toward norms and rules.

References to agency in sociology proliferated in a context where overblown and unsubstantiated deterministic accounts of human activities had flourished, and needed to be challenged. Assertion of individual agency was the rhetorical device employed for that essential task. Perhaps it would have been better if some other device had been used, but given the way that history has actually transpired it makes sense to continue with existing practice, and to speak of human agency, albeit in a cautious and naturalistic way. Caution is necessary because 'agency' is a notion with important functions both in everyday discourse (in the guise of 'free-agency'), and in non-naturalistic forms of social theory as we have seen. Indeed, before making further use of the term here, it is important to shake off some of the associations and connotations that it has acquired in other contexts. What currently gives the use of 'agency' a degree of theoretical coherence is not an agreed sense of what it denotes, but a common evaluative perspective in those who deploy it. It is used to celebrate the independent power of the individual human being as a good, and its use in that way has evolved within a specific tradition of thought about the nature of human beings. One way of confirming that this is indeed the case is to ask whether human beings have agency in relation to their rationality. The question is perfectly meaningful – strong rational choice theory, for example, would answer a clear 'no' to it – but it has a strange ring to it nonetheless. This is surely because 'the individual' said to possess agency is widely assumed to be constitutively rational, and agency in relation to rationality is, for her, power possessed over and against her very self as its possessor. The concept of agency, in other words, has been closely associated with a tradition where it was thought of as a power of reason over and against causes, a very deeply dualistic tradition. If the term is retained as a way of speaking only of our independence from specific forms of control or determination, then this association from the baggage of its history becomes misleading and needs to be set aside.

The case against individualism

Human beings are complex active creatures and there is something to be said for keeping that prominently in mind with references to their agency. But it is a mistake nonetheless to regard them as possessors of stably constituted independent powers and capacities, as those who speak of individual agency generally do. Let us pursue the point by discussing rational choice theory, which offers what amounts to a specific, precise account of the nature of individual agency. There is a good reason for focusing on this account. Most of the time, in the course of their social life, human beings treat each other as responsible agents, possessed, so the dictionary says, of rationality and free will and hence of the capacity for rational conduct. If we put an individualistic gloss upon these formulations they imply that responsible agents possess stable individual powers to reason and to choose, and that they are thereby able to behave as independent, autonomous human beings. In effect, an individualistic understanding of the responsible agent of everyday discourse renders her as the independent individual of rational choice theory. Rational choice theory offers an individualistic model of the powers of the responsible agent, and then tries to explain her behaviour as the exercise of these powers.

Despite the widespread respect which this model commands, however, it is well known to be wholly inadequate as an account of how human beings actually behave. Let us look first at rationality. Even in everyday life it is easy to identify empirical instances of non-rational behaviour. We are creatures with emotions, and we recognise our occasional tendency to act non-rationally, out of fear or anger, for example. We are creatures possessed only of a limited reason, and we recognise that our best efforts at calculative rationality may fail, as when we play chess, for example. Some of us are academics, and can ponder the problem of irrational colleagues, as when forthright economists scornfully proclaim to sociologists: 'people are rational, stupid'. But systematic empirical studies, and psychological studies in particular, go well beyond what reflection on these kinds of example might reveal, and indicate that in the normal way of things individuals are not rational, or at least not in the way that rational choice implies. Accounts of the general features of human reasoning based on the results of psychologists' experiments indicate that it radically diverges from 'rationality' in the sense of consistency and deductive propriety, and to an extent also from rationality as sensible induction.[3] And indeed the experimental work involved here is interesting both for the magnitude of the 'irrationality' it has revealed in individual inferences, and for the revelation of the ease with which we can identify it and regret it when reminded of accepted norms of good reasoning. (It is interesting how even technical work narrowly focused on individual inference, like so much else relevant to the criticism of rational choice, points reflection on rationality away from 'the individual' toward the contextual and the collective.)

Psychological studies also raise questions about how far actions involve the exercise of independent individual powers (whether of choice or agency). Certainly, they suggest that the individual does not remain unaffected by proximate others in her calculations and subsequent actions. Indeed, there was a time when social psychology was dominated by work on the susceptibility of individuals to social influences and social pressures, and spectacular demonstrations of this, by Asch, for example, and Milgram and others, remain widely known throughout the social sciences.[4] There are, too, many studies of co-operative interaction involving calculation; and the results of these consistently clash with rational choice and game-theoretical predictions. Individuals in these studies fail to optimise their own returns from interaction, but by no means always because of irrationality and flawed reasoning. The tendency in these studies is for individuals to be systematically more co-operative and more concerned for the good of the other, or the joint good of both, than rational choice individualism would predict. In these, and in related experiments in social psychology, it is probably fair to say that the 'freely choosing' independent individual fails to put in an appearance.[5] Whilst the precise details of what is going on may be debatable, it seems clear that people are being profoundly influenced by others in their judgements and their actions. They do not calculate in isolation and act independently: they constantly take account of other people. It is true that there is a sense in which even wholly independent individuals must take account of other people. Other people, after all, are a part of the environment. But in these experiments other people are not taken account of only in this sense, like adverse weather or dangerous animals might be taken account of. The influence of other people (whatever it may consist in) is exercised through symbolic communications lacking any substantial threat or menace. Individuals are revealed to be profoundly mutually susceptible through communicative interaction.

Experimental studies are of great value in exposing the limitations of rational choice individualism, but they do not represent the only means of calling it into question on empirical grounds. Another way is to point to universally encountered and evidently indispensable forms of social activity that independent individuals with the powers envisaged by rational choice could not engender. One important form of activity of this kind is that involved in the creation, transmission, acquisition and use of knowledge. Rationally calculated actions make use of knowledge, but knowledge is a trans-individual resource, collectively generated, evaluated and standardised, and made available to individuals who for the most part take it on trust as the knowledge of 'their society'. This must be allowed for in our understanding of the nature of calculative action. Suppose that a fund-manager seeks to act rationally and responsibly by investing funds in the best way. A calculation is made and the funds are disposed accordingly. But the calculation of the 'best' investment will have required a vast stock of knowledge, of both the physical and the

social environment. And whilst there are many ways of acquiring knowledge, it must surely be that the greater part of any such stock must be
acquired from other people, in processes involving trust and the recognition of authority. The fund-manager who invests rationally will turn
out on detailed examination not to be an independent individual using
an internal capacity but a member of a collective utilising a shared stock
of knowledge beyond the capacity of any (rational) individual to evaluate. And if challenged to do so the manager will be able to make the
investment accountably rational only by reference to the specific shared
and trusted stock of knowledge that informed the calculations she made.

Calculative actions are not mere manifestations of the rationality of 'the
individual'. Reflection on the role of knowledge in calculation may enrich
our understanding of what is involved. Stocks of knowledge are carried
by collectives as part of their culture, and different collectives carry different stocks. When an individual makes a rational calculation, the
outcome will depend on which stock of knowledge is drawn upon, how
much of it has been assimilated, how it is utilised. The calculation will
reflect not the fixed and given rationality of 'the individual' but her contingent involvement in specific social relations and social processes.
Moreover, because of this involvement, routine reference to a calculated
action as a freely chosen action is no longer possible. Or rather, it is no
longer possible unless free choice may properly be imputed to an agent
who, far from acting independently, acts rationally only by acting as she
is authorised to act as a *member*.

It is sometimes argued on behalf of an individualistic understanding
of these matters that the use of knowledge does not compromise the independence and rationality of the individual who uses it. The individual
may check the knowledge herself – relearn it, as it were, from an examination of what it refers to. But the very activity of learning is itself impossible to represent as rational action. In the final analysis, it cannot be that
people learn because they have calculated that it is rational to do so. In
the final analysis, people are only in a position to calculate what it is
rational to do when they have acquired knowledge. Knowledge acquisition is in that sense prior to any individual rational calculation. And so
too, by the same argument, must be the acquisition of language, symbols,
procedures and all the rest of the shared culture that permits individual
reasoning. These acquired elements are essential preconditions for the full
manifestation of individual calculative rationality and the processes
wherein they are acquired are not themselves individually rational. They
are rather processes of communicative interaction in which people
engage, and through which they learn, without any prior calculation.[6]

It is important to recognise as well that knowledge and culture do not
come as fixed and unalterable packages: learning is never completed. The
bodies of knowledge that inform individual calculation constantly
undergo change, not least as the result of the real-world learning of individual persons. Indeed, these bodies have no inherent stability and left

to themselves, as it were, would fragment into a chaos of private memories, perceptions, impressions and similar individually possessed units of information. That they do not do so (and it is everywhere apparent that they do not) must be due to activities that sustain shared standards and paradigms across collectives and bring individual understandings into alignment with them. Members must constantly provide for each other accounts and displays of their understanding of knowledge and culture, constantly evaluate each others' accounts, and constantly seek to move in the direction of uniformity and agreement in accounts, if knowledge and culture are to continue to exist. But, again, as part of what precedes calculation and generates that which calculation makes use of, it is implausible to regard such activity as the product of calculation. If we do not so regard it, however, we are led to a picture wherein streams of calculative actions must be intimately associated with streams of non-rational communicative interactions necessary to support them.

It is important to be clear that the 'problem' constituted by the collective basis of knowledge arises in relation to both knowledge of natural order and knowledge of social order. In the first context, it has been a recognised problem for sociologists of knowledge ever since Durkheim (1915, pp. 146–7) made his famous contrast between individual perceptions and collective representations and asked how the varied, vague and fluctuating character of the former was to be related to the uniform, definite and persistent form of the latter. Durkheim indeed provided a vivid and dramatic account of a problem which the members of all actual societies invariably manage to ignore or to suppress. Characteristically, we choose not to remark on the different positions from which individuals monitor the world, the different instruments both natural and artificial that they use, and the invariable lack of identity between the observations of one individual and those of another. Instead we act on the presumption of an inherent coherence in the ways of seeing different individuals, and in the ways that they apply existing knowledge: it is an individualistic presumption, the taken-for-granted character of which offers stunning insight into how profoundly human beings are constituted as social agents.

The same problem arises in relation to social order, where shared knowledge is frequently knowledge of rules or norms. Again the presumption is that individuals, somehow, have identical perceptions of a given rule and its implications, and that the rule can accordingly be regarded as shared by so many independent individuals. But this rule individualism represents an even more remarkable assumption than that implicit in an individualistic conception of natural knowledge. For where the latter is concerned there is at least the possibility of referring to material objects, the existence of which is indicated by the coherent testimony of the different senses of an individual, to legitimate the notion that something external accounts for a uniformity of perception between individuals. With rules, there is no external something. Knowledge of rules is self-referring knowledge, sustained by a collective, with nothing external to point to as an explanation of why allegedly independent individuals should all know the same thing. With rules, determined individualists have to allege the existence of an essence, a true or intrinsic or essential meaning of a rule, that individuals separately encounter, and by this happenstance come to share 'the same rule'. All that then remains is the lesser matter of understanding why they should be disposed to act alike in accord with it.

All that is manifest with rules is examples of their use. To act in accordance with (knowledge of) rules is to proceed using such examples as precedent and analogy. And given that the examples differ in detail from each other, and that what constitutes proper analogy with them is always contestable, it is clear that uniformity in the following of a rule cannot be understood by reference to some manifest property of 'the rule itself'. In order to generate a continuing sense that there is a rule there, implied in all the examples, and to define 'the' right way of extending the rule to future cases and situations, all the various attempts at correct rule use across the collective have to be considered. A sense of which of these attempts are right and which wrong has to be agreed. And a shared sense of how to move from agreed 'right' instances to new applications has likewise to be sustained.

Diverse individual inclinations in the definition of and application of rules must be ordered into a coherent collective practice. Without such agreement in practice, there will be no sense that one way of continuing to follow a rule is better than another, and hence no rule. But independent individuals have no obvious incentive to do the work of evaluation and standardisation constantly necessary to sustain a sense of 'what the rules are'. It is necessary to postulate that non-independent individuals do this work, individuals who are active and independent in relation to rules but not in relation to each other. Mutually susceptible individuals, affecting each other implicitly, causally and continuously in their communicative interaction, may co-ordinate their understanding and their actual implementation of rules in a way that independent individuals cannot.[7]

Rule individualism is untenable: it fails properly to describe and make intelligible what is involved in recognising the implications of, and hence in following, rules. At least, this is true if one evaluates rule individualism naturalistically and does not allow it to pluck the 'true meanings' of rules out of thin air. As visible phenomena, neither the learning nor the uses of rules are intelligible as so many separate encounters between independent individuals and 'rules themselves'. This is a criticism not just of rational choice individualism, but of any version of rule individualism, even including that in the social theory of Talcott Parsons, wherein not just knowledge of rules but pressures to enact them arise from separate individual encounters with them. Indeed, the criticism extends to many theorists who do not count as individualists in the usual sense, and to any theory that accounts for uniformity in actions as the result of separate encounters of individuals with rules, or norms, or principles, or traditions, or meanings, or whatever else.

Consider, for example, those sociological theories which take social systems to be sets of enacted social practices produced and reproduced by knowledgeable human beings. Neither Anthony Giddens nor Pierre Bourdieu, who are perhaps the best-known proponents of such theories, is commonly thought of as an individualist; indeed they have both striven to avoid individualism and especially individual/society dualism. But both describe macro-order as constituted by individual persons who separately orient themselves to the same rules, or give expression to the same principles, or unfold the same competences. In Giddens (1984), individual agents all draw upon the same set of rules and resources as they act and thereby reconstitute the set as a shared 'social structure' and an associated social system as a particular expression in practice of the structure. In Bourdieu (1990), there is a correspondence between social structures and mental structures. A 'habitus' of 'durable transposable dispositions', of 'principles which generate and organise practices', is deposited alike in individuals as a mental structure and disposes them to act alike. This habitus is the product of a 'field' of relationships between social positions – a set of objectively given relationships with structural or systemic properties. At the same time the field itself is continually reconstituted as the practices of particular human beings oriented by habitus. In these recent reflections on the relationship of macrocosm and microcosm, order at the macro-level ultimately derives from an isomorphous order immanent in the mind and/or body of each individual. Admittedly, it is stressed that individuals may adjust or creatively interpret rules and principles. And social interaction is acknowledged as important. But there is no clear recognition of the *essential* role of interaction in the constitution of order. Routine practices constitute systems because they are enacted by individuals within each of whom the same templates, whether in the form of principle, or disposition, or rule, or knowledge of how to go on, are to be found. Macro-order reflects the existence of similarities between individual human beings, not the interaction that overcomes the differences between them.[8]

Attention to instances suggests that the routine practices of collectives are *not* analysable into the routine performances of individual persons, and indeed that routine at the one level is incompatible with routine at the other. The successful execution of routine social practices always involves the continual *overriding* of routine practices (habits, skills) at the individual level. Think of an orchestra playing a familiar work or a military unit engaged in a march-past. Any description of these activities as so many agents each following the internal guidance of habit or rule would merely describe a fiasco. Individual habituated competence is of course necessary in these contexts, but so too is constant active intervention to tailor individual performances to what other participants are doing, always bearing in mind the goal of the overall collective performance. As well as being of interest in themselves these examples will serve as metaphors for the operation of an entire social system. It is not the product of some trans-individual entity – whether a constellation of rules, or a habitus – acting on or in particular individuals. It is the product of interacting social agents constantly adjusting and aligning what otherwise would be non-identical and incongruous individual performances. It is the continuing consequence not of sameness and aggregation, but of difference and sociability. Where there is social order on a large scale there is agreement in practice amongst participants in the order. But that agreement is not the happy coincidence of the individual practices of appropriately socialised or informed agents, nor the fortunate consequence of their separate access to identical rules. It is rather the creation of agreement out of difference as a continuing ubiquitous project. The agents who successfully engage in this project must be actively oriented to any (instances of) rules they relate to. But they may not be independent individuals with no particular inclination to co-ordinate their actions with others, and no incentive to engage in the communicative interaction necessary to keep shared rules shared. Social agents are necessary here, agents with a prior non-rational inclination toward agreement and co-ordination, agents who by virtue of this inclination possess collective agency. There is no place here for agents who will interact only when they have calculated that it is profitable, and make that calculation only if that also is to their benefit, and consider the extent of that benefit only. . .

The problem of what is involved in learning and acting in accordance with rules is a profoundly difficult one, and controversy between rule-individualism and rule-collectivism is ongoing. The case for understanding knowledge as a collective possession and for rejecting individualistic accounts of its acquisition and use is less contentious, but it is still far from being everywhere accepted. There are, however, other areas of human social activity which pose more straightforward and widely acknowledged difficulties for an individualistic perspective. There are even familiar forms of calculative instrumental action for which rational choice individualism, and indeed any form of individualism which envisages agents acting separately and independently, can offer no convincing account, even if the knowledge involved is taken as given. An empirically important class of actions of this kind is collectively rational actions – instrumental actions undertaken as a means not to an individual end but to a collective one. Relevant examples here might include actions for the good of an ethnic group, or a nation, or a gender; or actions which serve as sanctions to enforce social norms or standards, to keep social institutions operative, and hence, as it is often put, to maintain social order. These last kinds of examples are particularly interesting because they suggest, rightly, that collectively instrumental actions are not merely manifest in our social life but necessary to its persistence: social order is a collective good that is a necessary good.

Collectively beneficial instrumental action is indeed individually irrational, and its existence faces rational choice individualism (indeed, individualism *per se*) with what is everywhere known as the problem of
collective action. It arises in a particularly extreme form when joint
actions for the good of very large groups are considered – strikes, upris-
ings, demonstrations, votes and so forth. Individual members of such
groups would decline to participate in such enterprises if they were independent rational calculators, since it is better to leave others to pay the
price for success and an individual contribution would make no difference anyway.

The existence of collective action poses profound problems for individualism, since it calls into question not merely assertions of self-interest or self-regard but the fundamental postulate that individuals are
independent calculators. Consider how, for an uprising to succeed, very
many people may have to risk their lives in participating – as occurred,
for example, in Romania when Ceauşescu was overthrown. The fundamental problem here is not why altruism should have overcome self-
interest and led to participation, but why persons whose *individual*
participation was a drop in the ocean nonetheless did participate.
Collective action is scarcely well-described as irrational, since it may be
exquisitely calculated and highly effective instrumental action, but it
cannot be rationalised by reference either to altruistic or self-interested
individual goals. Indeed, as so many individual actions it cannot be rationalised as instrumental to any goals at all; for in the last analysis each
such individual action is a futile irrelevance even though their totality is
a potent force. The manifest existence of collectively oriented instrumental action constitutes a fundamental problem, therefore, just so long
as it is assumed that individuals operate independently and evaluate the
consequences of their own individual actions separately in terms of the
difference they make to the overall flow of events. The problem of collective action arises directly and entirely from the postulate of 'the independent individual' calculating and making choices in isolation. And the
existence of collective action implies that the postulate of such an individual, sufficient unto herself, unconnected to a larger context save only
through expediency, is incorrect. Indeed it implies, just as other critical
suggestions in this section have done, that in order to understand the
actions of an individual attention should be directed beyond her, toward
her relations with others.

The entrenchment of individualism

Independent individuals are incapable of constituting themselves as
knowledgeable collectives. And even if they were so capable they would
still be incapable of the kinds of joint and collective action in which
members of such collectives must and do engage. The agents who are

capable of these things must be understood as social agents. This, however, is not everywhere acknowledged. To be sure, there is some recognition that individualism clashes with clear evidence from sociology, psychology and biology; and even in its strongholds in political science and economics there are those who acknowledge the dominant rational choice individualism to be not merely false but radically at variance with what is known of human behaviour (Friedman, 1996).[9] Its proponents, however, continue to characterise it as a remarkably successful account of human behaviour notwithstanding, and point to its domination of the social science disciplines in the USA, and of economics almost everywhere, as a sign of that.

Individualism has indeed become increasingly dominant in the thought of the social sciences just as it has in the world of everyday life. One way of appreciating how deeply entrenched it has become is to reflect on responses to work that has challenged it. A lot of social psychology has done just this. The work of Stanley Milgram certainly did so. In his famous experiments, carried out in the USA in the 1950s, individuals proved willing to inflict severe electric shocks on a fellow human being, to his apparent great distress, in obedience to the requests of a scientific experimenter, or, in other versions of the experiment, at the behest of peers.[10]

Milgram's experiments suggested that massive modifications of individual patterns of behaviour could be elicited by apparently modest levels of external prompting and interaction, and pointed to the conclusion that individuals are readily influenced by each other in symbolic interaction and communication. In the context of a culture inclined to account for actions by reference to the motives of supposedly independent individuals, this was an unexpected conclusion and an unwelcome one. Certainly, Milgram's results were unexpected; both lay and academic opinion were wholly unprepared for them. Milgram demonstrated this himself by describing his experimental set-up to audiences and inviting them to predict his results: neither the wider public nor professional social scientists came remotely near to predicting the levels of obedience that Milgram observed. But if audiences were surprised, so too had been Milgram himself: he had initially expected individual subjects to manifest much greater autonomy, and when he moved on to attempt to account for his anomalous results, he continued to think in an individualistic framework, albeit a slightly modified one.

Milgram conjectured that when they entered his experimental situation (most) individual subjects shifted from an autonomous to an *agentic* state. They were induced to switch off their independent faculties of judgement and become *agents* in the sense of persons acting under the control of someone else. (Notice the intriguing difference between this variety of common usage and how 'agent' and 'agency' are used elsewhere in this book.) It was in this agentic state, with their ability to distinguish right from wrong inoperative, that individuals became capable of the cruel and inhuman actions observed. What had hitherto gone unrecognised, and needed to be recognised according to Milgram, was how very easily individuals might be induced to switch into an agentic state.

Notice how the problem has been framed and defined here. An individual has acted abnormally and immorally. The question is: what in the social situation, what externality, can have acted to neutralise the autonomy of the individual and thereby to make the immoral act intelligible? This remains a common way of framing the problem created by work like Milgram's, but it is nonetheless a very odd way. Autonomous individuals fly into social situations that pose a danger to their autonomy and make them liable to act immorally; after a time they fly off again and resume their normal, autonomous and hence moral state. Surely it is closer to the truth that individuals spend their lives moving from one social situation to another. This invites the thought that in one respect at least Milgram's subjects were behaving in his experimental setting just as they were wont to behave in any other setting: they were coping with a situation by taking account of, and largely acting in accord with, the expectations encountered within it. Expected to engage in inflicting GBH in the laboratory they largely obliged. Expected to refrain from such behaviour on returning to the street, they duly refrained. But a radical contextualism of this kind seems never to have been adopted in the interpretation of Milgram's work, even though micro-sociological studies, by Howard Becker (1970), for example, have long been available as models of what would be involved.[11] A convention of attributing normal moral activity in normal social contexts to the independent agency of individuals has generally been followed.

Orientations to Milgram's findings, including his own orientation, have manifested the familiar 'biases' identified by the attribution studies mentioned in Chapter 3. Audiences have been predisposed to relate the actions of subjects to internal antecedents, and to underestimate the role of externalities. And they have also been inclined to make a link between strong and stable internal individual characteristics and action that is reasonable and morally acceptable, as they have interpreted the experiment. This is very much the approach of most current modes of individualistic thinking, wherein the instigator of normal morally acceptable action is paradigmatically the independent stably constituted individual person.

It is this individualistic scheme which is threatened by the work of Milgram and more generally by the long series of studies of social influence that have been carried out by social psychologists. It would be wrong, of course, to imply that it takes the special techniques of social psychology to generate consciousness of our sensitivity to others. This is a part of our informal awareness. We do recognise our lack of independence, and indeed many of us come through reflection to recognise a continuing essential dependence on relations with other people. But this recognition is inadequately expressed in our shared culture. Contradictory conceptions of ourselves as dependent yet independent somehow co-exist in our thought, and it is the latter conception which is most commonly endorsed and given explicit public expression. We are able to accept the validity of studies like those of Milgram, or some of us are, but we tend to set them apart and refuse to allow them to affect the mainstream of our thinking. It remains a convention of everyday discourse to treat the other as an autonomous agent, although work which indicates that the opposite is the case is readily incorporated into the training of personnel managers or counsellors or therapists, or others of the vast and increasing numbers of professionals now involved in the repair and overhaul of human capital. Were we routinely to acknowledge the ubiquity of the effects of social influence, it would be deeply disturbing to intuitions which value above all else personal autonomy and integrity, and regard susceptibility to others as a serious human weakness.

Even today, first encounters with work like Milgram's rarely fail to surprise and disturb. In being surprising, they reveal the independent individual as the stereotypical source of social action in much of our thought. In being disturbing, they suggest that stereotypes of what is tend also to be stereotypes of what ought to be. The natural, the normal, the acceptable, the valuable need not elide in our thinking, but in practice they do: revelations of abnormality almost invariably grate against both our empirical and our moral expectations. In the world of our imagination, the independent individual tends to be our ideal source of normal, natural, acceptable, valuable actions. She exists in many versions: there is the rational individual of economics, the moral individual of philosophy, the creative individual of the arts and sciences, the active individual of some forms of sociology, and the prototype of them all, the responsible individual of everyday life. The independent individual is the source of most of the actions that constitute our ideal vision of society.

All this stands as testimony to the extreme individualism of our current everyday culture; and yet the distinctiveness of this modern individualism should not be exaggerated. Everywhere and always cultures have recognised the independence and autonomy of members to some extent, and it could well be asked (although it appears not to have been) whether all have not tended to underestimate the extent to which their members are bonded together and mutually susceptible. It is intriguing to note how in practically all the great world religions the soul is an individual essence, often one that will receive its own individually tailored reward or punishment in some conjectured afterlife. And of course all the great issues of free will, the nature of individual reason, the problem of determinism and the rest were investigated with unsurpassed penetration long before what Durkheim referred to as the emergence of the cult of the individual in our own recent history.

It may be that a certain individualistic bias tends to inhere in all forms of everyday discourse because of the work that it does. This is not, by and large, the work of displaying action as the product of antecedents, but much more that of defining and affirming statuses and assigning rights and responsibilities to them. When the duellist requests her opponent to choose weapons, she does not pretend to knowledge of the extent of her opponent's autonomy or of the causal nexus around her: the request simply signifies acknowledgement of a right proper to the opponent's status and holds back the unfolding drama of the situation until the call for swords or pistols is heard. The ideal recipient of a right is a clearly identifiable unambiguously bounded object. Similarly, when the duellist is later held responsible for the duel, the causal nexus surrounding her then becomes an inconvenient complication threatening the attribution. The ideal carrier of responsibility is an uncaused cause of whom it may be said: it was you, and you alone, who did it. Even if in reality the individual is but a speck of dust trembling on a spider's web, it may be that all that matters is her location, and that the numerous elastic silk threads attached to her are best ignored.

Social theory, however, should not ignore such threads; it should be concerned to understand actions in terms of their antecedents, and sequences of actions in terms which include the continuing pressures and influences bearing upon those who perform them. Hence, the treatment of persons as independent units, or pure positions, that often expedites the work of everyday discourse can lead social theory astray. If social theory takes from everyday discourse a functional conception of persons as independent units, it cripples itself as far as the pursuit of its own proper and distinctive purposes are concerned.

Social theory, like the whole of the social sciences wherein it belongs, needs to orient itself to human beings naturalistically, and to seek to understand in this sense how they behave and how that behaviour can be related to its antecedents. In doing this it will inevitably find itself attending to a wider range of contingencies than are routinely taken account of in everyday life, given the different pragmatic concerns predominant therein. At the same time, however, its conclusions may usefully feed back into everyday concerns and even conceivably alter the moral and evaluative perspectives of everyday discourse. Thus, responses to Milgram's work indicate the existence of an accepted framework of moral understanding based on the stereotype of the independent individual: independently chosen actions are normal, good and moral, and social influences on action are potentially causes of lapses from what is normal, good and moral. Social theory surely performs a useful task if it highlights the naturalistic inadequacy of this stereotype. Equally, it does so if it keeps in play the utterly banal but often ignored arguments against treating such an individual as a moral ideal. Moral agents must presumably be capable of sustaining social life, but it is hard to imagine how social life would be possible in the absence of something to move the individual in the direction of the collective. Without this, idiosyncrasy would run rampant not just in action but in understanding as well. An individual who will defer to others, and not for her own good reason but for theirs, is essential not just to the existence of moral order in the collective, but to the existence of linguistic and epistemological order as well.

Notes

1 In the study of culture the dominant picture is now of human beings actively mobilising and deploying cultural resources as suits their purposes. In the sociology of knowledge, human beings are held to be actively oriented toward their collective representations. In the mainstream of sociological theory they are active in relation to rules and social norms, and social life is characterised by rule reflexivity. And all this has been an unequivocal good, since the view it proposes is substantially correct and the one it has superseded was not. It needs to be admitted, however, that the extent of the advance that this has represented in the context of sociological theory is partly a function of the depth of the hole that theory had dug for itself previously. It is interesting how rational choice theorists, who were rightly unimpressed with the powers of rules and norms in the past, are not much given to talk of agency and activity at present, even though their views could easily be expressed in this idiom. It is perhaps not sufficiently acknowledged that rational choice theory implies the agency of individuals in relation to rules and norms. In so far as such entities exist, rational individuals will orient to them calculatively and instrumentally, just as they orient to all other entities, including each other. They will take account of them and make use of them, to satisfy wants and achieve ends.

2 Those theorists with the greatest fondness for ontologies tend also to be fallibilists, but how ontologies are to be thought of as fallible remains unclear. Natural scientists can be more straightforward about their conventions and tactical commitments. The central dogma of molecular biology was the commitment of a status-secure specialty. And it was soon abandoned.

3 See Hogarth and Reder (1987), Kahneman *et al.* (1982), Lea *et al.* (1987), Mullen and Johnson (1990), Tversky (1969), Tversky and Kahneman (1981). Although the focus of the argument in this book is sociological, these mainly psychological studies are nonetheless valuable in showing the disciplinary tension between psychology and rational choice economics, in displaying the monumental empirical inadequacy of the latter and in thereby offering insight into the kind of entity rational choice theory is. Those who regard it as a catch-all sense-making system, such as Marxism was of old, have a point.

4 Social psychology is riven with controversies into which I have no desire to enter. Different perspectives, all of which may look interesting and valuable from the outside, quarrel with each other. All I want to assert, and it will be obvious from the text in any case, is that I see enormous merit in the old influence studies in this field, and indeed in other older 'scientific' approaches, notwithstanding that they are often rejected and intensely criticised by current practitioners.

5 Marwell and Ames (1981) is a study of great symbolic importance here. Some of the best general insights into the limitations of theories that postulate an independent individual come from rational choice theorists themselves; for

example, Elster (1989), Hardin (1995). See also Turner (1991).

6 There is a great deal of muddle in this area because it is thought that individuals must aquire knowledge either from interaction with the world or interaction with others. The correct picture is of person–person–object interaction. See Kuhn (1977, pp. 307–19) on scientific training, and Trevarthen (1988) on 'secondary-intersubjectivity' in the learning of extremely young children, for two interestingly different descriptions of this.

7 The locus classicus for debates about rules is Wittgenstein (1968), who is interpreted in a collectivist sense by Kripke (1982), and Bloor (1997). Rules as ongoing collective accomplishments and the fundamental deficiencies of individualistic accounts of them are discussed again in Chapter 8, and the self-referring character of knowledge of rules is returned to in Chapter 9.

8 An extended criticism of this aspect of the thought of Bourdieu and Giddens, and indeed of this form of thought wherever it appears, is given in Turner (1994). But Turner is even more of an individualist than they, and dismisses 'habitus' and 'structure' as referring to imaginary unitary objects when all that is actually there to be referred to is a myriad of individual habits. Using the traditional individual–society frame, Turner never considers the third possibility here, that social practices are neither unitary objects nor individual habits but collective accomplishments.

9 See Thaler (1991) and Lane (1991) for economics, and Green and Shapiro (1994) for political science. This last has elicited a number of responses, from both critics and defenders of the theory, gathered together in Friedman (1996). The collection is an invaluable compilation of evidence against rational choice, cited by its critics, and philosophical arguments on its behalf, assembled by its defenders.

10 Milgram's experiments have probably attracted more criticism and controversy than any other set of studies in the social sciences; see, for example, Milgram (1974), Miller (1986), Mixon (1989), Pigden and Gillet (1996), although there are many other equally relevant sources. An ethical ban now prevents work of this kind, although not assertions about what the original work did not imply, or about what anodyne interpretations ought now to be foisted upon it. The ethical ban raises fascinating and difficult issues. But the technical criticisms of Milgram are excessive, and the tendency to 'explain away' his results perverse. As Pleasants (1999) has shown, in an impressive defence of Milgram, his work and its results merit enormous respect, although of course no empirical findings, and no interpretations thereof, are beyond criticism. Some people, it would seem, simply cannot handle the results, and the implications they invite us to consider.

11 This is not to say that Becker (1970) is necessarily right on the relevant issues, but merely that his and Milgram's studies ought to have been linked together and the empirically well-grounded theories of the former used to generate possible interpretations of the equally well-grounded findings of the latter. Perhaps this has been done somewhere.

5

TRANSCENDING INDIVIDUALISM

Accountability and susceptibility

Human beings are not independent individuals; they are social creatures. More specifically, they are interdependent social agents, who profoundly affect each other as they interact. Individualism, and in particular rational choice individualism, is false. But if this is the case then the individualistic gloss that rational choice puts upon everyday voluntaristic discourse is called into question. If we are social agents then this discourse, with its references to rationality and free will, must be applicable to such agents and their actions. The objective of this chapter is to suggest, in a very rough and ready way, how it is so applied and to point to the interesting consequences of its being so applied.

To realise this objective it is necessary to move on from criticism of asocial individualism, and to reorder the evidence against it into a positive account of the nature of the sociability and interdependence of human beings. As such a positive account is developed, it ought to become clear how individuals' own self-descriptions as responsible agents fit with it, and what the cues are that prompt them to employ voluntaristic notions in those descriptions. However, only a stopgap account will be given here, to symbolise what could perhaps be constructed by those with the appropriate expertise. The intention will be to show that the substantial body of work on the sociability of human beings, and on how they treat each other as more than mere objects in instrumental calculation, could be used to specify a social agent capable both of intelligible communication and of collective instrumental action.[1] But the present discussion should not be mistaken for what it points toward.

First of all, then, let us consider social life as ethnomethodologists describe it. They think of collectives as so many competent members. Such members expect their routine encounters to be with other competent members – members who will give them intelligible accounts of what they have done, and are doing, using shared language and shared knowledge.[2] Ethnomethodological studies suggest that members' expectations of each other are related to rules. But it is not necessarily conformity to rules that is expected; it is rather accounts of actions that intelligibly relate them to rules, whether by counting them as applications of rules, or as deviations from them, or as whatever else an action may routinely be in relation to a rule (Heritage, 1984). More generally, members expect, not necessarily the standard story of why a course of action was taken, but some story constructed from the routinely available cultural resources and recognisable as a plausible story. In brief, the basic competence members presume in each other is that of *accountability*, of being able to give an intelligible account of what has been done. This basic mutual expectation informs communicative interaction, and propels it along as a series of matter-of-course exchanges, not as the calculated means to any particular end. The result of the interaction is that things unfold as retrospectively agreed understandings of what has just happened, using members' shared knowledge.

The merits of the overall picture of social process provided by ethnomethodologists need not concern us here. What is immediately interesting is their pinpointing of accountability as a taken-for-granted expectation between members, and the way that their case studies confirm both its importance and its ubiquity. Ethnomethodology, it would seem, may be done anywhere: mutual accountability appears to be a universal feature of the relationship between a human being and the fellow members with whom, always and everywhere, she is associated. In all social contexts, members continually provide each other with an intelligible commentary on what they are doing, utilising shared symbols, and knowledge with collectively recognised modes of application, as a matter of course.

Many ethnomethodologists appear to be averse to generalisation, and some of them might perhaps take exception to the account of the cross-cultural applicability of their ideas given above, but this is far from being the most radical generalisation of the significance of their work. Elsewhere, it has been treated as a contribution to the understanding of human beings as inherently communicative creatures. The psychologist Colwyn Trevarthen (1988, 1989; Trevarthen and Logotheti, 1987), for example, has suggested on the basis of cross-cultural studies of very young children that the general communicative competences described by ethnomethodologists are native endowments. Human beings are born communicators, who actively seek out the culturally specific symbolic and cognitive resources necessary to becoming actual communicators in specific settings. They actively turn themselves, that is, into the local variety of ordinary member. Accountability and other essential attributes of membership are not thrust upon new members or socialised into them, but are sought out and demanded of existing members by new arrivals, who from the start, with a vengeance it might almost be said, are in this sense active agents (Trevarthen, 1988, pp. 37–9).

Accountability might possibly be described as a characteristic of an individual member, but only of an individual-in-setting, not of an individual *per se*. Like status, or weight, accountability is a property *located* at a point in a system of relations but *constituted* by the system as a whole.[3] It emerges through social interactions that allow new arrivals access to shared language, knowledge and culture, and enable them to become the local variety of competent member. And it is kept in existence only through continuing social interactions, since the language, knowledge and culture essential to it are located in the collective and constantly being changed by the interacting agents of the collective. By no means is accountability a stable independent internal power.

How now does accountability relate to responsible agents, capable of rational conduct? It is necessary to ask again what rational conduct entails. The dictionary tells us that rational conduct may be conduct based on 'reason', which has not been altogether helpful, but it also tells us that rational conduct may be that which is found sensible and judicious. And this immediately suggests the relevance of the external judgements of fellow members, made by reference to shared ways of living, on the basis of accepted bodies of knowledge and culture. This conception of rational conduct is easy to exemplify, but is difficult to formulate in general terms. When reifications give rise to difficulty it is a useful strategy to move from noun to verb. What is it, not to be rational or possess rationality, but to rationalise? Perhaps the most important of the senses of this term is that of explaining *ex post facto* how what has been done was rational. To rationalise is to make an action intelligible as reasonable, sensible or judicious. If a responsible agent possesses rationality in this sense, she possesses the ability to give others intelligible, acceptable accounts of her (not necessarily acceptable) actions. If rationality is expected of her in this sense, then it is accountability that is expected. Members who align their relations with each other on the basis of this expectation will engage in communicative interaction and thereby sustain shared language, knowledge and culture. But when individualism cuts the links with others implied by accountability, and hypostasises rationality into an internal power of an independent individual, it forfeits its ability to grasp the nature of communicative interaction and to account for its products. It is then forced to take them as a mysterious 'given' backdrop to the calculative rationality that is its major concern. And this can sometimes lead on to a form of selective perception in which communicative interaction fails to appear altogether.

Members actively align and co-ordinate their accounts, and hence their language, knowledge and cognition, with those of others, in the course of communicative interaction. Of course, this alignment always involves more than 'mere talk'. It emerges from talking and doing, and involves the co-ordination and standardisation of practical actions. Agreement at the level of language requires and implies agreement at the level of practice, a co-ordinated understanding of what is being done as well as what is being said. The disposition to achieve such co-ordination is indeed normal and natural to human beings if work like that of Trevarthen is to be believed. And human beings acknowledge their accountability, and expect it of others as a matter of course, as part and parcel of the activity that secures and maintains co-ordination. It is important to recall previous discussions of this activity here, and particularly to keep in mind that it is never a matter merely of 'finding' existing knowledge, or shared understandings or meanings. The co-ordination implied by these terms has to arise out of interaction itself: it has to be collectively accomplished as ethnomethodologists tend to say. And as the co-ordination being spoken of is the condition of continuing mutual intelligibility, the interaction that secures it cannot be understood as a rational dialogue wherein mutual intelligibility had already been achieved and is no longer a problem. It is necessary here to understand the relevant interaction causally, and to recognise that members affect each other therein in a causal sense. Agents who are disposed to co-ordinate their understandings with others have to be agents who are affected by others.[4]

Mutual accountability implies co-ordinated understanding, which implies agents who affect each other. It implies, we might say, mutual *susceptibility*. To be capable, as a matter of course, of agreeing in their practice the members of collectives must be understood as mutually accountable and mutually susceptible. But it is important to recognise as well that the co-ordination that is actually achieved in specific collective settings may, and indeed invariably does, extend well beyond what is implied by reference to agreement in practice. Members may agree in how they do things and how they describe what they are doing, yet disagree about what specifically ought to be done. Or they may agree on what ought to be done, yet fail to implement it. Or again they may agree what ought to be done and manage to get it done. Success in this last sense implies co-ordinated collective instrumental action, a form of action that is necessary in all collectives, as we saw earlier, but one that involves much more than shared understandings and accountability. In order to solve this problem of collective action it is necessary to think of situations where satisfactory communication exists, and to consider our susceptibility to the evaluations which communications typically contain, and the effects they have upon us.

One particularly interesting account of the nature of mutual susceptibility is that of the sociologist Erving Goffman. Goffman used various images and theoretical vocabularies in attempts to throw light on social interaction, but his most widely known and perhaps most satisfactory account employs the concepts of *face* and *face-maintenance* (Goffman, 1967). On this account, participants in social interaction have an overriding concern with their face or standing in the eyes of others. They constantly assess how successfully they are keeping in face by monitoring the responses of others to what they do. They have regard to signs and signals of acceptance, recognition and deference, or, conversely, of rejection and disdain, and adjust their actions accordingly, although they may not themselves recognise that they are doing so. Thus, out of concern for face, individuals will act in ways that, rather than being rational expressions of their own fixed preferences, reflect the evaluations of others, and thus the preferences of others. But concern for face is itself far more than a mere individual preference: individuals are solicitous of the face of others and will act co-operatively and collectively to protect and repair it. Goffman's account of face is occasionally misunderstood as ironic commentary on the weaknesses or strange preferences of calculative individuals, but when systematically examined it proves wholly incompatible with an individualistic account of human behaviour.[5]

Like the ethnomethodologists, most micro-sociologists have been averse to generalisation, and Goffman was no exception. But a valuable systematisation of his ideas has nonetheless been provided by Thomas Scheff (1988). Scheff discerns a general theory implicit in Goffman that links actions to a universal 'deference-emotion system'. As an individual interacts, she monitors the evaluations, usually implicit, fed back to her in the communications of other people, and thereby the extent of the deference others extend to her. This feedback of deference moves the individual to and fro along a continuum of emotional states, from a state of pride, engendered by high levels of deference, to a state of shame, the product of loss of deference and negative evaluations. Since states of pride are desired and shame is avoided, the system will serve as a device whereby individual action is modulated by the evaluations of others implicit in their symbolic communications. Although the existence of the system is rarely acknowledged explicitly, and may indeed in some cultures be something never spoken of at all, it is nonetheless a cultural universal, operative everywhere. Indeed, just as Trevarthen naturalises ethnomethodology, so Scheff is not afraid to do the same for Goffman. The deference-emotion system is, he claims, a 'biosocial system that functions silently, continuously and virtually invisibly, occurring within and between members of a society' (Scheff, 1988, p. 405).

Scheff describes the general form of the deference-emotion system but, needless to say, all actual instances of the system will have characteristics specific to cultural context. Members will be differentially susceptible to those particular forms of communication originating from fellow members. But the form of the system will be much the same everywhere. It will be constituted of agents who, of their nature as it were, are both susceptible to the evaluations of others and disposed to offer such evaluations to others. These will be agents to whom verbal and symbolic communication is normal and natural, and on whom the evaluations implicit in such communication will have effects. Like accountability, susceptibility in the context of the system may be understood as an individual property, but only as a property of an individual-in-setting, not of an individual per se. And what is important is that it is a ubiquitous property; for that means that the members of any interacting collective will routinely affect each other through the mere fact of their interaction, and achieve in their collective instrumental action much of what they set value upon in their shared discourse.[6]

What, though, is the present relevance of the deference-emotion system? How is our mutual susceptibility to be related to the activities of responsible agents, capable of exercising free will and making choices? As we have noted in earlier chapters, this aspect of responsibility raises great difficulties: we have so far found no way of distinguishing free agents and chosen actions from agents and actions of other kinds. Consider, however, the overall picture of interacting human beings that has now emerged. The responsible agents referred to in everyday discourse are capable of rational conduct and of making choices: they are rational and have free will. The responsible agents who use that discourse are capable of making their actions mutually intelligible and of pressing each other into collective action: they are mutually accountable and mutually susceptible. But the two sets of agents just referred to are the same agents. And we have just equated the rationality of the former with the accountability of the latter. The direction in which the analogy points is accordingly unmistakable. It invites us to equate the free will of the former with the susceptibility of the latter: to have free will is to be susceptible.

How an action could have been otherwise

The hypotheses we have arrived at are these: our sense of the free will of an agent derives from her susceptibility to others, the kind of susceptibility implied in accounts of the deference-emotion system; our characterisation of an action as chosen identifies it as the kind of action that is open to modification through use of the system, that is, through symbolic communications and the evaluations they convey. Clearly, if these are correct hypotheses, then individualistic accounts of free will hypostasise features of social relations and social processes into fixed internal powers, just as similar accounts of rationality do. And a properly formulated conception of responsible agency can restore proper awareness of human sociability in both respects. However, the hypothesis is far from being clearly and obviously correct, and may even be found counter-intuitive. It remains to be shown that there are grounds for taking it seriously.

First of all, it is worth clarifying the hypothesis in a way that may lessen its counter-intuitive character. We have many sensible intuitions about will as an individual power. We imagine it allowing us to overcome physical adversities, or inner urges, or temptations hung before us by other people. It is easy to become directly cognisant of this power in operation – by holding a breath, for example, and introspecting for a while.[7] And it is routine to impute different amounts of this power to others, as when a group seeks to give up tobacco, and some succeed in overcoming their drug-addiction whilst others do not. But will thus experienced is not what is at issue here. Will thus experienced operates in the implementing of choices, not in the making of them. For all that will is routinely characterised as the power of choice, will as we experience it comes wholly *ex post facto* to choosing: it is our individual power to implement a decision against resistance, when we have 'made up our mind' as we say. It is tempting to imagine that vast reserves of will power in this sense make us less susceptible to others, and hence that susceptibility is a matter of lack of will; but this is not at all the case. The possession of a strong will does not imply lack of susceptibility to others: Shakespeare's Coriolanus dramatises the point beautifully. References to will-power and strength of will imply nothing about susceptibility, just as they imply nothing about the capacity to make choices and freedom of will. Nor do references to lack of choice or free will imply an overriding or suppression of will-power: the landing of an aircraft under the duress of hijackers, for example, may involve every last drop of a pilot's will-power. It is important to be clear that the hypothesis at issue here concerns, not will-power, but freedom of will. It is that freely willed or chosen actions, as identified in everyday discourse, are paradigmatically those of human beings in a normal state of susceptibility to others.

Let us reflect now on the empirical plausibility of this. We have remarked a number of times on the apparent lack of any empirical means of distinguishing chosen from caused actions. Actions may be rendered as chosen, according to the institution of responsible action, or as caused, according to the institution of causal connection, and no fact of the matter seems to show which institution is better employed. Certainly, there are no evident features of actions themselves, or their antecedents, to indicate whether they could or could not 'have been otherwise'. There is only one past. Whether or not it could have been otherwise it was not, and nothing empirical hangs upon the could have been that was not. Members can make out actions as chosen or caused *ex post facto* to suit their expedient ends, safe in the knowledge that nothing is going decisively to refute their favoured accounts of them. But at the same time it has always been clear that members do not regard the attribution of choice as wholly and legitimately an *ex post facto* activity. On the contrary, their presumption is that, in the normal way of things, something empirical, antecedent to actions, is relevant to their recognition as chosen, even if it is difficult to put a finger on what that empirical something is. Now we have a pointer to it: it is whatever indicates or implies that the action was performed by a normal, susceptible agent, and that it was accordingly an action possibly modifiable by symbolic intervention.

The thought that chosen actions are modifiable actions in this specific sense is certainly consistent with a good part of our everyday attribution of choice and causation. Causation may be attributed to courses of action precisely to indicate the futility of any attempt at symbolic intervention, as when the arachnophobe, or the vertigo afflicted, after some panic-stricken retreat, cites her condition to explain why 'there was nothing you could have said to make me act differently'. Conversely, the greater part of the 'chosen' activity of ordinary members is regarded as readily mod-ifiable through symbolic communication. The proposed walk easily adjusted to include a call at the shop (please, would you mind?), the cig-arette likely to be put out on request (there is a 'no smoking' sign over there!), and endless analogous cases illustrate the point. And between these two kinds of case is a continuum of instances that also seem to fit well enough. There are those obviously voluntary actions, for example, of which the agent may say: 'I'm sorry, I have no choice.' Here, we are likely to think, there is a choice, but only of costly alternatives. And the clear implication of this thought is that persuasion might just possibly succeed in modifying the action after all, but not easily.

What serves to persuade us, however, that an action is, or was, mod-ifiable, or that its performer is in a normal susceptible state? It is not, needless to say, that we recognise modifiability and susceptibility first and engage in symbolic communication second, but neither are those states or conditions mere rationalisations without an empirical basis. What happens is that we recognise the efficacy of symbolic communica-tion in modifying certain kinds or classes of actions, and we call further actions, recognised as of these kinds or classes, freely chosen actions. Often these actions will include all the routine actions of specific indi-viduals, which will also confirm us in our disposition to continue to treat those individuals as responsible agents. There is here a straightforward empirical basis for the attribution of choice to actions and free will/agency to their performers, but not one that identifies any common empirical characteristic shared by all such actions. To understand what is involved we have to think of life in a collective wherein members are constantly engaged in modulating each others' activity through commu-nicative interaction. The deference-emotion system will constantly be at work. And over time we can imagine terms, perhaps contrasting pairs like choice/causation, coming into use to record the efficacy of the system. As such terms come to be employed, they will lay down in the collective memory a record of two classes of action and agent. There may be very little in the way of empirical analogy to link the individual instances of these classes. Even so, the two classes may serve as the basis for ongoing classification independent of use of the deference-emotion system itself: new instances (actions or agents) may be classified on the basis of empirical analogy with particular existing instances within either class.

Notice that if the empirical basis of our attributions of choice has been adequately described here it immediately indicates the nature of the work that our contrasts of choice and causation do for us – their normal func-tion in our discourse as we might loosely say. The system of classifica-tions we are discussing serves to identify agents, actions or action-situations where activation of the deference-emotion system is or is not worthwhile, where the use of pressure or persuasion is judged (on an inductive basis) likely or unlikely to be attended by success. To this extent, the institution of responsible action and the institution of causal connection are not merely alternative sense-making systems for the *ex post facto* rationalisation of action. They are involved in the constitution of important parts of members' stock of knowledge. They facilitate the construction of theories with which to predict when and where in the future there will be pragmatic value in orienting to others through the medium of communicative interaction. In particular, they generate knowledge of how far agents may be treated as occupants of social statuses, sensitive to the expectations thereby directed toward them, capable of acknowledging responsibilities and exercising rights. Accountability and susceptibility are indeed just the basic 'states' essential to all status attributions, which is one reason, of course, for the strong back-pressure noted in Chapter 1 from status allocation processes to the attributions of state that should precede and justify them.[8]

It might be asked, in implied criticism of this hypothesis, why members do not explicitly recognise the empirical considerations that allegedly prompt them to attribute rationality and free will. There are, indeed, interesting methodological issues latent here. Ordinary members of society are not countless thousands of rational choice theorists, all profoundly mistaken about their own nature and behaviour as social agents, all getting by somehow nonetheless; but, equally, they are not proponents of the account advanced here. In proposing that account there is the implication that everyday activity may be described better from the outside than by those who enact it – better, that is, for some purposes. This is indeed so; it is true of all social practices that for some purposes there are better descriptions of them than those initially used by members themselves. Indeed, members routinely recognise as much and take it as a matter of course that it is legitimate to challenge each others' accounts.[9] The particular case in point here, however, is of special theoretical interest. Members' reflections on their own practices tend almost invariably to reify and render in an individualistic idiom much of what is most interesting sociologically about those practices.

In all cultures there are classifications the final empirical basis for the use of which lies not in the intrinsic properties of things considered in isolation but rather in how things are related to or affected by other things. Everyday examples are fuels, foods and medicines. More interesting sociologically perhaps are monies, permits and contracts. Members often have difficulty when they reflect on the basis of their own use of these classifications, and are puzzled by what inspires it. A common device is to take such classifications as referring to some invisible intrinsic characteristic – whether a propensity, an inner structure, a hidden object or an essence – and to rationalise usage on that basis. Thus, the potency of monetary tokens may get rendered by reference to what is intrinsic to their metal, or susceptibility in the context of the deference-emotion system by reference to invisible intrinsic characteristics like the power of choice. Such an understanding may be perfectly compatible with skilled use of the relevant notions as part and parcel of everyday activity, but it is nonetheless a potential disadvantage that it fails to grasp the actual basis of that activity. There is no need for an external observer to shrink from claiming a better understanding.

Many social theorists, rather than examining everyday voluntarism as social action, emulate it themselves, borrow its key concepts, and often intensify its tendencies to essentialism and individualism. This occurs because the distinction between the caused behaviour and the voluntary action of human beings is regarded as of very great importance in marking the special standing of individual persons as active powers or agents. The distinction reflects and reinforces the metaphysical distinction between actions that could have been otherwise and behaviours that could not. In contrast, the present approach weakens this distinction. Admittedly, it does point to an empirically viable way of distinguishing 'chosen' and 'caused' actions, as metaphysical accounts of the distinction do not, but it is a way that is perfectly consistent with a causal account of 'what could have been otherwise'. Indeed, it is even compatible with determinism, although it does not entail it. The conventional contrast between the chosen and the caused can be rendered as a contrast of two classes of caused actions on the present account, which account can be thought of as a sociological version of compatibilism.

For the complete determinist all events, and hence all actions, unfold in a 'could not have been otherwise' way, according to what causes move them. But this need not prevent her acknowledging that a course of action which is ongoing in a 'could not be otherwise' way, because of the operation of a set of constantly operating causes, might nonetheless be modified and continue otherwise if an *additional* cause is brought to impinge upon it. And intervention with persuasive communication may count as just such an additional cause, a cause which, if it leads to a variation in the ongoing course of action, leads to a variation which itself 'could not have been otherwise'. Thus, from a deterministic point of view the contrast of 'chosen' and 'caused' behaviour may correlate not with the presence or absence of causation, but with the degree of resistance of a caused process to variation. Consider how a leaf falls from a tree, and how a branch falls. Both are conventionally accounted as caused movements, but the slightest breath of wind will cause variation in the path of the leaf whilst leaving the branch moving pretty well as before. It is the kind of difference between the leaf and the branch that deployment of the institutions of free will and causation often stresses.

For all that a different account is offered here, it has to be acknowledged that empirical insight may occasionally be derived from current theoretical discussions of chosen actions and the way that they 'could have been otherwise'. In order to do so it is only necessary to read 'could have been otherwise' as shorthand for 'could have been otherwise if symbolic intervention had occurred'. At the same time, of course, much is lost in this 'shorthand'. The whole basis of the collective agency of human beings is thereby reified into an individual power, the utterances through which people affect each other are made visible as celebrations of individual autonomy, and the activities that give the most profound expression to our sociability become those wherein it is least in evidence.[10]

The status of the responsible agent

We now have the outlines of a sociological theory that will account for those crucial human activities previously shown to be beyond the grasp of individualism. This theory identifies human beings as complex active creatures, who are, nonetheless, social creatures. That they are social creatures is manifest in their interaction. First, they act toward each other as agents capable of giving an intelligible account of what they are doing and why; and often this is much the same thing as stating why what they are doing is right and justified. *Accountability* is required if agents are to co-ordinate their understandings, sustain a shared sense of what they are likely to do in the future and hold each other to account for the mutually recognised outcomes of what they have done in the past. Secondly, they act toward each other as agents sensitive to symbolically conveyed evaluations of their actions and potentially responsive to them. *Susceptibility* in this sense is necessary for the co-ordination of actions and their coherent ordering around collectively agreed goals. Clearly, susceptibility implies intelligibility, which implies accountability. Accountability and susceptibility are two closely intertwined components of responsibility, and together constitute a necessary basis for social interaction. Social life as we know it requires responsible agents who may be held accountable, and to whom it makes a difference that they have been so held. Of course, there are human beings who fall short of what is required. And there are countless occassions when normal responsible agents fall short of what is necessary in the way of accountability or susceptibility. Such failures are sometimes referred to as lapses from rationality or, where chronic, as signs of loss of reason or of impaired agency, but whilst these may be useful labels for many practical purposes the error involved in reifying rationality and agency into independent internal states has already been pointed out.

It is useful to remember here that no agent is ever regarded as the source of a pure stream of responsible actions. Typically, her actions will be described by means of the institution of responsible action and the institution of causal connection deployed together. Those of her actions that involve choice and those that do not will be distinguished pragmatically, and in so far as there is a consensus on the distinction it will always be a contestable one. This must be so; for there is no radical discontinuity in the actions an individual produces – only a continuum from those easily modified by symbolic intervention to those less so. For all that 'choice' documents susceptibility, the distinction between what is chosen and what is caused may be drawn very differently in different contexts and may be a matter of continual controversy in any or all of them. A sociology of 'choice' and 'causation' is not precluded by the position set out here. In so far as there is a settled form to the distinction drawn between them in any specific context, it will have the character of a convention therein, and represent, as it were, the agreed policy of members with regard to how they treat each other.

We can usefully think here of the responsible agent as the occupant of a social status, at once the most rudimentary and the most important of all social statuses. Accountability and susceptibility, albeit differently defined in different contexts, are the basic, ubiquitously encountered mutual expectations of occupants of the status. Specific deficiencies of accountability and susceptibility have the character of temporary failings in role performance, often accounted the consequences of causation overriding rationality or will. Chronic deficiencies may on occasion be taken as indications that the status is incorrectly imputed and hence as the pretext for its withdrawal. With complete withdrawal of the status, of course, the individual will no longer be held accountable/responsible and no longer evaluated via the deference-emotion system. Nor will she be able to hold others to account, or evaluate their conduct as before, or wield any analogous social powers or have any other rights associated with responsible agents. Human beings cannot function in a status, even if they have all the requisite individual competences, unless others permit them to. Status involves the 'collective intentional imposition of function on entities that cannot perform those functions without that imposition', and that they cannot do so is because 'we do not allow people to perform the function . . . unless they have been *authorized*' (Searle, 1994, p. 41).

An interesting general line of thought can emerge from regarding responsible agents as acting in mutually defined statuses in this way. If interaction of the simplest kind involves treating the other as possessed of a status, then even the simplest imaginable forms of bounded interactions, involving very small wholly undifferentiated groups of human beings, will have the character of social systems. In the simplest case, the system will involve just one status, the responsible agent, and the status order will define a single institution, the institution of responsible action. It will be clear how in this very simple case the systemic element is not external to the interaction but a feature of it. The institutional order is a product of interaction between members who know each other to be responsible agents. But having noted how this is the case in the simplest instance it is then possible to understand how it may be the case in any instance. The systemic features of the complex institutionally differentiated societies in which we actually live, with their elaborate allocations of responsibilities to many statuses, and the endless contestation of them, can be seen also to be the product of interaction, between members who know each other as having these various statuses.

When members interact in this way they do so through the medium of a voluntaristic discourse that is both a means of explicit communication and a series of speech acts with (non-rational) causal power. The causal power of their communicative interaction is indeed of crucial importance.[11] It may imply a lack of individual agency, but by way of compensation it engenders collective agency, such as is essential to the constitution of institutional order. Recall how economists, rational choice theorists and other believers in the autonomous powers of an individual reason typically begin their work by presuming a given order of statuses, rules and institutions, within which calculative action takes place. To have a genuine social theory, that given order is something that they must explain, and yet it is inexplicable as the creation of asocial rational individuals. Such individuals would leave everyone else to make the ordered society in which they lived, and no such society (such as everywhere exists) would be engendered. This is the problem that has plagued individualist theorists since the time of Hobbes, and there is a certain pathos in the recurrent efforts they have made to solve it. Bravely disregarding their own postulates, they have persisted in trying to show how independent individuals will act non-independently and self-regarding individuals altruistically, but to no avail.

There is no way that recourse to an autonomous reason will ever solve this problem, as the history of attempts to do so clearly shows. What will solve it is susceptibility and causation. Impossible to enact directly, the required collective action may nonetheless be induced indirectly by agents who are causally affected by each other. Indeed, being such agents, human beings actually solve the problem as a matter of course, with consummate ease, in the course of a communicative interaction that is as normal and natural to them as breathing. In breathing forth evaluations of the actions of others they call forth from them the requisite collective action, otherwise so difficult to produce; and in response to evaluations breathed forth by others they are moved to such action themselves. Thus, mutual susceptibility, liable to be scorned as human weakness in individualist social theories (and in much associated moral philosophy) stands revealed in this account as the distinctive strength of the species and the basis of its finest accomplishments. Most of the order in our social and mental life is sustained, in the present picture, by mutually susceptible responsible agents who press each other to do what is necessary to create it, continue it and change it. Communicating and evaluating, learning and suffering, in the course of their social interaction, their collective accomplishment far transcends anything that could be hoped for from autonomous individuals. It is this accomplishment which makes groups and collectives, offices and hierarchies, institutions and organisations recognisable as features of the landscape in which we live our social lives, and hence as loci of responsibility and accountability in their own right. In this way the full expression of the institution of responsible action as we know it becomes possible, and the complex and elaborate systems of practice we recognise as those societies in which we presently live. The simple institution allows the elaboration of the larger society: the larger society is the simple institution elaborated. And voluntaristic discourse is the medium through which all this is achieved and sustained, the characteristic form of communication in which the inherent sociability of human beings is so potently expressed.

Notes

1 Some proponents of the positions recommended here may very well take a negative view of the overall argument of this book and the use it makes of their work. This would not, needless to say, make the work any the less interesting or relevant.

2 The following discussion will be relaxed about the use of terms like 'knowledge', 'understanding', 'cognition' and so forth, even though exception could be taken to such invocations of inner states and invisible theoretical entities. Even ethnomethodologists have been known to use such terms.

3 It is interesting to reflect on the concept of 'weight' (as opposed to 'mass'), since it is typical of many concepts with delocalised and relational referents in routine use in the natural sciences. These are concepts that create problems for some of the stereotypes of concepts of nature diffused through the social sciences.

4 It is necessary to move away from ethnomethodology at this point because it never uses the institution of causal connection in accounting for human actions and most of its practitioners seem deeply averse to doing so. The aversion, which seems to be widespread amongst micro-sociologists as well, sometimes results in accounts imbued with an oddly individualistic and rationalistic flavour through metaphorical use of terms like 'negotiation', 'work', 'accomplishment' and so forth.

5 Barnes (1995, Chapter 3) gives a detailed argument for the 'irreducibility' of Goffman's kind of sociology to individualism, and against theorists like Coleman (1990) and Heckathorn (1989), who have tried to incorporate 'social pressure' into a rational choice framework.

6 Some detailed suggestions concerning how collective instrumental action emerges from communicative interaction, and what conditions and circumstances favour this, are offered in Barnes (1995, pp. 83–5). The problem is one of very great theoretical interest but the details are best omitted here.

7 There are good grounds for the taboo enforced against introspectively based knowledge-claims. But it can be interesting to break taboos occasionally, if only to remind ourselves of why they are there. Take a breath and hold it for as long as possible. At the end of the procedure there will be an individual experience to describe. Something is there inciting one to breathe: partly it is pain but it may be more than that – maybe it is something causal. Against it, something is inhibiting breath. The something seems to be associated with thinking; intense concentration seems to be necessary. And the something seems to have odd side-effects, tensing irrelevant muscles, inducing peculiar movements and facial expressions. Maybe this something is will-power. Consider, however, the initial decision to hold the breath. Intuitive awareness of the use of will-power only arises after that decision, in the course of imple-

menting it. In general, will-power is introspectively experienced as the power that brings about the implementation of an action, not as the power that decides to do it. We could ask if there is a second will with the power to make decisions, lying behind a first will that has the power to implement them. But we have no intuitive awareness of this second will, as we may conceivably have of the first. Introspection on mere decision-making yields us little or nothing. Nonetheless, if we seek knowingly to influence another person into deciding something in a certain way, we treat them as having free will in the making of the decision, as a matter of courtesy. The crucial etiquette of free will and choice is never more in evidence than at such times.

8 Strictly speaking, there will be a set of status attributions that do not demand these things; for human beings always count as something, and there is always a residual category.

9 Some theorists are deeply devoted to the impossible task of sustaining members' accounts of their own practices as the only acceptable ones. The task is impossible because practices are joint accomplishments and to sustain the account of one participant in the joint enterprise may inevitably require rejecting that of another. The rejection of 'external' accounts of practices is currently legitimated by spurious arguments that imply the rejection of members' own accounts as well.

10 Social theorists, from Kant, through Marx and Durkheim, to Habermas, have always been moralists, and moralists act upon others precisely through symbolic communication. Is it a coincidence that just this is rendered invisible in the shorthand formulation? Or has there been a subconscious unwillingness to recognise communication as the engagement of myriads of wills to power, including their own?

11 It is true that other social theorists, notably Jürgen Habermas, have ceased to focus theory on the individual human subject, and stressed the importance of the communication between persons, yet, despite that, have not moved to a causal mode of analysis. Habermas has spoken instead of communication that is based on propositions and that implies a commitment to rational argument as the appropriate means of evaluating propositions as truth claims. In truth, however, this kind of theory is but the last redoubt of individualism. Its understanding of communication as propositional presumes a finished language of determinate meanings available to the individual, and completely ignores the need for language to be sustained as a shared communication system wherein the actual use of terms is kept, somehow or other, tolerably well aligned and co-ordinated. This is yet again to ignore what independent agents cannot do and what mutually susceptible, co-ordination-seeking social agents are needed to do in and through their communicative interaction. Through treating communication as propositional, this theory passes over the fact that communications are not abstractions, but actual occurrences, with particular sources, expressed in particular styles, with all kinds of contingent accompaniments, in particular contexts, and that it is as such occurrences and not as abstractions that they affect their recipients. The point receives further discussion in Chapter 8.

PART 2

SPECULATIONS AND EVALUATIONS

Voluntaristic notions do work for individual human beings in the course of their social interactions. But to understand what work they do, and how, it is necessary to understand something of the human beings who deploy them. If human beings are modelled as interdependent social agents, then a very different conception of what underpins the form of voluntaristic discourse emerges from that implied if human beings are modelled as independent rational individuals. In the first part of this book the case was made for accepting the former model, and rejecting the latter. The first model, needless to say, remains an idealisation, like the second, and inadequate to that extent, like the second. But the suggestion is that it is nonetheless a satisfactory idealisation – that although wrong in the way that the second model has always known itself to be wrong, it is right in the way that the second model has tried and failed to be right. As such, it is recommended as a replacement for the individualistic model; and in this part of the book its possible utility in that role is explored. It is asked how far a picture of human beings as responsible agents, affecting each other through the medium of a voluntaristic discourse, can assist our efforts to understand social life on the large scale.

Since a great deal has been said about individualistic rational choice perspectives in the foregoing, the emphasis will now be placed on more discursive strands of social theory, and particularly on theories used in macro-sociology, many of which currently give great prominence to the notion of individual agency and to the supposedly increased importance of individual choice in the context of modern differentiated societies. Chapter 6 deals directly with these macro-sociological theories. It is critical of this body of theory, first for so frequently proceeding without even a rudimentary model or conception of individual human beings, and secondly, when it does make use of such conceptions, for misusing them. It is particularly critical of selective references to active agents, in narratives of social order and social change with much of the teleological character of myth – narratives less concerned with naturalistic adequacy than with reinforcing particular evaluative visions of life in our currently highly differentiated societies. At the same time there is a positive dimension to the argument. It is shown that a conception of human beings as social creatures could be the basis of a viable macro-sociology, and that it could even assist theorists in their traditional project of understanding the great ongoing secular trends of social change. In particular, it is suggested that *consistent* acknowledgement of the collective agency of persons in relation to rules and norms – its acknowledgement as something possessed by human beings everywhere and at all times as an essential element of their nature as social creatures – would advance understanding in this context.

Chapter 7 broadens the discussion by reflecting on the rise of the new human biotechnology, an area that, as well as being of considerable substantive interest, is formally intriguing because it can bring causal and voluntaristic accounts of human behaviour into confrontation with one another. The main concern of the chapter is to show through examples how causal accounts deriving from biological naturalistic theories are perfectly compatible with members' own accounts of each other as free agents and of their actions as chosen ones. If references to choice and so forth are references to the accountability and susceptibility of social agents and the degree to which their actions might be modifiable in social interaction, then there is no clash with accounts that relate the same actions to causal antecedents. It is worth adding that, if the argument of this chapter is correct, it is not just sociologists and social theorists who fail to understand what is going on here but biologists and geneticists as well.

There is more to be said of these two chapters, and the criticism they offer to the main body of macro-sociological theory. It is worth noting in passing how, in focusing first on social differentiation and then on technological innovation, they address the two secular trends commonly cited by theorists as both the major components and the mainsprings of social change, and thereby engage with the key substantive interests of macro-sociology. But of deeper interest here are the apparently conflicting theoretical orientations of the two chapters. The first chapter accepts that there is a sense in which it is legitimate to speak of the agency or activity of human beings in relation to the rules and norms which some theorists are inclined to cite as explanations or even determinants of their actions. The second chapter acknowledges the existence of causal, 'biological' antecedents of human behaviour, and even agrees that they could conceivably feature in wholly causal and fully sufficient explanations of voluntary actions. Loosely put, to understand how causation can be defended against citations of agency, but agency defended against alleged determination by rules, is to understand the form of the compatibilism advocated in this book, and much of its sociological import.

The third chapter of the section considers the role of a naturalistic sociology in debates that explicitly address moral and ethical issues. Debates of this kind, about the nature of moral action and the possibility of a good society, run through the whole of social theory but are recognised as the central concerns of political theory and moral and political philosophy. In these fields, the autonomous rational individual has long featured as a regulatory ideal. But recently, particularly in the familiar context of the continuing liberal/communitarian debates, more and more theorists have accepted that human beings are irreducibly social agents, and have attempted to draw out the moral and ethical implications of what for them is this new perspective. What is suggested here is that the move to social agency has usually been too timid, and does not represent a genuine renunciation of the earlier individualistic view. Indeed the tendency has been to regard human beings, not as accountable and susceptible social agents, but as independent rational individuals encumbered with social selves. In particular, human beings have been thought to encounter moral rules and ethical standards as entities with well-defined implications that the reason of the individual can grasp; whereas if the argument given here is correct they can only relate to rules and standards collectively. To understand our relationship to rules and standards in this alternative way, it is suggested, permits some of the more strongly contested issues in the liberal/communitarian debates to be seen in a new light.

In the concluding chapter of the section, which also serves as the conclusion of the book as a whole, renewed consideration is given to the thought that human beings are interdependent agents who orient to each other as occupants of independent statuses. After some further analysis of the relationship between the individual human being and the status she occupies, the implications of this thought at the macro-level are addressed. Among other things, they hint at a possible solution to the problem of relating 'structure' and 'agency' that has long been of absorbing interest to sociological theorists.

6

'AGENCY' AND 'RESPONSIBILITY' IN SOCIOLOGICAL THEORY

A glance back to Weberian sociology

Sociologists and economists have long differed in their basic approaches to the study of social order. Economists have built macro-theories from a model of the individual human being as an independent, rational calculator. Sociologists have rightly refused to accept such a model, but more contentiously some of them have declined to employ any model of the human being at all in the development of macro-theories. They have addressed macro-patterns directly, without regard to the individuals who have engendered them, rather as physiologists initially addressed macro-features of the human body without regard to the nature of the cells involved. On this basis they have produced insightful accounts of modern societies as systems of interdependent social institutions, and offered a vision of institutional differentiation leading to more and more complex societies over time, rather as differentiation has led to more and more complex biological organisms evolving over time. Even today, when reservations are routinely entered against these holistic visions of classical macro-sociology, their continuing value merits acknowledgement.

There is no doubt that macro-sociology can make headway without any elaborated model of the nature of individual human beings. It evidently has done so. Nonetheless, it would have proceeded still better with an adequate model – a model that systematised and made explicit the intuition that human beings are social agents.[1] Sociological theory needs to be relentless in its insistence on the intrinsic sociability of human beings. Explicit recognition of that sociability can both offer positive guidance to macro-theory and protect it against inadvertent lapses into individualism. A good way of developing this point is to give brief attention to the macro-sociology of Max Weber; for Weber, great sociologist though he was, took little interest in the empirical characteristics of human beings and was content to regard them as suppliers of all the various kinds of actions he identified and classified, and enactors of the many institutions he catalogued and described. If anything, Weber tended a little too much toward individualism in his thinking about human beings, as is particularly evident in two of the most important areas of his work – his account of status and class, and his discussion of bureaucracy and administration. It is interesting to revisit this work possessed of a model of human beings as responsible agents, in the sense developed in the first part of this book.

Weber says somewhere that throughout history societies were predominantly ordered on the basis of status. Only in the unique conditions of the market capitalism of the last two centuries has class become more important and true 'class societies' replaced earlier 'status societies' (Weber, 1968, pp. 302–7). This is a profound insight that is very nearly right. Only in relation to a couple of centuries in thousands of years is it mistaken. The nature of the mistake, however, is extremely interesting. Status groups are constituted of agents who know each other as members and who are able to generate instrumentally oriented collective action through communicative interaction with each other. They were indeed long the basic constituents of social order, as Weber states. But classes, as defined by Weber, are aggregates of individual persons who have similar economic opportunities by virtue of being in similar 'class situations': such individuals need not know each other, or of each other, but they may nonetheless act alike through making independent rational calculations on the basis of similar economic interests. It is in terms of calculations of this kind that the orderly stratification of 'class societies' is reckoned to be produced, and their stability understood. Weber is incorrect here and importantly so. Separately calculated rational actions cannot be genuine collective actions, and only genuine collective actions will keep the internal and external boundaries of macro-society constituted, since these boundaries are collective goods not individual ones. Neither these boundaries, nor indeed any fundamental feature of social order, can be based upon class relations in the way that Weber implies. To look away from status toward class, and hence (on Weber's definition of 'class') from groups to aggregates, connections to categories, memberships to similarities, is to cease to attend to the true basis of macro-social order, and to the inherent sociability of the persons who constitute it.

Weber's mistake has had unfortunate consequences in a long tradition of sociological studies of class and class structure, wherein it has incorrectly been presumed that individuals may be moved by the collective interests associated with class position to undertake significant kinds of social action. Theorists have been slow, and often deeply reluctant, to take full account of how most instances of supposed 'class action' are actually products of the collective agency of status groups or of localised interacting communities, even though this has long been evident from the work of historical sociologists.[2] And even today, for various complex reasons, there remain enclaves of research concerned with 'class analysis' that perpetuate the error, and only avoid the associated problems through lax definitions that conflate the notions of 'class' and 'status' that

Weber rightly distinguished. Indeed there has long been great confusion in the use of 'class' and 'status' in macro-sociology, as John Scott (1996) among others has documented.[3]

Weber himself, of course, was aware of the fundamental difference between 'class situation' and 'status situation', and that class, unlike status, would only become a significant basis for social action in particular conditions. He spoke of 'social classes' as sets of class situations between which mobility was easy and frequent, and conjectured (on grounds that he never properly clarified) that stratification in modern societies might be understood in terms of such classes. But it is clear that he continued to think of class action as an aggregate of individually rational actions resulting from the coincidence of individual interests. Only quite recently has a different approach emerged in the context of Weberian sociology, in the shape of Randall Collins' observation that 'Status group organisation is the natural form in which economic interests can act socially' (1986, p. 129), and an account of the status group as an economically oriented unit peculiarly well-suited to the generation of collective action (Barnes, 1992, 1995).

A particularly interesting footnote to Weber-inspired treatments of modern societies as class societies is provided by the work of Ulrich Beck (1988). Beck rightly points out that many of the orderings of so-called class societies have in truth been status-based orderings that developed in antecedent, 'pre-modern', 'traditional' societies, or even earlier. He claims that these status arrangements are now eroding, in a process of 'detraditionalisation', and that this places increased demands on the individual, who is left to face the rigours of the labour market and the consumer economy without the support of the old status order. There are obvious limitations to this account,[4] but much of what it has to say about status rings true. What Beck may actually be sensitive to, however, is not the erosion of status *per se*, but the decline of the old status order in the face of a newly arising one. After all, work itself continues to be strongly structured by status particularism in modern industrial societies (Granovetter, 1974; Collins, 1979), and consumption is intimately related to the signification of group membership and the expression of status claims. What Beck rightly stresses is that even in so-called class societies individuals always lived their lives as responsible social agents. What he does not draw attention to is that this is how people continue to be. When this is recognised the question is no longer what happens when independent individuals become uncoupled from the status order: it is rather in what way responsible agents are currently reconstituting status relations, in societies which continue to be ordered on the basis of status as they have been since time immemorial.

Implicit in these remarks, of course, is a general view of how best to advance the project of macro-sociology. Its attention should focus upon status as the key to an understanding of macro-order, and particularly perhaps upon the boundaries between status groups and the social relationships of members within and across those boundaries. Indeed the study of status and status-maintenance in the macro-context ought to be recognised as the appropriate parallel to the study of face and face-maintenance in the micro-context, in any sociology that seeks to embody proper recognition of the inherent sociability of human beings.[5] For all its importance, however, this suggestion can be no more than an aside in the context of this book, and it scarcely counts as a relevant reflection on Weber that he himself did not propose it.

What is relevant is that there is an unresolved tension in Weber between his accounts of 'class' and 'status' that he might perhaps have recognised. As Weber chooses to define the concept, 'class' refers to an objectively apparent individual property, and explanation by reference to class sits well with individualism, especially rational choice individualism. His notion of 'status' is fundamentally different. Statuses are collectively constituted and recognised by interacting memberships, and explanations that refer to status sit well with accounts of members as social agents. Thus, Weber's notions of 'class' and 'status' evoke two fundamentally opposed conceptions of the nature of individuals, and only a theorist with little interest in human beings at that level would with equanimity regard them as alternative foundations of social order as he does. There is in Weber a truly brilliant analysis of status, status groups and the competition between those groups, which is of fundamental sociological importance and offers insight into the understanding of macrophenomena in all societies. But there is not the kind of engagement with what moves individual actions in those groups that would have permitted Weber to display this fundamental importance, and to recognise the way that this work on status was actually incompatible with his own work on class. In this way Weber's work is diminished even as macrosociology by its lack of genuine concern with individual human beings and of any plausible model of them as actors.

There is a further disadvantage associated with Weber's exclusive focus on macro-phenomena. Because he cleaves to no developed model of what moves individual social actors his work is easily assimilated into ordinary informal modes of thinking about action, and provides no basis for a challenge to them or a dialectical engagement with them. Yet we can scarcely rest content with our informal modes of thought here, if only because they are themselves internally conflicting and inadequately rationalised. Indeed, informal reflection is like the thought of the social sciences in its equivocation between a conception of human beings as social agents and one that renders them as independent individuals. The tendency to an individualistic conception is particularly hard to resist when we reflect on economic and administrative activity. Financial and bureaucratic transactions bring us into contact with the two great classes of stranger-members of modern societies. Our paradigms of relationships with these members are precisely of wholly impersonal, mechanical transactions: the fixed-price purchase over a counter; the dessicated exchanges, with purely formal courtesies, between member and official, perhaps through a sheet of unbreakable glass. It is easy to perceive the other in relationships of this kind as a mere instrument, operating purely calculatively, and coupled purely by self-interest to some distant impersonal power. And indeed, in our folk theories, such an other is often rendered as the paid instrument of external powers, powers that may be referred to as 'them' or 'the system', and that may be addressed, much as natural powers and forces are, as fixed externalities to be taken account of and adjusted to.

Weber's theoretical sociology is unfortunately close to this form of reflection, and it is easy to read his account of rational instrumental action and forget that it is social action at all. This is particularly the case when rational action in bureaucracies is discussed. Weber appears to describe a completely atomised system devoid of social relations altogether, and constituted entirely of independently calculated actions. His ideal type of the rational impersonal bureaucrat is very close to the everyday stereotype of the stranger-member. And his account of a hierarchy in which individuals are decoupled from social relations in order to operate as part of a 'reliable mechanism',[6] a vast human machine or instrument, corresponds nicely to everyday ideas of 'the system'. Weber's theory even includes an analogue of the threat posed by 'the system'. His ideal type of bureaucracy not only operates rationally, instrumentally and impersonally internally, it enforces this mode of operation externally upon whatever activities it seeks to subject to an 'orderly domination'. Bureaucracy is not merely 'rational', but a source of societal rationalisation: it codifies and systematises the responsibilities it grasps to itself and in that form is able to impose them on others and control them, thereby inspiring a secular trend to more reliable and predictable patterns of activity.

It is interesting to notice how, over time, sociological research has identified more and more difficulties for the individualistic elements of Weber's account. It has demonstrated the need for power and discretion to reside at every level of the hierarchy, to overcome information bottlenecks, to deal with the 'unforeseen circumstances' that are actually normal circumstances in all bureaucracies, and to carry out the 'staff' functions that Weber neglects as well as the 'line' functions he highlights. The need for discretion in the interpretation and application of supposedly 'impersonal' rules is especially obvious in work of this kind. It makes it clear as well that bureaucrats have the capacity to act instrumentally for their own collective good as bureaucrats, a capacity strikingly documented in study after study of 'bureaucratic politics'. And it is evident from the same studies that bureaucratic and administrative organisations are not so much mechanisms as cultures, which opens the way to seeing them not only as instruments of rationalisation but as targets of it. In general, empirical accounts of bureaucratic administration are consistent with its being the accomplishment of responsible agents, not isolated individuals (Barnes, 1995).

Agency as a component of dualist myth

Whilst empirical sociological research on bureaucracy has pointed to the need to mitigate the individualism of Weber's account, there is, notwithstanding, work that goes the other way and intensifies it. Thus, the incurably dualist thought-style of Jürgen Habermas leads him to exaggerate precisely what is most unsatisfactory in Weber. In *The Theory of Communicative Action* (1984, 1987), instrumentally oriented (purposive-rational) action ceases to be social action altogether, and the contrast between *non-social* action of this kind and social action is given a decisive importance. Habermas assumes not just that agents may act 'non-socially' but that entire systems of instrumental (purposive-rational) action can be sustained as non-social patterns of task performance, ordered and controlled impersonally and externally. He fails to acknowledge the necessity, *everywhere*, of that continuing co-ordination of instrumental actions, and continuing stabilisation of the understandings that inform such actions, that is only possible for interacting responsible agents. Although he stresses the importance of what he calls communicative action in everyday life, he does not recognise it as a necessary feature of the settings of all organised activities without exception. Instead he identifies the economy and the polity as differentiated systems wherein human actions are to be understood and explained in quite different ways from those appropriate to the social actions that constitute the 'lifeworld'.[7]

Habermas' famous contrast of 'system' and 'lifeworld' is, of course, the basis of a powerful political vision. 'System' menaces 'lifeworld'. In the form of ever-increasing instrumental control and regulation by administrators and technical professionals, it threatens to encroach on a 'lifeworld sphere' currently the realm of communicative action and human agency, and to 'colonise' it. This theory has obvious resonances with the everyday stereotype of 'the system' that presses upon everyday life from without. And, like much sociological theory, its mythical form and implicit moral message are congruent with those of the everyday stereotype: 'system'/'power' opposes 'lifeworld'/'agency'; so that 'system' is easily cast as villain, and 'lifeworld' as hero, in a drama of conflict.[8] It is indeed an unwritten rule of sociological theory that 'system' is evil and 'agency' good, just as it is a characteristic 'attribution bias' of ordinary members of society that externalities are evil and inner states are good. Thus, it is easy to understand the enormous attraction of Habermas' account and the way that it has been used to make sense of practically every kind of concerted effort to resist dominant forms of economic and political power. And yet the account, artfully constructed and indeed valuable though it is as myth, does not pass muster either formally or empirically when considered as theory, as indeed has long been widely recognised (Baxter, 1987). It is actually the product of a transparent and systematic partiality.

Habermas creates the sense of different kinds of action residing in separate spheres simply by the selective deployment of two different theories. By fiat, as it were, actions in the lifeworld are ordinary social actions
generated by the agency of interacting human beings. And, again by fiat,
actions in the differentiated systems are non-social actions, generated by
individuals oriented not to each other but to control exercised through
money and power: here there is no mention of agency, only of external
causation. Of course, money and power are only media of control, not
sources of control, and one might expect Habermas to say something of
the people who wield money and power and control others through
them. But in fact he says no more of the agency of the controllers than
of that of the controlled. He changes the frame of explanation altogether.
Money and power engender action, he says, that accords with the 'functional imperatives' of the system as a whole. It is not that human agency
is manifestly absent from the differentiated systems but rather that
Habermas arbitrarily refuses to make any reference to it within them: it
is entirely and wholly artefactual that in the differentiated sub-systems
of instrumental action no human agency is to be found. By switching
whenever expediency requires between intentional/voluntarist and sys-
temic/functionalist accounts of action, in effect between accounts of
human beings as social agents and accounts of them as impoverished
asocial individuals, an illicit contrast of 'system' and 'lifeworld' is con-
jured into existence, albeit one that can claim spurious justification from
its correspondence with much informal thinking.

What is actually needed here is a monistic account. It goes without
saying that individual human beings act in radically different ways at
different times and in different contexts, but they do not act sometimes
as social animals and sometimes as asocial individuals. In roles as bureaucrats, administrators and technical experts they remain responsible
agents.[9] Of course, some bureaucratic/administrative actions may be
coerced or financially induced, but this will be through the actions of
other responsible agents. Indeed, to follow a chain of inducement back
from administrative actions will typically lead away from a 'lifeworld situation' through one link to another and another, and back to the 'lifeworld' again. The allegedly external pressures of 'system' will then be
made visible as pressures transmitted from one social context to another
through the mediation of administrative and expert roles. It is via these
roles, as it were, that the various factions and memberships of differentiated societies quarrel with each other and bat responsibilities back and
forth, including the factions that are themselves administrators or experts.
Needless to say, this implies the abandonment of myths of 'the system'
as a threatening externality.

Historically, such myths have carried credibility because the financial
and bureaucratic resources of the state have been at the service of some
in society but not others. Certainly, administrators and expert professionals in the course of their rise in the nineteenth century stressed their

potential as controllers, regulators and indeed rationalisers of the greater part of society on behalf of the state and those in immediate control of it. But subsequently there has been a continuing empowerment, so that 'the masses' (to use one of Habermas' favourite expressions) are now having increasingly important effects on bureaucratic and administrative practices, both through the media of money and power and by other means. In these circumstances, rationalising projects may be conceived of and sustained in the communicative interaction of 'lifeworlds' themselves. And because there is strong interdependence, and the products of economic activity are substantially redistributed by the state in these societies, everybody may gain an interest in the accountability and the effective working of everyone else and the support for rationalisation may become very widespread.[10] It is interesting to note how in Britain over the last three decades there has been a very substantial 'rationalisation' of the work of administrators and expert professionals, accomplished by coercive political action with substantial, if by no means overwhelming, public support. There are several examples of this kind of rationalisation impinging upon legal, medical, educational and other professional settings and scarcely less so on the work environments of bureaucrats and administrators in government departments and elsewhere.[11] If there is an ongoing process of 'colonisation of lifeworlds', then it is they above all perhaps who have been colonised.

In *The Theory of Communicative Action* there is a strong tendency for approved actions to be credited to agency and individual autonomy, and deplorable actions to constraints and externalities (just as is commonplace in everyday life). A simplistic voluntarism is selectively used to articulate a *dualist* vision that valorises one part of the social order at the expense of another. Habermas also uses much the same strategy to valorise the present in relation to the past. Here dualism is expressed as evolutionism, a teleological and historicist version of evolutionism that exemplifies what has always been, and remains in macro-sociology, a widely used way of conceptualising social change.[12] Evolutionism of this kind focuses on some valued feature of our present society, presumes that it was absent in the past, and infers a progressive social evolution from past to present wherein it comes into being. Thus, moves from undifferentiated to differentiated societies, pre-industrial to industrial ones, or traditional to modern ones, are rendered as progressive developments, at the cost, some have said, of rendering societies antecedent to our own in ways that bear scant resemblance to how they were as a matter of history. In the case of Habermas' evolutionism, the valued state is the individualism of modern differentiated societies. These societies, it is assumed, are made up of increasingly autonomous individuals faced with substantial individual responsibilities and possessed of independent powers. And hence it is inferred that the societies from which they evolved were made up of linked individuals faced with fewer such responsibilities and lacking in independent powers.

Habermas (1992) marks out modern individuals as distinctive in being possessed of agency and rule reflexivity. These individual powers have evolved in the course of social differentiation. Individuals have progressively gained agency in relation to rules over time, so that, rather than passively enacting the responsibilities rules lay upon them, as formerly, they are now becoming capable of adopting a critical, active and reflexive orientation to them and thereby taking individual responsibility for their own lives. There is a clear contrast to be made between the convention-bound human beings of undifferentiated traditional societies and the rule-reflexivity characteristic of individuals in our own societies today.

The increasing autonomy of individuals in relation to rules must be understood as part of a process of *individuation*, and individuation as itself an evolutionary correlate of social differentiation. Individuation is the outcome of a socialisation process of a kind found, in its most developed form, only in highly differentiated societies. In these societies, individuals are expected to plot their own unique courses through many different social roles and institutional locations. They are required to evolve their own plans and make their own decisions in the face of problems too complex to be resolved merely by following the tramlines of custom and convention. They find themselves routinely expected to deviate from routine expectation, in situations where conformity is innovation. There is no way of successfully responding to the expectations associated with life in a differentiated society, with its complexity and conflicting demands, other than by taking responsibility for one's own life history and treating the future as the outcome of one's own active agency. No 'conventional ego identity formation' can cope adequately with all this. Unlike members of traditional societies, individuals in differentiated systems face the challenge of moving to a stage of moral development where they become reflexively aware of the rules and responsibilities that bear upon them, and critically oriented to them. In so far as they respond to that challenge, they develop a 'post-conventional ego identity' in which rule-reflexivity is a crucial element (Habermas, 1992, p. 197).

It might be thought a curious kind of agency that actually evolves as a response to a socialisation process, and a peculiarly insipid and docile kind that actually arises from the efforts of individuals to fulfil the social expectations that bear upon them. It is indeed a nice symbol of the uncritical character of current so-called critical theory. But it is also a kind of agency that challenges the central arguments of this book; for emergent agency in relation to rules entails that persons may be bound to a greater or lesser extent by the power of rules, whilst here it is held that they cannot be so bound at all. There are, however, no grounds for crediting Habermas' account. By suggesting that in undifferentiated, traditional societies human beings exist in a convention-bound condition – that is, at a less 'advanced' stage of moral development than ourselves – he makes an empirical claim of considerable generality and importance, for which no evidence is provided. It stands more as an expression of faith in the relevant superiority of the present than as an empirical conclusion with any foundation in historical or anthropological studies. Like many theorists, Habermas appears to have generated his account of the nature of life in legendary traditional societies by the inversion of valued features of our own mode of life. And in doing this he has laid hands on a great swathe of history for his immediate moral and political purposes, without pointing to anything that demonstrates his entitlement to it.

What kind of empirical evidence would be salient here? How should we evaluate the claim that people in 'traditional' societies are more convention-bound than we are? Is it material to cite their, relatively speaking, high rates of homicide, the priority of calculation over custom in much of their economic activity, their creativity and ingenuity in the articulation of rules of kinship and descent, their capacity for laughter? And what of our increased tendency to take individual responsibility for our own lives and the decisions encountered in the course of it? Where is responsibility supposed to have lain before, and what shows that it lay there?[13]

Evolutionary perspectives on social change have long understood the rise of individualism as involving a move toward increased individual responsibility. In a famous essay, Sally Moore (1972) has criticised this view as expressed by legal anthropologists. These theorists spoke of simple societies as incorporating systems of collective responsibility, and imagined that individual responsibility became more and more pervasive and important as these systems slowly eroded with differentiation. On the face of it, this account is a plausible one, consistent with the modern aversion to systems of collective responsibility, but Moore has no difficulty in exposing the empirical inadequacy of its central claim, mainly by employing anthropological materials to convey a more balanced picture of simple societies. She is particularly insistent on the fundamental role of individual responsibility in all such societies. A key conjecture of her essay is that 'whenever an individual member can incur collective liabilities there are always rules whereby the collective may discipline, expel or hand over the offending individual' (1972, p. 89). And the conclusion of her survey of case study materials is that 'within a group or aggregate bearing collective liability, in the long run individuals are held individually responsible for their actions. Collective responsibility does not exclude or substitute for individual responsibility' (ibid., p. 93). This is indeed just the empirical conclusion to be expected, as far as Moore is concerned, for it is individuals that act and collective liabilities incurred by irresponsible actions are no disincentives, or but slight disincentives, at the individual level. The efficacy of institutionalised collective responsibility is attributed to the incentive it gives the collective to enforce individual responsibilities on its members, an attribution wholly consistent with an understanding of those members as active responsible agents, such as has been advocated in this book.

The model of the responsible agent proposed in this book itself amounts to a denial of Habermas' evolutionism. Nor is it merely a formal denial: it implies an empirical argument against the evolutionist view, even if it does not directly confront it with empirical evidence. It is a model of the kind of organisms we must surely be in so far as we are palpably engaged in a social life lived in institutional settings. And as such it is an account which makes all the vast range of empirical evidence that this is how we do live, and long have done, relevant to our self-understanding. Given that we do live in this way we cannot understand ourselves even in part as asocial individuals, whether as independent calculators or as automated rule followers: we have to recognise ourselves as responsible agents, affected by each other but active in relation to rules. The very fact that we live together and act together in ways recognisably related to shared rules implies agency and rule-reflexivity (and mutual susceptibility). These things cannot be understood as emergent in the course of social evolution since they are constitutive of what is allegedly evolving. They are well incorporated into a general model to symbolise their ubiquity and (in a certain sense) their necessity, and to remind dualist 'critical' theorists that they are not available for use in myths designed to valorise the present.

Sociological theorists have come routinely to acknowledge agency and reflexivity in relation to rules, but only amongst members of differentiated societies. Instead of exploring the consequences of extending and generalising the insight, some of them have chosen instead to make it the basis of yet another assertion of difference between modern differentiated societies and the legendary 'traditional society' from which they evolved. An implicit conviction of the superiority of the modern seems to have induced a misplaced inference to the superior reflexivity of the modern individual. If the argument of this book is correct, individual human beings do not systematically differ in this respect between societies, or in any other aspect of responsible agency, and this has implications for how we should understand our own history. There is no need to discard the intuition that there is much to celebrate in the modern condition; but there is a need to remain aware that the modern condition is the product of the reflexivity of the ancestors. We are their creative accomplishment.

Changing patterns of responsibilities

Despite what has been said in the previous discussion, there have always been sociological theorists who have recognised a particular responsibility to treat human beings as social agents and to keep this at the forefront of their thought. This book is written in support of that position, and seeks to give it uncompromising expression by characterising free action as the social action of mutually accountable and susceptible agents, and the associated voluntaristic discourse as the medium through which such agents affect each other. If this position is accepted, then the great secular trend to individualism, that sociologists also regard themselves as having a particular responsibility to elucidate, has to be rendered as changes in the culture and the institutional arrangements of societies of social agents. And a great part of this will be change in the institution of responsible action itself, and the attendant distribution of specific responsibilities, intelligible as the product of collective agency and oriented to the collective good.

Sociological theory and macro-sociology offer several different accounts of the rise of individualism and the nature of its intimate association with the ever-increasing differentiation of society. And whilst some extraordinarily disparate pictures of what is involved exist in the sociological literature, as testimony to how not even the availability of a vast supply of relevant evidence will settle conflicts between different ways of seeing, this does not detract from its importance as a source of insights. Curiously, however, discussions of responsibility are thin on the ground in this context, despite its crucial relevance to an understanding of the changing institutional order; and the attention that sociologists have recently been giving to it represents something of a new departure.

As we have seen, Jürgen Habermas attributes an emergent individual agency and rule-reflexivity to the fact that individuals have to take more and more decisions independently and are increasingly required to 'take responsibility for their own lives'. There does indeed seem to be considerable support for the view that responsibility is increasingly being reallocated to individuals, and important arguments exist to support it. It is said, for example, that institutional complexity and a very rapid rate of institutional change require the high level of flexibility only available in systems where responsibility is maximally devolved. And supporters of 'the detraditionalisation thesis' argue that the removal of traditional kinds of social and institutional support results in responsibilities impacting directly on the individual as they previously did not. In evident contrast, it has already been argued here that human beings everywhere, in all kinds of social context, bear very substantial responsibilities and are held individually responsible for their own actions, even whilst being constitutively sociable and non-independent creatures. But if the thesis of a transfer of responsibility to individuals is rejected on these grounds, the need arises for an alternative account of the secular changes that have occurred in the institution of responsible action and the distribution of responsibilities. For the intuition that differentiation and the consequent rise of individualism have found expression in changes at this level is surely sound, and cannot be ignored.

What will be suggested here is in some ways the opposite of the current view. The proposal is that differentiated societies are remarkable for how little they rely upon individual responsibility in the usual sense (although the attribution of individual responsibility remains as important as ever), and how much and how successfully they have come to rely, not upon collective or group responsibility as usually understood, to which they are indeed averse, but upon *institutional* responsibility, and in particular institutional response.

References to a development of this kind are implicit in the familiar story of the emergence of specialised occupational roles in modern societies, and the proliferation of administrators, skilled professionals and technical experts. Many responsibilities hitherto located in the family have been passed to them: most of the responsibilities attendant upon birth and death are in their hands, as are those relating to the health, education and basic well-being of children; and they share responsibility, so to speak, for the basic economic provision in family units. Nor has this been merely a transfer of responsibility from one social role to another of just the same kind; for the responsibilities which administrators and professionals take on their shoulders, in return for appropriate emoluments, were formerly associated not with kinship roles so much as with persons through those roles, and many of them were inalienable. Indeed, we continue in everyday discourse to account individual actions in family and informal community contexts matters of inalienable personal responsibility, perhaps as revelations of 'personality', whereas in occupational settings such attributions are far more equivocal.

It might still be argued that the shift of responsibilities cited here is by no means radical, since what an individual is released from in one context is merely taken up by another individual elsewhere, in the relevant occupational role. But this is to overlook how, for those in occupational roles, the *response* element of their responsibilities is covered not individually but institutionally, by employers, or employers' insurers, or government agencies. Individuals in occupations are tending to become millions upon millions of micro limited-liability companies, and the limits in question to become smaller and smaller. Moreover, if we turn back to those responsibilities that remain vested in individual persons directly, it is clear that from them too most of the *response* element is being removed. Again through the mediation of administrative skills and practices, the liabilities incurred by failures of individual responsibility are being transferred to institutions. Whilst the attribution of responsibility at the level of the individual remains necessary, it can become of but slight significance to the actual individual involved and more a marker for use in financial transactions between institutions. Individuals' liabilities are increasingly being converted, with or without their knowledge and/or consent, into institutional liabilities. A concerted and systematic extension of the insurance principle figures amongst the most important of all secular trends in the modern world. It is through this institutional device that modern societies are giving practical expression to the value they place upon the individual. They are celebrating her unique worth by minimising the magnitude of her responsibilities, and the extent to which they have now managed to do so in many societies represents an extraordinary collective accomplishment.

The suggestion is that, in differentiated societies, institutional arrangements have diminished the weight of the responsibilities faced by their members to what is, historically, a remarkably low level. This is neither a radical nor an unprecedented proposal. It is unlikely, for example, to strike anthropologists as revelatory, since their studies have long identified responsibility evasion as a continuing counterpoint to its allocation and enforcement. There is a collective interest in enforcing responsibility and response, so that members may be freed of the risks implicit in the lapses and failings of others; but there is an individual interest in avoiding responsibilities and in evading response when they are not met. Human beings everywhere recognise both interests and search for strategies and institutional arrangements that might somehow reconcile the two. The solution to this universal problem that marks the signal achievement of the collective agency of members of modern societies is remarkable only for the extent of its success.

If the anthropologists are close to being there already in their studies of simple societies, then so too are the communitarians in their account of the here and now: to proclaim the weakening of individual responsibilities is just to echo the communitarian lament. The precise form of that lament, however, is interesting. You cannot have increased individual rights without accepting increased individual responsibilities, so it goes. But the very frequency with which the claim is made tends to confirm that it is false. The trick has been performed by displacing responsibilities, and, even more, response, onto institutions. What communitarians in fact lament is the *actual existence* of increased individual rights without correspondingly increased responsibilities. For many and various reasons, according to which locus of communitarianism is addressed, its proponents don't like living in that way. They hold that it isn't good to live in that condition. And as far as that is concerned they could conceivably be right, even though those burdened with the more substantial demands that fall upon individuals in less differentiated societies might perhaps regard such a condition as an enviable one.

Although what is being claimed is consistent with anthropological studies, and reconcilable with communitarian philosophy, it would seem nonetheless to go against much of the currently accepted wisdom of social theory. Habermas speaks of individuals being forced to take more and more personal responsibility, and having to make more and more decisions on the basis of their own independent judgement. Others agree with him in speaking of a world of lifestyle choices, and of an identity politics wherein individuals seek independently to realise their own personal plans and projects. Conceivably, however, what has been proposed above might be reconciled even with all this. In the docile, normalised collectives of modern societies, life is more peaceful, predictable and risk-free than almost ever before. Because of the shift of liabilities to institutions, the individual costs of acting in one way rather than another have been radically reduced. In comparison with the life-or-death consequences of many decisions that have to be made in simple societies, about when precisely to sow seed or where to trek to find good grazing, for example, the penalties exacted for unfortunate individual decisions in modern societies are generally trivial. And it is just when alternatives differ little and the risk inherent in choice is consequently slight that individuals will be inclined to say that they 'have a choice' and to regard what they do as more than an obligatory response to circumstances. Then it is notable as no more than a feature of language that a society replete with choice and diversity may equally well be rendered as one of insipid uniformity, and vice versa.[14]

To return to the main line of argument, it is worth being a little more precise about just what the displacement of individual responsibility onto institutions involves; for a key theoretical claim is implicated here, which underpins the entire argument of this section. In no society does a member face demands for response in isolation. Always, when she has to meet such demands, there is a backdrop of social relations via which the necessary resources are channelled to her, and thence to those to whom she has liabilities. In many societies the relevant social relations are those of family, kinship, friendship and other kinds of close-knit social network. But in modern societies the suggestion is that the relationships are more with large, 'impersonal' social institutions. This is a crucial difference. Close-knit networks can generate an extremely strong reciprocal pressure on those they are called upon to succour and rescue – this is one important message of Sally Moore's paper. Large institutions, on the other hand, wherein and whereby liabilities are spread very widely over great numbers of individuals, may generate little or nothing by way of such reciprocal pressure. The theoretical rationale for this is that the logic of collective action, as worked out for independent individuals, applies also even to responsible agents in large numbers: the wider a given cost is spread, the less becomes the incentive, and the greater the difficulty, of organising to eliminate it. Thus, as the price of lapses in the meeting of individual responsibilities is more and more paid by institutions, the collective interest in their strong enforcement is radically weakened. And this surely has been the secular trend, even if it has involved many ups and downs, and proceeded at markedly different rates in different contexts.

The move to institutional response involves the insurance principle spreading through society in a variety of guises, engulfing one area of activity after another, lessening the stresses and pressures of individual responsibilities, offering security against the risk represented by lapses from responsibility on the part of others. And, of course, there are other happy consequences of the spread of the principle. Should the physical environment fail to meet expectations, the safety net is there just as it is when people fail to meet expectations. Equally, the provision of security in the face of risk may be the provision of a context for risk-taking. The insurance principle allows the acceptance of projects of enormous risks and potentially massive benefits: it produces societies of unique and extraordinary courage, for all that their individual members may be strikingly timid in comparison with those of many simpler societies. However, in arranging the institution of responsible action to minimise personal responsibility and personal risk, it may conceivably be that members of modern societies have inflicted conditions of too little responsibility and insufficient risk on some of themselves. Indeed it may even be that (due to collective action problems) they have created these conditions for most of themselves. Certainly, how to cope with few responsibilities and low risks are among the more interesting of the problems currently studied by sociologists.

The problems of living with few personal responsibilities are amongst the staples of sociology, although they are addressed via many and various terminologies and schemata. Where responsibilities are attenuated, interdependence is weak and the strength of commitments is correspondingly low. This happy condition of the modern individual was interestingly analysed long ago by Howard Becker (1970) as the condition of the child, prevented from falling into binding commitments and able to continue to live life as a form of play. But the alleged ease with which lives of this kind may come to be perceived as drained of meaning and devoid of proper satisfaction has been a focus of reflection in most traditions of sociological theory, where many writers have wondered whether personal fulfilment might not perhaps entail the fulfilment of responsibilities to others. And the thought running through this book, that in the last analysis responsibility is a privilege, leads on to related forms of reflection.

Risk is the other side of the coin from responsibility, and as with the one so with the other it seems that social changes are reducing them beyond the level that 'in an ideal world' would be desirable. Nobody wants to pay the price when they fail to meet their responsibilities, or when they take a risk and run out of luck, but this does not mean that people thrive if the price is reduced or eliminated. The collective action problem here is especially clear in the case of risk. Modern societies have devoted enormous resources to risk reduction through regulation, insurance and the use of specialised expertise in efforts to engender a safer and healthier environment. Every disaster is liable to drive the process further forward, via inquiries, reports, batches of yet more regulation and legislation. Those burying their dead need, so it is said, deeply to believe that that particular disaster 'could never happen again'. Those unaffected remain indifferent to the very widely spread costs of the necessary adjustments. Levels of risk in societies are institutionally sustained and the same levels must serve for everyone. For many, possibly most, people the levels seem to have become too low, but the institutional ratchet continues to turn nonetheless. Safety is now churned out in vast quantities by a combination of the awesome productive power of modern economies and the enthusiasm with which their associated polities command it via fiat and regulation, indifferent to genuine demand. And as with other over-produced commodities, its satiated consumers increasingly seek to get rid of it, or convert it to something else (Adams, 1995).[15]

Conclusions

The aim of this chapter has been to relate the naturalistic and monistic ideas developed in the first part of this book to the attempts to understand human actions, and secular patterns of change in them, made by macro-sociologists and sociological theorists. As far as social change is concerned, it proposes to regard it, as is normal in macro-sociology, as institutional change. It conceptualises the rise of individualism, for example, in terms of unchanging social creatures inhabiting a changing institution of responsible action. It goes on to suggest that institutional change of this kind should be intelligibly related to the goal-oriented activities of the relevant social creatures. And finally, it claims that in understanding social change in this way, as in all other efforts to understand social action, a naturalistic model of the fundamental features of human beings as social creatures may be of great utility. Reference is made to Max Weber's sociology to illustrate what may be lost if such a model is dispensed with, and to Jürgen Habermas' social theory to indicate the importance of treating such a model as a naturalistic one capable of guiding and disciplining theoretical thought, and not as an evaluative ideal put to use *ex post facto* to express and rationalise that thought.

Needless to say, the discussion not only advocates the use of a naturalistic model; it offers one. On that model, our sociability is expressed in and through the medium of our voluntaristic discourse, and the patterns of use of most of the key concepts of that discourse are related in their basic form to features of our nature as social creatures. Hence, if voluntarism is used as a template for an academic, theoretical account of human beings, or voluntaristic concepts are borrowed for use in such a theory, it should be a theory of the characteristics of human beings everywhere. 'Agency', 'will', 'responsibility' in the sense of the individual capacity for rational conduct, are not going to be of use in referring to characteristics present in some human beings in some contexts but lacking in others elsewhere. On this basis, the work of Habermas has been criticised.

This criticism is, of course, relative to a specific naturalistic model, and any naturalistic model is fallible, and liable to be modified as we learn more about ourselves. However, even if criticism of the naturalistic adequacy of Habermas' voluntarism is for this reason less than decisive, the deeper criticism, that he does not in any case deploy his models and theories in an appropriately naturalistic way, remains. Habermas deploys voluntaristic notions selectively, not to capture observed differences in the ways that human beings act, but to project an evaluative standpoint.

More than anyone else today he is able to create powerful dualist myths as rationalisations of moral judgements of great scope and generality, and he deploys voluntaristic notions in the construction of such myths. But voluntarism in this work is not an ontology that allows an illuminating description of states of affairs to be provided; it is rather a resource selectively deployed in a morally biased way – a way that does violence to its nature as an ontology, as it were, and that shows insufficient respect for readers of the myth as makers of moral judgements in their own right.

Habermas' work will serve as a symbol of the way that voluntaristic notions, and particularly 'agency', are now being very widely used. Certainly, in sociology, at practically every level of theorising, instances can now be found where it is the extent of approbation or disapprobation of actions that seems to move imputations of agency. Given this, it might be asked why so much attention has been devoted to Habermas rather than to more modest accounts of human agency, and why his large historicist and teleological conceptions of social change have been reckoned so important. Is it not the case, after all, that very general sociological narratives, redolent of what in other ages would be identified as myth and story, are now passé? Are not the particular and the context-bound now the obsession of the literature? The answer is that this is only partly the case. Certainly, very general visions of history, whether accounts of its gradual evolutionary progress or the alternatives of Marxian eschatology, have lost much of whatever credibility they once held. But the shift in cognition involved has been superficial. Theorists remain incurably Hegelian in their accounts of social change, and their concepts remain steeped in historicism and teleology. Indeed, the recoil from generalising and synthesising narratives evident in sociological theory, far from encouraging a naturalistic interest in the particular such as elsewhere has often manifested itself as some form of empiricism, has actually generated yet more debate about just how best to describe the present 'stage' in the development of society. In sociology there exists a tradition of theory rooted in the genre of comedy, and in this particular respect it shows no sign at all of any inclination to change.

Notes

1 Sociology has benefited from its independence of the inadequate models of economics, and scarcely been helped by some of its own fundamentally individualistic models, so it is not surprising that the case for doing without any model at all is widely regarded as a strong one.

2 Calhoun's (1982) study of class in England in the nineteenth century has been of major importance in this context. Needless to say, Calhoun's position is accepted here, both as history and as theory. See also Barnes (1995, Chapter 7).

3 It would have been inappropriate to cite those who put forward the 'death of

class' hypothesis here, since the view being put forward is that the supposed corpse was never a living body in the first place. The 'death of class' perspective is an instance of the undesirable practice of excusing the failings of social theory by holding that the circumstances it was designed to apply to have changed. In truth there never have been class societies. John Scott regards 'class' as a far more useful term than I do, but his understanding of the issues is indisputably impressive, and has the respect even of someone like myself who disagrees with him even on the significance of his own work.

4 The problems raised by the notion of 'detraditionalisation' should become clear in later discussion of Habermas. It is perhaps also worth asking here whether individuals are not now more strongly supported in their relations with the labour market and the consumer economy than ever before.

5 All this is set out more extensively in Barnes (1988, 1995). Exemplars of what is recommended can be found in work by Randall Collins (1979, 1986) and Michael Banton, whose *Racial and Ethnic Competition* (1983) has been unjustly neglected in the context of social theory. I was long guilty of underestimating the importance of this remarkable book myself, having misunderstood Banton's references to rational choice theory.

6 This is an instance of what Wittgenstein (1968) calls the use of the machine as symbol: it is a symbol of reliability. It goes without saying that all actual machines are to an extent unreliable.

7 An empirical and not an analytic division is clearly implied when Habermas contrasts the system and lifeworld spheres. Giddens' contrast of structure and agency is quite different, even though it has the same resonance for many readers.

8 Habermas has denied that this is so, but the correlation of the descriptive and the evaluative in the relevant material is overwhelming.

9 During 1998, widespread indignation was directed at medical and legal authorities in England for resorting to the forcible imposition of surgery upon unwilling recipients, particularly pregnant women who refuse permission for the Caesareans regarded by medical professionals as essential if they are to give birth safely. The example has a special interest in that it has involved recourse to powers of compulsion available under the English Mental Health Acts for use in cases of mental illness: if they don't want the surgery they must be crazy, so the argument seems to have gone, so let's section them. As an example of Catch 22 there is nothing better, even in the annals of the old Soviet Union. Not only in authoritarian societies do powerful professionals feel entitled to make use of law as plaything in pursuit of particular moral or evaluative agendas. It is true that these same events may also be represented as efforts by sensitive and well-meaning authorities to save people from the devastating consequences of their own temporary aberrations of judgement – twiddles and extemporisations on the law, as it were, in spur-of-the-moment attempts to save life. But the point of the example is merely to illustrate agency in relation to laws and rules, not to pass judgement upon it. There have been innumerable other widely publicised illustrations of the point, many scarcely less spectacular.

10 There is an obvious analogy here with the kind of argument made by Michel Foucault, whose account of power can be thought of as an interesting development of Weber's tragic vision. That both writers were influenced by the philosophy of Nietzsche is of course well documented.

11 The legal system is plausibly cited by Habermas as an important instrument of societal rationalisation (or 'juridification', as he calls rationalisation involving the codification of permissible activity in law). But it is interesting to notice the strong 'lifeworld-based' pressure currently being exerted for the 'rationalisation' of allegedly unreliable and inefficient legal procedures, as well as the way that the associated conceptions of the reliable and efficient administration of justice tend to clash very strongly with those of legal professionals themselves. Indeed, there have recently been moves in Britain to circumvent legal professionals and develop more reliable and effective do-it-yourself approaches to law enforcement. Recent innovations on this front include the blazoning of the names and photographs of 'unconvicted murderers' across newspaper front pages, and the naming of an alleged but unproven school-teacher/paedophile as the lead item in the BBC news (the predictable suicide of the individual involved followed within hours). Neither of these instances of a new kind of media helpfulness in this context have elicited any significant public expression of disquiet, and indeed legal institutions seem to be pre-empting populist criticism by moving in the direction of this kind of approach themselves.

12 For the sake of clarity, it is worth noting here that evolutionary accounts of both technological change and social differentiation are defensible even in the context of a naturalistic perspective on social change. A notion of contingent variation with selective retention of advantageous variants can be deployed in addressing either of these trends. But, of course, sociological theorists generally follow accounts that regard evolution as a progression toward something, and an idea of evolution as an undirected, meaningless process is still not sufficiently familiar in this context. Thus, for example, whilst the exquisitely detailed historical accounts of technological innovation and change given by George Basalla's *The Evolution of Technology* (1988) would probably evoke admiration from most sociologists, its extremely restrained (Darwinian) conclusion might possibly be found surprising by some of them: 'A workable theory of technological evolution requires there be no technological progress in the traditional sense of the term. . . . In its place we should cultivate an appreciation for the diversity of the made world' (p. 218). It is not this kind of perspective that is criticised as 'evolutionism' in what follows.

13 There is in Habermas' view of tradition, and in that of other similarly inclined rationalist macro-social theorists, a tendency to confuse repetition and repro-duction at the level of the life-cycle with their existence in individual lives. In truth, individuals in so-called traditional societies may routinely have to face the most extraordinarily profound changes, such as members of 'modern' societies would regard as traumatic in the extreme, and be routinely called upon to manifest remarkable resourcefulness and flexibility just to continue the status quo. There is no need to cite 'normal' circumstances like plague, starvation or warfare to make the point here. Think simply of the marriage of a woman in a 'traditional' patrilocal system. It is hard not to be irritated by the treatment of tradition in this kind of literature.

14 It is probably expedient to stress all the many barriers that modern individuals jump over, in writing of this, and not to point out how very low the barriers in question are. It is pleasant, after all, to feel free.

15 Every year in Britain a small number of broken bodies are removed from the foot of cliffs and precipices, and give rise to tiresome debate about the safety

problems presented by climbers and mountain walkers. It cannot be admitted that it is these very deaths that give the cliffs their lure as sources of hazard and danger, and condition the very perception of these physical features as inspiring and beautiful, but to an extent it is so. The deaths sustain an edge of hazard that for those who remain can be part of the very essence of what they do: in that sense they are a necessary sacrifice to the collective good. It is increasingly common, however, under the impetus of the obsessive institutionalised risk-aversion that characterises our culture today, for rock-faces to become spattered with bolts and pitons and similar accoutrements. As a result, people find themselves forced to put their lives at risk to remove the offending artefacts and restore the rocks to their original beautiful and hazardous condition.

7

AGENCY, RESPONSIBILITY AND NEW HUMAN BIOTECHNOLOGIES

The background

There are many fields of enquiry that seek to understand human beings and their activities, and although in practice they may take little account of each other, their different approaches and conclusions should ideally be compared and brought into some kind of consistent relationship. The fundamental aim of the discussion here is to relate an understanding of human beings as responsible agents with the very different ways of understanding them to be found in genetic and biological sciences. In practice, this entails consideration of whether and how the conception of human beings appropriate to social theory and those associated with the new human technologies and genetic engineering can be reconciled with each other. The discussion here will largely be a formal one, and will not attempt to engage with any of the spectacular recent developments, announcements of which have continually punctuated the writing of this book. Indeed, it will be more concerned to cite relatively ordinary and familiar examples, in order to show how the cognitive resources we already possess will serve to orient us to much of what the future may bring in these fields.

To suggest this, however, is emphatically not to imply that satisfactory connections have already been made between biological accounts of human beings and those of sociology or social theory. Consider that technological and scientific change stands alongside social differentiation as one of the two great secular trends that constitute much of our history and promise understanding of a good deal of the rest of it. And note how the natural sciences supply our paradigms of naturalistic understanding and explanation, and technological artefacts our familiar examples of causally connected systems. Clearly, the cultures of technology and science should figure amongst the main foci of interest of the social sciences. If one seeks them there, however, one finds little or nothing. Indeed, it is extraordinarily difficult to describe how the mainstream of macro-sociology and sociological theory is oriented to science and technology, because there is very little evidence that a coherent orientation currently exists.[1]

For detailed discussions of the relationship of biological and sociological forms of explanation it is necessary to look backwards. Indeed, it is best to begin three decades or so ago, when sociology was still consolidating itself as a discipline. At this time, itself aspiring to be a recognised science, it took the methods and causal modes of inference of the natural sciences as its own ideal. Even so, its relationship with adjacent sciences, like biology and psychology, was often tense and equivocal, because many sociologists were repelled by the way that these fields addressed human beings as causal systems. Sociologists at this time could be found opposing nativist accounts of the distribution of conditions as diverse as intelligence and schizophrenia, and challenging the 'hereditarian' forms of causal explanation favoured by socio-biologists, Darwinians and geneticists. But it is clear that *internal* causation, by fixed states causally linked to behavioural tendencies, was the major focus of criticism, and not causation as such. Because such states were inaccessible, and hence unchangeable, their effects had simply to be accepted and endured – or so it was thought. And this was taken to imply a fatalistic and reactionary perspective on the human condition and an acceptance of inevitable 'natural' inequalities between individuals. Against this, many sociologists insisted on the consideration of environmental and contextual causes as explanations of behaviour, not least because of their belief that *external* causation implied the possibility of intervention in causal processes and amelioration of their adverse effects. Thus, for many years, the explanation of human behaviour and behavioural dispositions was attended by controversies between hereditarians and environmentalists. And whilst these so-called nature–nurture controversies were often complex and subtle, they revolved around a conflict of different forms of causal explanation, one of which relied predominantly on internal states and the other upon externalities.

This preference for external causal explanation was also evident in the orientation of sociologists to technology. Technology was widely cited in causal accounts of human behaviour, precisely because it was perceived as an externality. At this time, too, sociologists tended to regard their major theoretical task as the explanation not of social order but of social change, then generally thought of as cumulative and irreversible and hence as explicable only by reference to some independent externality which itself changed cumulatively and irreversibly. Technology appeared to many to be just such an externality. History gave evidence of a progressive accumulation of technological resources over time, and also seemed to indicate the independence of technology, its progression through an internal momentum apparently beyond direct human control. Thus it was an attractive conjecture that technological change explained social change, that the latter consisted in institutions, practices and ideologies adjusting to the former. This is the thesis of *technological deter-*

minism, once widely accepted as the basis of general 'theories of history', and still not wholly bereft of defenders.[2]

Needless to say, both its inclination toward an externalist form of causal explanation and its self-conception as a science inclined the sociology of this period away from voluntarism. Indeed, at one point any reference to what was internal to the individual, whether to a power or to a cause, was likely to be regarded as a suspect appeal to 'subjectivity', and criticised as both unsociological and unscientific. It is here that a great change has occurred in recent years. Unmistakably, in Britain and Europe at least, the role of naturalistic causal accounts of action has been radically downgraded; perspectives like technological determinism have lost their allure; and there has been a renewed stress on the individual and her independent powers. However, this change has not resulted in any systematic effort by theorists to understand individual actions scientifically from the inside, as it were; for this new form of individualism, whilst careful to remain respectful of the sciences in their proper place, has seen no role for them in this context. Indeed its references to individual agency feature it as something to be valued, not as something to be studied, and serve primarily, as was described in Chapter 4, as means of decoupling human beings from what otherwise might have been regarded as causes of their actions. By such means agents have been rescued from structural and cultural determinants, and they would no doubt have been rescued from genetic and endocrinological determinants as well, save only that in this context they had never been captive to them. Indeed, at the extreme, the meaning of 'agency' has acquired an 'in flight' character, as the term has been used to celebrate the victory of the individual not just over technology, or structure, or biology, but over all naturalistic causal accounts of action however rich and complex. References to agency have served to assert the fluidity and unpredictability of human nature against a 'reductionism' which allegedly is constantly seeking to fix and hypostasise it. And, given that explanatory references to the internal, intrinsic characteristics of individual human beings are generally perceived as 'reductionist' in this context, there has been even less inclination to consider their possible merits than before.

At the very time that this transformation in sociology and sociological theory was occurring, however, the basis was being laid for a reinvigorated understanding of human beings through internal causal mechanisms; this was the period of the emergence of the new human biotechnology. There is room for argument about just what is new here. Biotechnology is as old as technology itself. Many major recent advances associated with it, brain-scanning techniques for example, do not currently amount to new technologies of intervention and control. And whilst genetic engineering, conventionally taken to date from 1973, is indeed a new technology in this sense (and often taken as definitive of the 'new' biotechnology), nearly all its important industrial and economic applications currently relate to the non-human realm. What definitely is new, however, is how this field has become part of what we take to be the leading edge of technological change, and how, thus conceived, it is constitutive of the myth of a technology which is capable of turning back upon its users and subjecting them to inexorable analysis, control and transformation. A crucial change has occurred at the level of myth, if not yet actuality; but at the same time the myth is very far from being a fantasy. It highlights the extraordinary possibilities latent here, and it draws attention to a changing reality as well. The technical basis of an unprecedentedly potent human biotechnology is indeed taking shape in the relevant scientific and technical fields, and those involved in the process, needing vast funds and facing intense competition for them, are projecting the products of their imaginations with enormous energy.

Even so, the emergence of the myth has been quite extraordinarily rapid. This may be something to do with the way that political interest has fastened upon this emergent technology as the possible basis of a new phase of long-term economic expansion, and has heeded and amplified its publicity accordingly. But it is also perhaps that the collective imagination, which can usually run far ahead of practice, was here held back, and is now making up for lost time. For much of the perceived significance of the new human biotechnology is its eugenic significance, and the association of eugenics with the perversions of the Nazis long placed it beyond the pale, particularly at the level of ideology. Today, all Western societies routinely practise eugenics, in strict moderation as it were, but the reintroduction of appropriately laundered conceptions of the potency and value of human biotechnologies has needed very careful management.[3]

That the reintroduction has been strikingly successful is now, however, surely unquestionable. One area where its effects can be clearly discerned is in perceived contrasts between 'biological' and 'sociological' accounts of human behaviour. A quarter of a century ago the nativist and hereditarian accounts of behaviour associated with the biological sciences were widely regarded as fatalistic and reactionary. As described earlier, many sociologists felt obliged to oppose them with more 'optimistic' environmentalist and contextual theories. But today it is environmentalism that is the more vulnerable to the charge of fatalism: better that your behavioural problems are innate and not acquired, it is now sometimes said, because at least there is then the hope that something can be done about them. Indeed, in the imagined future of biotechnology there are limitless possibilities for transformation. The Enlightenment vision of human emancipation so dear to many social theorists is now invited to define itself in relation to a human nature thoroughly subject to human control: technology and its users threaten to become bound in a tight loop that might appear not only to vitiate all extant accounts of their relationship but to erode the meaningfulness of the categories themselves.

The proliferation of biotechnology

It is important to be clear that the resources of the new biotechnology do not currently find extensive application as ways of intervening in the bodily processes of human beings. Only a modest 'progress' has currently been made in this direction.[4] However, there is no question that inroads are being made into our lives, that is, into our practical activity and not merely our abstract thought, at another level. Ahead of new techniques of manipulation and intervention have run new techniques of diagnosis and classification. It is these that are now in the van of an advancing human biotechnology and that have already made close contact with the entrenched practice of everyday life. All manner of new distinctions are being generated by the encounter. Human differences never before remarked upon are being identified and institutionalised. And these are differences marked in a causal frame, for use in causal discourses. At this growing point of contact, the language of causation and that of choice and agency are being brought into a closer and more intimate relationship than ever before.

Even though they do not involve genetic engineering and scarcely count as a full expression of what the new field involves, the pervasive diffusion of new diagnostic techniques, in conjunction with widespread knowledge of what the future promises to bring, is ensuring that the new biotechnology becomes part of the routine awareness of a much larger proportion of the populations at least of the highly industrialised societies, and acquires a vastly greater credibility than anything that preceded it. Consequently, it is no longer going to be a realistic stance to deny the salience of internal individual differences in nature or state. Already that salience is proclaimed by numerous inexpensive and simply applied tests of individual characteristics capable of being applied to populations of millions of people, tests that seem sure eventually to acquire a reputation for utility and reliability. DNA fingerprinting is perhaps currently the most widely known of such tests, and whilst it has no predictive value in the usual sense it conveys with unparalleled clarity the key message that every individual is unique and different from every other. Biotechnological tests for diseases and disorders do have predictive utility. They can diagnose incipient pathologies, both congenital as with Huntingdon's Chorea and post-natally acquired as with most cases of AIDS, years before their physical expression. Indeed, the enormous practical potential of tests of immediate state is beginning to be realised in everyday life. Recently, for example, a miniaturised, highly portable monitor of sex hormone levels has been marketed as a form of natural contraception. Already the device is being used by many thousands of women willing to trust the information it offers and to act upon it, and future sales could run into millions.

What response should be made to the enormous boost of credibility that is accruing to biotechnology and its internal, causal style of explanation? One thing that sociologists might wish to supply is a note of caution against over-confidence and the making of inflated claims, and scepticism in the face of the flow of popularisations of the subject. Another is assistance in appreciating the seriousness of the issues raised, and the great potential for good or ill even of imminent and relatively minor biotechnological techniques. Thus, whilst it will be useful to call into question the work of the hacks and opportunists who are increasingly going to be talking about a gene for crime or a gene for flower-arranging, it will be even more important to reflect, for example, on the growing availability of genetic profiles, and the possibility that features of such profiles will correlate with behavioural tendencies or dispositions. There is no shortage of current examples with which to bring out what could follow on from this. In Britain, for example, there is currently intense pressure for the introduction of wholly prophylactic forms of incarceration – pressure, indeed, to which legal and political institutions have already started to succumb. Given that this seems to be gaining some acceptance as an end, it is not unrealistic to have some slight anxiety about the predicted proliferation of the required means.[5] Nonetheless, when they address the new biotechnology, scepticism and the drawing of cautionary tales from history should not be the only, or even the primary, responses of sociologists. As trusted assertions, biotechnological diagnoses of individual natures and states are going to lead to claimed links between variations in these natures or states and variations in manifest individual characteristics and behaviours. And, for all that they will inevitably be accompanied by a penumbra of scientistic nonsense, there are going to be more and more claims which are not only accepted as valid but rightly so accepted. There is a need to reflect on the possible significance of valid claims of this kind.

It has been suggested that even now, at the mainly diagnostic stage, the new human biotechnology is bringing about profound changes in the accounts we give of our own activities – that it is engendering or intensifying more *individualistic* and *deterministic* forms of self-understanding (Nelkin and Tancredi, 1989). Two factors account for this, so it is said. First, the new diagnostic biotechnology is permeating our lives and insinuating itself into our institutional arrangements to an unparalleled degree, transforming even routine, personal activities. Secondly, it is encountered as a deterministic account of individual natures and individual differences, by users whose contact with the technology is through individual diagnoses and causally framed accounts of their significance. Even if there is nothing inherently individualistic about the theoretical thinking of biotechnologists themselves, even if their genetics, for example, is given a misleading individualistic gloss by commentators biased by the individualism of the culture in which they live, it remains the case that this is how biotechnology is actually experienced, and, even more, how it is going to be experienced.

The empirical generalisations put forward in Nelkin's and Tancredi's invaluable study are extremely plausible, and can be supported with any number of additional examples. Consider the personal contraceptive device previously mentioned. It is at once one of the most striking examples of the great potential of biotechnology, and a massive understatement of that potential. What may become part of the daily routines of millions is in truth a very highly sophisticated hormone monitor which currently fails to use most of its own capacities, and which even so is but the first primitive accomplishment in a whole chain of possible further developments. Miniaturisation to wrist-watch size is a perfectly realistic thought. Extension to other hormones, adrenalin perhaps, or testosterone, suggests itself. Perhaps indeed, in a decade or so, monitors will be capable of providing a whole battery of readings, an immediate hormonal profile on the basis of which to plan one's day. Hormone levels correlate with behavioural dispositions and tendencies, and probably operate causally to create them. Even the information provided by the simple fertility monitoring device may correlate with behavioural tendencies, so that it could currently be used to predict PMT, for example, or to give warning of whatever other conditions and tendencies a sensitive user learned to associate with given readings of state, or rate of change of state. Such warnings could be used to avoid social interactions, or important encounters, or particularly demanding obligations, at given future times. Evidently, even now, immediate knowledge of hormone levels could be used in the detailed day-to-day planning of everyday activities. Knowledge of the causes of one's behaviour could be used, as it were, in choosing it. Here is an interesting alternative route through which hormone levels are capable of affecting human behaviour.

It is easy to construct yet more exotic future scenarios, and to extend the discussion from hormonal to genetic profiling. But the significance of all this must be kept in proportion. There is nothing unprecedented here, nothing that cannot be adequately assimilated to existing paradigms of understanding. Certainly, there are existing precedents and analogies for everything alluded to in the preceding paragraph, and none of them is found at all problematic at the everyday level. Diabetics have long monitored their immediate hormonal state and adjusted their day-to-day lives to take account of it, knowing how it is liable to affect their behaviour. Drug users, that is, most of us, are very well aware of the behavioural correlates of internal levels of these substances and make allowance accordingly. Such cases present no problems to the robustly compatibilist discourse of everyday life. Revelations of the causal impact of internal states on how we behave have long been available and long been taken account of, which somewhat calls into question the conjecture that further such revelations will have any profound significance.

Left to itself, biotechnological research will confront our internal states, as it were, in three ways. It will diagnose them, and relate them to our actions and behaviours. It will develop means of modifying them, perhaps with the goal of modifying the related actions and behaviours.

And it will perhaps eventually find itself with the means of modifying them so profoundly that the very relationships between 'us' and 'our inner states', and between the different 'individuals' who constitute the 'us', are thrown into confusion.[6] Of this last nothing specific will be said here, although the book as a whole offers an implicit message on the matter, in the shape of its account of 'us' and the relation of status and state in that account. But in so far as the diagnosis and description of inner states is concerned, and even the modification of those states, the suggestion is that nothing unprecedented or even especially unfamiliar is involved. Having said this, however, it is immediately necessary to add that when the same kind of point is made as part of the rhetoric of reassurance that now surrounds biotechnology it is often advanced in a completely unacceptable way. The claim that there is nothing fundamentally new here is liable to become the claim that there is nothing new here at all, in this context, and legitimate anxieties to be dismissed as mere irrationality. In truth, there are sensible grounds for these anxieties and it is even possible to offer thoroughly practical rationalisations for many of them – rationalisations intelligible even to those so impoverished that their only notion of rationality is utilitarian rationality.

Many biotechnological procedures are going to be applicable in areas that so far have been subject to little systematic control and scarcely any external regulation – areas where the ordering of conduct into collectively tolerable patterns has hitherto depended on the lack of knowledge and power of those engendering the conduct. As power becomes available where power previously was not, this basis of existing co-ordination may be eliminated and a profound problem of social order created – precisely the kind of problem that generates anxiety and a sense of moral and ethical disorientation. The point is easily illustrated by reference to existing diagnostic resources. Single individuals may become empowered by the advent of such a resource, and the empowerment of individuals is liable to create problems of collective action. The parent with access for the first time to techniques for selecting the sex[7] of a child is able to act for her individual good, and without regard for the collective good, in a way that before was impossible. This empowerment has arisen in a context where individual discretion has traditionally reigned supreme. Before empowerment the exercise of that discretion could engender little in the way of collective harm. After empowerment the capacity for collective harm is enormous: widespread use of the relevant powers, say to guarantee the conception of male children, could be disastrous. It is important to recognise also that the provision of 'abstract' knowledge may empower, just as much as the direct provision of new technique. On being given knowledge of her state, the carrier of a deleterious gene is put in the same position as the parent given the means of selecting the sex of her child. By knowing that she carries a recessive allele for one of the heritable anaemias, for example, an individual is empowered to act with regard to her own good and without regard to the collective good, or vice versa, as previously she could not do. And the partner of the individual, or her doctor, or the biotechnologist who makes the knowledge available, may be placed in the same kind of position by its possession.

Needless to say, being constituted of responsible agents and not independent individuals, societies will often move quickly to solve the relevant collective action problems by subjecting individuals to social influence, regulation or control. But anxieties about the dissolution of existing forms of order may well reasonably extend to the question of the kind of order that will replace it. That the assimilation of new techniques always implies a reconstitution of social order is not always appreciated by technical experts themselves, who may expect to be as powerfully placed in any new order as in the old, but for others it is a major area of unpredictability and hence anxiety. Even as new human biotechnology offers individuals new powers, they will find themselves facing claims from various competing sources, all seeking to regulate and control their behaviour. In such case studies as currently exist, claims of this kind have been made by peers, by informally accepted authorities in the social setting, by semi-autonomous professional experts, and by bureaucratic creatures of the state. And the studies record both highly beneficial and deeply tragic consequences of the imposition of all four kinds of control (Wilkie, 1993). What kind of control becomes dominant, if any, in the future use of biotechnological techniques remains to be seen. One inductively plausible conjecture is that their diffusion will be accompanied by greatly intensified medical and bureaucratic intrusions into the relevant areas of human activity, although this is not the only conceivable scenario.

Biotechnology and the explanation of action

The rise of the new human biotechnology is engendering anxiety, and rightly so. But whether that anxiety is linked, as some suggest, primarily to its challenge to our notions of individual agency and integrity, and the larger ideological frame in which they are set, is another matter. The assertion of such a link, so often advanced in the context of abstract debate, is difficult to square with the manifest ease with which everyday discourse combines voluntarism and causal forms of understanding, even causal accounts of the voluntary behaviour of human beings. Given the easy-going compatibilism of most everyday discourse, it seems more likely that the causal internalist explanatory schemes of biotechnology and genetic engineering will be assimilated to it, or accepted by it, without any profound adjustment being entailed either in practice or in cognition. People will continue to deploy voluntaristic notions to orient toward other people, to acknowledge their status as carriers of rights and obligations, and to interact with them. And they will continue to use a repertoire of causal accounting to link what they do to antecedents and to anticipate their possible future actions.

To say this, of course, is little more than to assert a prejudice in favour of the account of ordinary discourse given in the first part of this book. That account characterised their voluntaristic discourse as the crucial medium through which human beings affected each others' actions. It was an account in no way inconsistent with actions having causal antecedents, whether external or internal/biological. And it provided a sensible rationale for the acknowledgement of such causes, even within a discourse that retained its voluntaristic idiom notwithstanding, and continued to treat those participating in it as responsible agents.

It is interesting to ask how this account might be related to the kinds of causal/explanatory claim that will surely proliferate as the new human biotechnology is extended. An example is necessary here, but it is not necessary to look to the leading edge of genetic science for something that offers clear illustration of the necessary points. Brief mention was made in the first chapter of this book of a case where the possibility of a causal link from inner nature to 'chosen' behaviour has already been widely entertained. Let us return to this example, and ask what might follow if variations in sex-chromosome complement are causally linked to variations in how people behave. It does not matter that the particular connection proposed in the example is now largely discounted, perhaps indeed that is an advantage: in its form it exemplifies a whole class of cases wherein the possibility of this kind of link arises, and indeed its only relevance here is as a vehicle for discussing the general problems raised by such cases. What the truth is about sex chromosomes and how we behave is immaterial here.[8]

Having emphasised the irrelevance of the details of the example, it is perhaps still worth indicating just how very complex they are. The number of sex-chromosome complements (karyotypes) identified in living human beings runs well into double figures, and there are in addition persons whose body cells have a mosaic pattern, with some being of one complement and some being of another. Chromosome complements are in any case only extremely coarse indicators of variations in genetic material, and they give no information as to what of that information is active or 'switched on' and what is not. The correlation of the complements with phenotype is also far from straightforward: there are known 'XY females' and 'XX males', and what counts as phenotypically male or female itself shows considerable empirical variation. Finally, of course, there is further variation between instances in terms of ascribed gender status and preferred gender role. Clearly, a serious discussion of actual states of affairs would demand an entire book in itself, and as far as empirical matters are concerned any brief account can be little more than drollery.

The case mentioned earlier was in fact two: that of carriers of the XYY chromosome complement as compared to the XY, and that of the XY as compared to the XX. The first comparison is possible because of post-war developments in biological science: the XYY complement was identified in the 1960s and conjectures about its possible behavioural significance followed very soon after as a result of what prima facie were surprisingly large numbers of carriers in certain custodial institutions. The second comparison has been possible for much longer and serves as a reminder of how little is new under the sun: it offers much stronger evidence of a correlation between behaviour and chromosome complement than the first, although not of genetic causation. Possessors of XY and XYY chromosome complements generally occupy identical gender statuses; the XY and XX complements, in contrast, correlate very strongly indeed with the different gender statuses of male and female, permitting an alternative explanation of behavioural differences between their possessors in terms of external causation.

Let us recall the formal features which make these cases interesting. There are, we assume, two groups of people different in aspects of their nature. A 'normal' (N) group of XX females may be compared with a group of XY males, or a 'normal' group of XY males may be compared with a group of XYY males. We can allude to both cases by speaking of an N group and a Y group, with the first including individuals of N-nature and the second those of Y-nature. Secondly, the difference in nature is associated with differences in voluntary behaviour: it may be, for example, that Y-nature is more strongly associated with violence than N-nature. Finally we assume that the difference in nature becomes accepted as the only plausible way of accounting for the difference in behaviour, and that a causal link relates the two.

There are many existing social contexts where male/female behavioural differences, including different propensities to violence, are accounted for causally by references to natural difference. And where this is done in the realm of everyday discourse, it is normally done as a routine and unremarkable mode of accounting that does not affect the standing of men as responsible agents. Yet from some perspectives such accounting raises serious problems. In particular, if chosen actions are liable to blame and caused actions do not attract it, then the acknowledgement of 'chosen-caused' actions is not merely inconsistent at the level of ideas but a serious problem at the level of practical action. In order to avoid this problem, it is necessary to insist on a rigorous incompatibilism, and radically to restrict the scope either of causal explanation or the imputation of blame. Both these alternatives buy consistency at a heavy price. If the first is implemented, then all the available resources for understanding voluntary actions in terms of causal antecedents have to be renounced, including the present and future resources of the new human biotechnology, and all preferred explanations from that quarter have to be rejected *a priori*. But the consequences of adopting the second possibility are still more far-reaching. The causal accounting of a biological-genetic perspective is not merely a mode of understanding what is abnormal or variant. It is a comprehensively causal orientation: in so far as it offers a causal account of behaviour linked to Y-nature, it offers the same form of account of behaviour linked to N-nature as well. Thus, if one accepts the genetic causation postulated by biotechnology and holds that where it is operative there is no room for blame, then there is no scope for the institution of blame at all.

In practice, we are a society willing neither to pay the price of restricting the scope of causal and naturalistic accounting, nor to forego use of the institution of blame. Hence, whatever incompatibilism is to be found in our practical life is typically sustained in a formally unsatisfactory form, as is the case, for example, in many legal contexts. Among the strategies commonly employed to 'reconcile' references to choice and causation is that of understanding the former in an incompatibilist sense, but allowing that features of human nature, or else immediate contingent features of a human body, may causally affect the conditions which constrain our power to choose. Then actions remain potentially blameworthy, with the degree of blame depending on the precise extent to which free will is supposedly constrained by the givens of human nature. Sadly, however, measurement of the relevant 'constraints' is still a little difficult. And the thought that access to a genetic profile, plus a range of hormone tests, is the least that is required as the prelude to any attribution of blame or fixing of responsibility is one that legal authorities seem (very sensibly) so far to have failed to think.

Nobody is in a position to demonstrate that it is incorrect to use 'choice' and 'causation' as opposed and contrasting notions, and nobody can dismiss out of hand proposals to abolish the institution of blame or vastly to increase the resources for genetic profiling and hormone testing. Nonetheless, consideration of these options can lead to an increased appreciation of the merits of everyday informal compatibilism, and of formal arguments against a presumed contrast of what is caused and what is chosen. If such arguments are accepted, then 'the solution' to the problem implicit in our example is simply to do as everyday discourse so often does, and allow that the differences in the behaviour of groups N and Y may be both caused and chosen, both entirely due to natural causes operating in the context of given conditions *and* voluntary in character and liable to blame. There is no need to withdraw imputations of choice, or even agency, in order to accommodate to expanding causal accounts of human behaviour, nor need we refrain from blame as we learn more of the causal antecedents of voluntary actions.

But if voluntary actions have causal antecedents sufficient to account for them, what is it about them that makes them voluntary? The form of the answer has been given already in Chapter 5: kinds of actions designated as voluntary are generally those we believe to be modifiable by symbolic intervention, perhaps through the operation of the deference-emotion system. If this is correct, then in the last analysis violent assaults are commonly regarded as voluntary actions because verbal intervention, persuasion, calming the person down, and so forth, offer hope of forestalling them, even where men are involved. And such designations would not be called into question by research showing that those afflicted with XY chromosome complement are far more prone to engage in violence: indeed, we know as much already. Nor would they be called into question by evidence of genetic causation – or indeed by evidence of environmental causation. Basically we treat male violence as voluntary, and its sources as responsible agents, as part of the business of engaging with those agents, in the belief that a certain mode of engaging with them might have efficacy – that it might result in their 'acting otherwise'.

Let us look at this matter of the responsible agency of men in another way. In our society men are much more prone to violence than women are. Let us assume that a causal story can be given of this. Perhaps it is something to do with men's Y-nature and the endocrinological states associated with it. Perhaps those of Y-nature will act violently in a much wider range of conditions and circumstances than those of N-nature. It is also the case that in our society members are expected to desist from violence. It is an expectation which falls fairly equally on everyone but which evidently places a greater burden upon men. Men constitute the vast majority of those imprisoned for violence, and the majority of the violent criminally insane. They incur more blame and disapproval, more liabilities, more costs, on account of institutionalised injunctions against violence, than women do. And one can only guess at how much additional work they have to do by way of controlling and dissipating rage and anger, subduing tantrums and fits of temper and so forth. Should we not sympathise with the plight of men in the face of oppressive impersonal institutions which seem to take little account of their peculiar inherent limitations and difficulties? Admittedly, some legal systems do quietly offer them some small reliefs: manslaughter laws may make some allowance for their relative lack of self-control, and the notion of the crime of passion may cater for some of the causes which make them prone to murder their wives or their lovers. For the most part, however, they face the formal rigours of the law and the informal evaluations of others much as other members do, even though they may be less well equipped by nature to meet the relevant expectations. Yet no systematic attempt is ever made to tell causal stories on their behalf, in an effort to exculpate them or to secure special institutional arrangements for them. Why is this? Plausible causal stories are available. Why is no use made of them?

There are two fundamental options open to those who face difficulties coping with the expectations associated with a given status. One is to perform in status nonetheless, and to accept whatever in the way of honour and contempt, praise or blame, one's performance attracts, along, of course, with whatever more substantial sanctions might exist. The other is to take up whatever available causal stories will serve as the basis for a plea of impaired agency. A plea of this kind may be successful in modifying the expectations of others, and hence in bringing the individual more praise and less blame for a given performance. But to offset this gain there will be a corresponding loss. The individual who successfully claims impaired agency is liable to be moved to a lower, less honourable status – in the extreme case to lose the basic status of responsible agent altogether and be assigned some special lesser alternative. By analogy the collective that successfully claims impaired agency is liable to see its collective status category moved down the ranking of statuses and its relative standing diminished. A successful claim of impaired agency avoids the penalties of status incompetence through status degradation. The dangers of blame diminish but those of stigmatisation increase.

Responsible agents evaluate each other through acknowledgements of status and through acknowledgements of competent performance in status, and the balancing of the one and the other is an important part of the drama of everyday life. Even in our own society the tension between the two things is apparent, notwithstanding that many of the gradations of status it implies are not supposed to exist. Thus, at one painful extreme, practically every group explicitly defined by impaired agency, whether the impairment is physically or mentally based, complains of stigmatisation. The mentally handicapped and the mentally ill, the palsied and the paralysed, the burned and the facially deformed, all find cause for dissatisfaction in their treatment by a population all nowadays aware of its duty to relate to them correctly and anxious to do so, but less than clear what such a relationship should consist in. The same is found at the other extreme experienced by the numerous beneficiaries of the ubiquitous practice of *making allowances*. It might be thought a simple matter of common sense and adaptability to make allowance for the other in social interaction, but every such action is liable, nonetheless, through its studied avoidance of blame, stubbornly to retain something of the quality of a miniature status degradation ceremony. Certainly it seems easier to make allowances for others than to acknowledge that others are making allowances for us. Anyone magnanimous enough to pass over the less than competent social performances of others, and not skilled enough to disguise what she is doing, is liable to stir that special form of indignation reserved for those who patronise and condescend, and who thereby imply our status inferiority. Indeed, even when the making of allowances is accomplished with great skill, as, for example, in many of the situations that Goffman so perceptively described, the hidden injuries to self-esteem can be serious.

In effect, it has been asked above whether we should not make allowances for men, and the implicit suggestion of status degradation should have been clearly heard in the very question. The question was a rhetorical device to draw attention to the strength of attachments to status. Recognition of status is in practice always of far greater importance, both individually and collectively, than recognition of any particular level of competent performance in status. Only in extremis will individual men seek status degradation. Even when possessed of highly credible stories of the causal antecedents of their actions, they will generally avoid giving prominence to them or making them the basis of claims to impaired agency. And at the collective level not even the possibility of such claims is going to be contemplated.

Collectively, there are expectations which men are going to meet less often and less adequately than women; for example, the avoidance of violent behaviour. In interactional contexts men will accordingly be blamed more and suffer more for behaviour some of which, it could be said, they couldn't help. But it is worth considering whether this is not a reasonable price for men collectively to pay for the privilege of being treated as responsible agents. Indeed, it is even worth asking whether men, with their tendencies to violence, should not welcome those social pressures and communicative interactions which keep these tendencies at the lowest possible levels of expression. And if this is so, then why should men do other than acknowledge fault and blameworthiness on those occasions when, through whatever cause, they lapse into violence notwithstanding?

Implicit in the discussion here is an important general point about the character of social institutions. We deceive ourselves about the basis of our own behaviour if we regard them as no more than oppressive externalities. Participation in institutions, for all that a burden of expectation may be involved, is fundamentally a privilege, and the status under which one participates confers an inherent dignity, as well as making one a potential recipient not just of blame and disapprobation but of praise and honour as well. This is true even of the rudimentary social status of the responsible agent that represents the default position in our dealings with others. Unless there are positive indications to the contrary, we assign responsibility to the other and thereby a certain basic human dignity. The assignation implies a voluntaristic orientation and a presumption of accountability and susceptibility in interaction, and it serves further as a kind of licence permitting participation in the more specialised roles and statuses sustained in and by the collective. It is a licence which may be extensively endorsed and qualified but which is normally withdrawn only with very great reluctance and via ritual procedures that are not particularly easy to arrange.

In a given collective, licence-holders will be individual persons with different natures, in different and varying states, loci of different causal processes, possessors of different skills and competences, talents and abilities, susceptibilities and vulnerabilities. But institutional expectations communicated in an ongoing voluntaristic discourse will bear down in ways that take no specific account of these individual differences, that treat all the occupants of a given status as very much alike. Thus some individuals will be blamed more, coerced more, made answerable more than others. From an individual point of view, some will pay a higher price for retaining their licence than others, although scarcely any will think the price not worth paying. From the point of view of the collective, on the other hand, some licence-holders will contribute less to the collective good than others, and cost more to influence and control, although scarcely any will merit disqualification. From the point of view of the collective, nearly all will be accessible through communicative interaction and to some extent susceptible to others in that interaction; to that extent they will be counted as responsible agents, possessed of rationality and free will, whatever causal antecedents are believed to bear upon their actions.

What the new biotechnology is in the course of doing is identifying greatly increased numbers of such causal antecedents and implying the existence of many more, yet to be identified. In this way it is increasing our understanding of how individual human beings are prone to act, and our awareness of the extent of individual difference and diversity amongst human beings. But none of these revelations of difference need be taken as grounds for denying specific persons the licence permitting their participation in the institution of responsible action. And such participation precisely involves their social interaction through the medium of a voluntaristic discourse, discourse in which others orient to their actions as chosen ones for which they are accountable. Indeed, it is precisely interaction in this voluntaristic idiom that allows the orderly social life in the context of which we exist to be enacted by the remarkably diverse organisms that we are.

Conclusions

In everyday discourse we have no difficulty in giving simultaneous expression to the thought that, as individuals, people all differ in their nature, and as responsible agents, accountable for their chosen actions, they are all somehow the same. It is those engaged in the systematic study of human beings who have difficulties with the resulting picture, because of the problems that are thrown up by attempts to give it detailed and rigorous expression. And the difficulties are intensified by the narrowing of vision attendant upon specialisation. Thus, when geneticists and biotechnologists extend their causal explanations to encompass human behaviour, it can be perfectly natural and forgivable for them to consider that their accounts face competition from 'voluntaristic explanations'. Voluntarism is thus encountered, not as the largely performative discourse of a vital institution through which human beings affect each other, but as an explanatory theory of individual behaviour.[9]

Biotechnologists are not always well equipped to deal with encounters with the institution of responsible action, but it may perhaps be that sociologists are no better equipped to deal with inherent individual differences. Historically, their concern has been with shared characteristics and ways of acting, rather than with what in individuals is idiosyncratic and differentiating. It is a standard point of epistemology that empirical phenomena are indefinitely complex and that all systems for their classification suppress vast amounts of information on the basis of which further distinctions and discriminations could always be made; but it is a point that sociologists have rarely had to take into account. A sense of rich difference, yet to be elucidated, is not routine for them; and the thought that social expectations bear alike upon individuals all with different natural powers and susceptibilities, many unobserved and unclassified, is rarely explicitly formulated. Indeed, there have been sociological theorists who have rendered individual persons simply as so many identical creations of institutional context, all fully interchangeable between equivalent points of a given set of roles. And there have been others who have baulked at the idea of inherent, context-independent kinds of individual difference because they have believed it to clash with the aim of securing genuine equality in society.[10]

It is true that there has been a move away from these modes of thought. In recent theories human beings are said to possess, in individual agency, an independent power that allows them to sustain difference in the face of external pressures making for normalisation and homogeneity, even if they only make sparing use of that power. But these theories do not address internal causation, and their insistence that all human actions 'could have been otherwise' identifies them as examples of just the kinds of theory with which a thoroughgoing causal biology would be liable to clash. The contrast between these forms of theory and the account offered here is fundamental. In them, the language of voluntarism is borrowed to emphasise how individuals are able to sustain difference and to make a difference. Here, the normal use of that language is identified as what allows responsible agents to overcome difference and achieve co-ordination; and its use and its content are perfectly compatible with causal accounts of such difference, including biological-causal accounts. This compatibilist view suggests how sociology, biology, and indeed any field seeking a naturalistic understanding of human actions might relate their perspectives: they should consider a picture wherein responsible agents, who differ in nature and state, who differ in history and enculturating experiences, who communicate together through the medium of a voluntaristic discourse, act in ways to an understanding of which all these things are material, and at a level of co-ordination to which the last thing in particular is material.

Of course, a sociological compatibilist position neither implies nor recommends that imputations of choice and of causation proceed without any kind of connection between the one and the other. Causes which make actions impregnable to disturbance may and do sensibly prompt agreement that choice is absent; causal stories which imply that agents are chronically impervious to all symbolic intervention may still legitimate the withdrawal of the licence of responsible agency. The compatibilist perspective merely exposes such withdrawals as contingent evaluative decisions. They are not required responses to the manifest presence of causes or even to convictions that causes are present. They are reflections of policy in our orientations to other people. Needless to say, this is policy that could be varied very substantially, but this is by no means to imply any fault with how it stands at present. It is sometimes said that our legal system errs too far on the side of caution in identifying those individuals who 'can't help it', and indeed more 'understanding' policies can easily be imagined than those it currently pursues. Again, it is possible to point to systems more willing than our own to listen to the causal stories of therapists and psychiatrists, and to suspend or qualify normal expectations in the light of them. But perhaps our own relative reluctance to follow these paths represents a virtue not a failing. It is worth repeating that responsibility, for all the stresses and difficulties to which it may give rise, is in the last analysis a privilege not a burden, and one that should be suspended only with the very greatest reluctance. To make allowance for the other may be to do harm to the other, as we recognise in our knowledge of the harm it can do to us. The right to be treated as a responsible agent is crucial to the living of a good life, in just the way that the right of a company to be sued is crucial to its ability to do business.

Notes

1 Science and technology are 'technical', and their technical difficulty is sometimes cited as an explanation of their neglect, but this seems unlikely, given that there are sociologists capable of reading George Friedrich Hegel and Talcott Parsons. And explanation by reference to technical difficulty fails to account for the way that science and technology *have* very recently become of some interest to the mainstream of sociology, and even begun at last to feature in the textbooks. Current introductions to sociology are beginning to discuss ecology, pollution and other dangers to the environment, and green issues. These are technical matters with a vengeance that require an understanding not just of the bases of scientific predictions but of the extent to which tiny errors are likely to arise in them. To encounter judgements on these issues, in texts that still omit any discussion of the main thrust of scientific and technological activity, is rather like reading technical discussions of the balance of payments, in an economics text that omits all discussion of exporting and importing as unduly difficult. To make sense of this strange state of affairs it is necessary to remember that sociologists often see theirs as a critical discipline, and that their interest in dominant powers and practices tends to focus exclusively upon their failings.
2 Technological determinism can often be found lying unacknowledged in some surprising places in current sociology and social theory. For a sophisticated defence of the position see Winner (1977) and for a recent overview Smith and Marx (1994).
3 The Reith lectures given by Steve Jones in 1991 are a useful marker here, and indeed Jones has continued to labour for the cause (1994, 1996).
4 It is worth taking note, as well, of the difficulty of predicting future developments here. On the one hand, simple projections from present rates of change risk underestimating what is in store, because they make no allowance for the

unpredictable radical innovations in techniques that are liable to occur, and that may increase their potency by orders of magnitude if and when they do. A good way of appreciating the immense importance of this kind of innovation is to read the extended study by Rabinow (1996). On the other hand, projections by apologists need to be treated with reserve because of the existence of so many incentives to exaggeration. It is important, as well, not to infer the future significance of the new human biotechnology from the extent of the resources being devoted to it. It is indeed a major enterprise, as the vast sums being devoted to the Human Genome Project nicely symbolise, but greater sums have been devoted to fundamental particle physics without vast consequence either for our economy or for our everyday culture.

5 The example of prophylactic incarceration, currently in the spotlight as people fulminate about paedophiles, is but a small illustration of a widespread enthusiasm for forms of sanctioning and control attracted not by what a person does but by what she is taken to be. Biotechnology offers immense potential resources to a future control-freak society.

6 Technical possibilities like those that permit corpses to become biological parents, or those that permit cloning, imply new kinds of relations between humans which some clearly find far more threatening than others. Techniques that allow the detailed modification of the information in human germ cells are more widely opposed because, it is said, they will disrupt our sense of individual agency and personal integrity. Even this kind of disruption has precedents, of course. Those human beings whose brains have been cut in two for medical reasons similarly challenge us to reflect on what personal integrity involves.

7 This is the correct word despite the ridiculous terminology of those medical professionals who now speak of 'gender-selection clinics'. Evidently the term 'sex' is now almost wholly restricted to describing kinds of activity descriptions of which sell newspapers. Talk of 'gender chromosomes' would seem the appropriate next step.

8 Chromosome 11 currently seems to be attracting more attention than the Y chromosome in this regard.

9 This perception of different theories competing for territory is, moreover, not just that of strong genetic determinists: it may also constitute an important element in the thought of their opponents: 'shallow genetic determinism is unwise and untrue. But society will have to wrestle with the question of how much of our make-up is dictated by the environment, how much is dictated by our genetics, and how much is dictated by our own will and determination' (Gilbert, 1992, p. 96). It is salutary to note how this well-meaning passage by an eminent biotechnologist parcels out our 'make-up' between two causal theories and a voluntaristic one, and thereby adds to what is already widely recognised as a wholly misconceived account of the relationship of genes and environment an analogously misconceived account of the relationship of genes and will.

10 Whilst few theorists of this kind have pretended to have a specific vision of what a genuinely equal society would consist in, they have been in no doubt that the existence of inherent individual differences would complicate the task of achieving it: if people differ in nature, then any institutional arrangement which treats them alike thereby generates an unequal distribution of suffering.

8

RATIONAL AGENTS IN DIFFERENTIATED SOCIETIES

Morals and ethics in a differentiated society

Neither sociological theory nor social theory more broadly conceived are well-defined and clearly demarcated activities. There is no strong boundary between social theory, political theory and moral and political philosophy, nor between descriptive and normative orientations to society in any of these fields. Social theorists have not merely described the changes attendant upon the growth of technological resources and the differentiation of society; they have also as a matter of course offered evaluations of them and of the changed patterns of choice and responsibility bound up with them. How the materials in this book relate to such evaluations will be the focus of the discussion in this chapter.

It might be thought that no extended discussion is necessary, since it is part and parcel of any truly naturalistic approach to how human beings live that it recognises its own irrelevance to moral and ethical questions of how they ought to live. Did not David Hume so effectively demonstrate the inability of reason to make a deduction from 'is' to 'ought' as to leave little more to be said here? It is true that Hume lamented the way that his contemporaries moved from 'is' to 'ought' without adequately grounding the move, and that he denied the possibility of a purely deductive grounding for it.[1] But it is also true that Hume himself moved easily from 'is' to 'ought': on the basis of his understanding of human nature, and the assumption that our actions ought to be conducive to human happiness, he made inferences about how we ought to act. Hume had a moral philosophy, and a specific conception of human nature was bound up with it. To that extent, a naturalistic account of human beings as social animals is relevant to any evaluation of Hume's moral philosophy. And the example nicely symbolises the general relevance of what has been set forth here to moral and ethical issues. It has little direct significance for these issues. But whenever moral or ethical arguments make essential references to how people are, it becomes relevant. And there is scarcely any area of moral or ethical debate where such references are not made.

The philosopher who famously insisted on a rigorous separation of 'is' and 'ought' was not Hume but Kant. For Kant, the features of the situations wherein moral judgements are made are of no relevance, and neither are their history and their connections with larger contexts of social experience. The natural characteristics of individual human beings are of no relevance either, not even those that are universal to the species and referred to as constitutive of human nature. Nor are the contingent consequences of moral actions relevant to their standing. All that is relevant is individual reason and individual will, oriented to a universal moral rule in the noumenal realm. Moral judgement is cut off from all contamination by the merely contingent. Even so, the credibility of such an account is going to depend on its being generally found consistent with actual, contingent features of human experience.

Kant's is a magnificent articulation of Enlightenment individualism as moral theory. It is also crucial in any reflection on current moral and ethical arguments; for it is at once almost irresistibly attractive, yet almost impossible to accept. What attracts is Kant's optimism. He had unbridled faith in the power of individual reason and believed it capable of identifying a single, true, substantive moral code. He believed that such a code, if followed, was capable of establishing right conduct and a good way of living across humankind as a whole. And he believed that human beings could reasonably be expected to follow such a code, that it could serve as the practical basis of conduct and not merely as an elusive ideal. As Jürgen Habermas (1990, p. 206) has put it, Kant was guilty of rigorism, and actually expected people to obey moral maxims.

What makes us unable to accept the Kantian view is our experience as members of a society of diverse moralities. Kant took it for granted that reason spoke with one voice, but in our experience it speaks with many. Kant imagined reason speaking of one morality, but in our experience it offers alternatives. Our experience is the product of our life in highly differentiated societies, wherein different moral frameworks exist, generally in peaceful accommodation. In such a context no single substantive moral order commands ubiquitous authority and respect. If justification for moral or ethical claims is sought, it is necessary to appeal to standards specific to particular moral traditions, carried by bounded sub-cultures, or else to look beyond all such standards for something abstract and universal that human beings everywhere might unknowingly share. The one possibility implies attention to what goes on within one or another of the moral traditions of the differentiated society; the alternative implies attention to what goes on across them, where interaction has necessarily to transcend their particularity.

Many moral philosophers, particularly those who work close to the edge of social and political theory, tend to accept a picture of this kind as the backdrop for their work. It is a picture shared by those who otherwise radically disagree, by Jürgen Habermas and Alasdair MacIntyre for example, whose work will be used extensively in this chapter to exem-

plify two opposed ways of developing a moral philosophy appropriate
in the context of a differentiated society. Habermas and MacIntyre are
both rationalist philosophers but rationalists of very different kinds.
Habermas has inherited the Enlightenment view of reason and sees it as
a force able to overcome tradition and transcend its limitations. It moves
human beings in the direction of the universal. In the context of a differentiated society it makes possible dialogue between those who initially
disagree on moral and ethical matters, and offers the hope of sufficient
agreement on the character of right conduct to permit of peace.
MacIntyre, in contrast, opposes the Enlightenment view and makes
reason subordinate to tradition. Only in the context of specific moral traditions, wherein clear inferences from shared objective moral and ethical
standards can be made and acted upon, will the use of reason lead to a
rational and fulfilling life for human beings.

In his very early account of *Secularisation and Moral Change* (1967),
MacIntyre remarks how *secondary virtues* are become the basis for orderly
social relations in a differentiated society encompassing distinct co-exist-
ing moral orders. Where the primary virtues upheld in these distinct
orders would otherwise clash, secondary virtues, such as tolerance, fairness or willingness to compromise, are invoked as a basis for peaceful
orderly interaction. But the import of MacIntyre's discussion is first, that
without commitments to primary virtues there is nothing for secondary
virtues to do, and, second, that if one has primary commitments it is not
logically consistent to espouse a morality of secondary virtues as well.
The thought is, for example, that if an abortion is wrong in being murder
it cannot at the same time be right as the expression of a compromise, or
as the practice of another sub-culture deserving of toleration.[2] Thus, life
lived on the basis of secondary virtues lacks rationality and authenticity,
and this is precisely the condition of life in modern societies due to the
contradictory demands placed on their members by different primary
moral codes. The fragmentation of society into different moral orders plus
the need for individuals to move between them and interact across them
is at the root of the problem. Even if individuals are in practice uncon-
cerned by the resulting moral inconsistency of their actions, they can be
criticised for it: this is valid immanent criticism that should be recognisable as valid by those to whom it is directed, given their own moral
assumptions and their standing as rational human beings.

MacIntyre's assertion that secondary virtues like fairness, toleration
and willingness to compromise have an especially prominent role in our
current moral and ethical discourse is surely correct.[3] Nor is it difficult
to understand why this is so. In differentiated societies, wherein 'reason'
conveys different moral messages to different people, to act 'authentically', without regard to such virtues, would mean war. It is a tribute to
the collective agency of the members of these societies that they have
evolved moral discourses centred on the secondary virtues, and thereby
devised a basis for social action that has made for peace. In whatever

particular contexts it has been possible, they have developed bounded patterns of action incorporating tolerance and co-operation. Act together where and to the extent that there is agreement, so the recipe has been, and keep institutional life constituted on that basis; refrain from acting where there is disagreement but allow both the conflicting positions their place in a private realm.[4] This seems increasingly to be 'the modern solution' to the securing of peaceful interaction, although it has long been associated with contexts where similar difficulties have had to be overcome – with trading centres, for example, or cosmopolitan cities, or élites in multicultural empires.

It is tempting to say that rationality has been *sacrificed* to peace in modern societies, but this may be to say too much. A fundamental issue arises here. Consider how the discourse of the secondary virtues today is not merely ubiquitous but also largely unproblematic and matter-of-course. Consider also how very smooth the move to compromise and a reconciliation of prima-facie opposed positions can be in differentiated societies. Actions are readily made out as compatible with whatever principles are expedient, and opposed principles are easily reconceptualised as but different expressions of some more general one, without any difficulties arising in the way of 'logical' inconsistencies. Peace may well be the object of changes of this kind, but whether agents actually subordinate their reason to it is another matter. Since empirical evidence of this is lacking, the belief that it occurs presumably derives from a prior conception of ourselves as rational agents in some strict formal sense. This is a conception that needs to be questioned. It could be, for example, that human beings everywhere are of their nature responsible agents, oriented to the piecemeal production of orderly interactions, and not individually rational agents oriented to the production of rigorous formal rationalisations of their actions. It could even be that the very idea of a rational agent in this last sense is incoherent.

In any event, the modern solution to what may as well be called the problem of social order is apparent everywhere in today's differentiated societies. This is the case at the level of individual morality, and even more so at the level of role. The two social roles whose alliance lies at the core of modern societies – the official and the advocate – also nicely symbolise the kinds of dissimulation crucial to their existence. The official must feign detachment from beliefs and moral orientations extrinsic to role, and address a diversity of members with the ritual courtesies appropriate to the stranger, in order, as it were, to represent the whole to the part. The advocate – not just as the lawyer theatrically dissembling in the courtroom, but as the intellectual who takes a position, or, increasingly, as the no longer independent technical expert who speaks for an organisation – must feign attachment to beliefs and moral orientations intrinsic to role in order to represent the part to the whole. The successful modern intellectual recognises a duty to represent a position. Concern for truth is considered less important than a fierce defence of the partial vision of things consistent with the position. And the technical expert can similarly cease to worry about 'the whole picture', secure in the knowledge that others in her trade will be presenting different positions in the same partial way. Truth, as it were, becomes structural. And the ordinary member of society has to cope with a world, not of endemic uncertainty as previously was normal, but of contradictory certitudes. Nor are these merely the certitudes of competing industrial organisations and government agencies. Today, vast multinational bureaucracies like Shell are infested with sizeable parasitic multinational bureaucracies like Greenpeace, which employ expertise against expertise with the active support of a range of 'lifeworld' interests. And it is possible to discern a certain poetic justice in the way that these parasitic predators evince a cynical virtuosity in the use of PR, image management, media manipulation, and the casual dissemination of expedient untruths, that exceeds even that of their prey.

Evidently, the modern solution is apparent both in the private realm of 'individual morality' and in the public realm of 'role performance'. But it is also a manifestation of the modern solution that we speak of 'both'. We go to work, in the factory or the laboratory or the nuclear power station, and return afterwards to the private realm, where (as we say) diverse moral and ethical considerations may bear upon our behaviour. We hand over some of the resources thereby acquired to government, and make use of the rest in the private realm, in the light of those moral and ethical considerations, with the resulting individual variation being converted, via the institution of money, into a uniform consumer demand. The existence of a separate 'private' realm of ethics and morals is indeed crucial to the implementation of the modern solution.

There are many ways of reflecting on moral action in societies constituted in this way. If their members are the rational agents of moral philosophy, then their actions are profoundly irrational and an extremely powerful immanent criticism can be directed against them. If they are the responsible agents of this book, then for all the piecemeal character of their moral and ethical practice that criticism is not available. But in actuality it is neither of these perspectives that has dominated our thought about ourselves. Differentiation affects cognition as well as action. The predominant trend of development from Kant's comprehensive individualism has been toward partial, specialised individualisms, lacking any vision of society as a whole and hence of individual life as a whole. In these perspectives 'the individual' has a way of appearing as a marker of the unknown, of the area of experience beyond the gaze of the specialised field. Thus, behind the uniformity of demand lies what for economists is the mystery of different individual wants, and behind production lies (or used to lie) so many unexamined, identical sources of labour. Similarly, behind the debates of a differentiated political theory there lies the individual as sacred object, for which justice and security are provided and on which rights are draped, a shell the existence of which is essential but the inner nature of which need be of no interest at all. The dominant liberal account of life in our modern differentiated societies is constituted almost entirely from these specialised individualisms. It is an account remarkable for how little attention it gives to the nature of its central theoretical entity: the individual. But it is this very neglect which makes liberalism the perfect analogue in cognition of the modern solution incarnate in our practice: where it is important that we refrain from acting, we tend also to refrain from thinking. The sacralisation of the individual in liberal thought has been a form of mind surgery that has made for peace.

Individuals and rules

The liberal form of self-understanding that now prevails in our differentiated societies is continually being questioned. A whole tradition of work has criticised its lack of wholeness of vision. The contrasts between 'culture' and 'civilisation' in nineteenth-century social theory were an early expression of this, as were the references to a legendary 'traditional society' so common in the conservative literature of regret stimulated by industrialisation and democratisation. Later, critical theory – the original critical theory, that is, not the ever-so-slightly critical theory of today – would insist that a rational life for an individual person was only realisable in a properly rational society, and deny the possibility of any understanding of the one that failed to encompass the other. But as well as provoking this sort of reflection, liberalism also elicits a more diffuse hostility from groups uncomfortable with life in societies embodying the modern solution. They see it as the justification of the pluralism, the negatively defined objectives, and the lack of concern with the private realm characteristic of the government of these societies. And hostile constituencies of this kind may at times come together with academic critics to create powerful challenges to the liberal orthodoxy.

The communitarianism so prominent in the USA over the last quarter of a century and now increasingly influential in Europe is one such challenge. Predominantly it is a reaction to specific kinds of lived experience and is expressed as criticism of particular institutional arrangements. Its supporters believe that individuals in their society have too many rights and too few responsibilities, that too little account is taken of mediating institutions like the family, that localised communities and sub-cultures are not properly valued, and that governments have an unfulfilled obligation to sustain social and collective goods. But communitarianism has nonetheless defined itself by its rejection of individualistic theories of human nature. Its most cited texts (not always themselves the works of avowed communitarians) deny that persons are independent individuals and that individual goods are the only goods. Instead, they offer a number of versions of persons as social agents. In Michael Sandel's account, for example, what an individual person is may be partly a question of what community she identifies with, and her good may in part be the good of that community. In Alasdair MacIntyre, who a person is may be a matter of what roles she plays in a given social order, and her good may derive from her enactment of those roles. In Charles Taylor, the self is socially constituted, and the importance of its dignity, the respect accorded to it by others, is one of its basic moral intuitions: how the self stands in the eyes of others is essential to its good.[5]

It is intriguing to note how mild the reaction has been to the communitarian attack on the notion that persons are independent individuals. In liberal political theory and moral philosophy there has even been a move toward acknowledging its plausibility. This may perhaps count as further confirmation that 'the autonomous individual' referred to by liberal theorists is primarily someone whose independence ought to be presumed and respected by external powers, and not an abstraction from the results coming out of psychology laboratories. Despite the strong historical association of liberal political theories with individualistic theories of human nature, the connection of the two kinds of theory is well regarded as entirely contingent and open to variation.

An effort to combine a liberal moral philosophy with an understanding of persons as social agents is made in Habermas' recent work on ethics and morals. This work looks back to Kant's philosophy with its rationalism and its stress on the role of universal moral rules, but it is of course well aware of the limitations of that philosophy. Indeed, Habermas frankly dismisses the Kantian vision of authentic living in a rational society as an unviable ideal for modern conditions. People today must be left to pursue their own conceptions of a good life in different cultural traditions and through different lifestyle choices. The most that can be hoped for is a general acceptance of some common rules of right conduct, running across traditions and lifestyles, sufficient to allow individuals in the different traditions to rub along peacefully together. And even this is to be hoped for only because people are not independent individuals. Kant's individualism has to be rejected as well as his ideals of rigorism and authentic rationality. Rules of right conduct common to participants in different cultures or lifestyles can only emerge to the extent that the communicative interaction and discursive argumentation of social agents across cultures are capable of securing a rational consensus for them.

Habermas' description of the human beings for whom this modest consensus is possible is, on the face of it, radically sociological. They are constitutively communicative creatures. The human ego is constituted in the course of communicative action and is intersubjective to its core. It is a fragile creation of collective life that needs the continual reassurance it derives from that life if it is to continue. The very individuality of the ego is constituted socially and is not a cultural universal: individuation is the product of socialisation and proceeds most extensively only in the most highly differentiated forms of society. Despite all this, however,

Habermas does not dare to dispense with the traditional picture of the human being as a rational and autonomous agent, and it is soon once more upon the stage. The communication in which human beings engage, so Habermas tells us, invariably and necessarily takes the form of *rational argument*. But in arguing we presuppose the equality of the other as a rational agent like ourselves, and her autonomy as one who may respond 'yes' or 'no' to our claims. This is something that is the case in all cultures and all discourse, both within and across moral and ethical traditions, and as such it can be made the basis of a universal, if modest, moral and ethical theory.

The theory is Habermas' well-known account of discourse ethics (1990, 1992). It amounts to a modification of Kant wherein a moral rule is initially addressed, not by an individual, but by a collective, and evaluated, not directly by the inner light of individual reason, but by the social agents of the collective in the course of communicative action and hence of rational argument. The central tenets of discourse ethics are that rules or norms need to be evaluated discursively and collectively for fairness, that the individuals evaluating them need to understand each others' circumstances and interests, and that only those norms which each and every one of them freely and rationally accedes to should become accepted as ethical norms. These tenets are intended to give explicit expression to the autonomy and equality of standing that human beings implicitly accord to each other whenever they engage in discourse and hence in rational argument.

According to Habermas, the hope of agreeing rules of right conduct peacefully, through discourse and communication, is available to us only because we are social agents. However, his conception of social agency is a very limited one. Crucially, whilst he envisages human beings enriching their knowledge and awareness by communicative engagement and empathetic understanding before they evaluate a moral rule, when it comes to the business of evaluation itself, that remains a matter for the individual and the rule, in one-to-one encounter as it were. Habermas (1990, p. 93) stresses this: each and every human being involved in evaluating the rule must freely and rationally assent to it. Such assent confers moral validity because it involves the operation within the individual of a reason that, at its core, is autonomous and context-independent (even if the self of the individual it inhabits is not). This is why Habermas is no communitarian, why indeed his moral and political theory is continuous with that of the liberal tradition. Substantially, it remains the individualistic rationalism of Kant, expressed in a rendering that makes the maximum possible concession to contingency, collectivity, culture and context. In the last analysis, despite the involvement of communication and argumentation, validity derives from the right kind of encounter between a rule and an individual human subject.[6]

The problems inherent in this approach will be addressed shortly, but first let us look at a different way of understanding human beings as social agents. Alasdair MacIntyre is much cited by communitarians, not for the early work already described, but for the later neo-Aristotelian discussion in *After Virtue* (1981). Unlike Habermas, MacIntyre continues, in his moral philosophy, to seek an understanding of how moral and ethical discourse relates to human life as a whole, and how it is conducive to the good of human beings. But, whereas Habermas passes over the particularistic ethics and morals incarnate in specific cultural traditions, dismisses their philosophical analysis as a hopelessly difficult task, and moves directly to the presentation of a wholly abstract and unexemplified discourse ethics designed to mediate between them, MacIntyre begins his investigations with just these very particularisms. For MacIntyre, moral philosophy entails the study of moral and ethical discourse in use, and it is used in the context of particular cultural traditions.

On the basis of this historical approach, *After Virtue* develops an account of the pursuit of the good life in the context of a cultural tradition both wonderfully insightful and rightly famous. In a cultural tradition is embedded a range of practices. To learn how to enact these practices, and to acquire the individual virtues which facilitate their enactment and development, it is necessary to attend to specific situated activities, not to universalisable abstract rules, and to have respect for those in the community already generally recognised as competent practitioners. It is assimilation of practices in this way that makes human beings what they are, and it is their continuing striving for excellence in practice which moves human beings closer to the good life and the realisation (both individual and collective) of their *telos*. All cultural traditions are made up of specific practices, and associated virtues the acquisition of which is conducive to excellence in their performance. Although some virtues, courage, for example, truthfulness, recognition of what is due to others, are probably universal, in the sense that they are conducive to excellence in the context of any practice, other virtues are relative to specific practices and cultural traditions. There is no external, context-independent basis for a ranking of the virtues or for identifying 'the best' of the many different cultural traditions within which excellence may be pursued. Certainly, such identification cannot be based upon comparisons of the effectiveness of different practices and traditions in providing goods for human beings, for a great part of what is good in human life is intrinsic to practices themselves and experienced as they are practised. It is the cardinal error of most forms of utilitarianism that they evaluate practice purely as a means to the achievement of some extrinsic good.

It is within the context of a tradition of practices that moral and ethical discourse is located and only in relation to that context can it be identified and appraised. Nonetheless such discourse does have some universal characteristics, as MacIntyre emphasises. First of all, it is *objective* in form: things are described as being good, not as seeming good to this or that individual as a mere matter of opinion. To say that something is good implies that it meets some objective standard of goodness, not that we like it or have a fancy for it or prefer it to alternatives. To convey liking or preferring we have a discourse of liking and preferring (in which we can intelligibly express a liking for wicked things). Secondly, ethical discourse routinely and properly describes things as good by virtue of how they are. The so-called naturalistic fallacy is no fallacy: valid inference from 'is' to 'ought' is possible; direct moves from description to evaluation can legitimately be made. The connection is a functional or teleological one. If we know what something is *for*, then we know how ideally it ought to *be*. And we can compare how it is with an objective standard of how it ought to be. Good coal is coal that burns well. A good farmer is one who manages the land well. Just to the extent that there is a shared understanding of *telos*, incarnate in objective standards of goodness or fitness, the use of evaluative predicates will be entailed by what is actual.

The picture painted in *After Virtue* is immediately recognisable: even its most radically 'unrealistic' elements are continuous with aspects of lived experience. Nonetheless, if this sense of congruity with experience were too strong and too widely shared, MacIntyre's own argument would be refuted. For his account of the living of a good life is the prelude to an account of why such a life is impossible in modern conditions. Today, he claims, standards of goodness and rightness are too diverse and variable, and not sufficiently widely shared. Indeed there has been so much moral and ethical fragmentation that they have ceased to exist. Individuals now make personal responses to moral and ethical questions, judging what is right and good by references to their own feelings instead of objective standards. Moral and ethical language is *collectively misused* in a way that cries out against its very nature as such language. A predicate like 'good' is deployed to express conformity not with shared conceptions of what is good but with mere tastes and preferences which may freely vary from one individual to another. The consequence is that moral and ethical discourse provides the context for endless irresoluble disagreements between clashing individual opinions, expressed in a language which falsely implies that there is some one thing, 'the good', which the arguments are about. This mode of use of moral and ethical predicates MacIntyre calls 'emotivism' and identifies as characteristic of the modern condition.[7] The violence done therein to the use of words is the correlate of our present pathological way of living. The only hope of retrieving the situation is somehow to create the basis for a good life in the form of a set of objective moral and ethical standards acknowledged by everyone.

Evidently, the relationship of an individual person to objective standards is crucial to MacIntyre's moral philosophy, just as her relationship to rules or norms is crucial to Habermas'. It is clear that standards in MacIntyre are different from rules in Habermas. MacIntyre stresses their

embeddedness in cultural traditions, their limited domains of application, and how they may only be intelligible to culturally competent
persons who encounter them in appropriate situations. Even so, standards must still be evaluated by those persons individually, and, moreover, by the *reason* of those persons, just as rules are in Habermas.[8]
Embedded or not, an objective standard has to be understood as something with definite implications that are accessible alike to the reason of
different individual human beings. It is to the relationship of individual
reason with rules and standards, and to the problems inherent therein,
that the discussion can now turn.

Lost insights of empiricism

Long ago, before clear boundaries existed between philosophy, science
and theology, all the thinking relevant to our present concerns would
have been philosophical. As such it would have been structured by long-
standing oppositions, between realism and nominalism, materialism and
idealism, rationalism and empiricism, and so forth. These remain with
us, but they rarely arouse the passion they once engendered, and in the
case of rationalism and empiricism it may be that we have lost a sense
that a conflict is there at all. What seems to have happened is that, in the
period following the Enlightenment, empiricism and rationalism, the previously conflicting forces of science and reason, became part of the progressive alliance against 'tradition',[9] and the opposition between them
was glossed over.

Before the reconciliation of rationalism and empiricism, the former had
always been the dominant position. Rationalism offered a story of a top-
down knowledge flow, by deductive inference from general principles
and laws. Empiricism kept alive the thought that the flow of knowledge
was from the bottom up, from particular sensory experiences and particular manipulative interventions through induction and analogy. These
references to 'top' and 'bottom' imply a ranking of knowledge wherein
the general is reckoned of greater worth than the particular. They indicate how rationalism stands higher than empiricism in a hierarchy nicely
congruent with the hierarchy of status and command in society, and no
doubt ultimately derivative of it. Even in a subordinate position,
however, empiricism could offer an epistemological perspective diamet-
rically opposed to that of rationalism, and thereby constitute a source of
reputable criticism of great potential value to rationalists themselves.
With what was, in effect, its incorporation and neutralisation, rationalists
no longer faced any source of opposition with comparable plausibility
– which was bad for them.[10] The ensuing loss of respect for an empiri-
cist perspective has encouraged disdain for what used to be called inductive reasoning and the gathering of data. And, worse, it has desensitised
rationalists to some important epistemological insights.

A question of particular interest here is that of how general knowledge is applied to particular cases; for this is at once an interesting phenomenon and a serious epistemological problem. This problem has been discussed already, in relation to the application of general rules, laws or norms, but it can now be addressed a little more systematically. General rules apply to the same states-of-affairs, and imply or prohibit the same kinds of actions. But empirical particulars, whether states-of-affairs or actions, are never unquestionably the same as each other. And neither, *ipso facto*, are the empirical properties or features of the states-of-affairs. Because they are *empirical* states-of-affairs, situated in an indefinitely complex world, they always differ from each other in some discernible way and are liable to differ further in not yet discerned ways. They are never identical. The basic problem here is sometimes formulated as that of the *intransitivity* of relations of sameness: if A is the same as B, and B is the same as C, it does *not* follow that A is the same as C. Thus, on opening the wine one can expect to have a bottle of vinegar in, say, a fortnight – something by no means the same, or even the same in taste, as the wine. Yet on drawing samples at half-hour intervals no taste-difference may be discernible between one and the next: successive samples may be in that respect the same. Between samples drawn at one-minute intervals (one second? one millisecond?) not even a spectrometer may find a difference. Yet a difference there must be. For if there were identity then the sameness relation would be transitive, and wine would be the same, and taste the same, as vinegar.[11]

That sameness relations are always intransitive is a claim that will not be rigorously justified here, but in truth it is scarcely controversial. What needs emphasis is its significance more than its validity; for whilst it is easily passed over by those who deal in abstractions, it is of great import.[12] Perhaps the example of the wine ought to be reinforced. Consider how best knowledge of sameness relations between human beings and cattle was radically revised after the BSE outbreak, and how the cost of trusting earlier conceptions, or rather of ceasing to trust them, has been several billion pounds, plus a little in the way of future uncertainty. Consider, too, that how far unborn and born children are the same is material in abortion debates, and endlessly contested therein.

If a sameness relation is intransitive, then its extension from case to case is not given by the world, and every extension that is actually made is defeasible and formally problematic. So, therefore, must be every application of a general rule or law or norm. The intransivity of sameness implies that rules cannot, as it were, apply themselves to particular cases. The move from general to particular, easily mistaken for a simple deduction from general category to particular case when considered abstractly, turns out to be much more than deduction once the question of whether that particular case truly belongs in that general category is addressed. This decoupling of the secure connection from the general to the particular seriously threatens the standing of deductive theories both in epistemology and in moral philosophy. In the latter context, it presents a serious challenge to the abstracting, generalising and universalising aspirations of discourse ethics, as Habermas himself has recognised:

> No norm contains within itself the rules for its application. Yet moral justifications are pointless unless the decontextualisation of the general norms used in justification is compensated for in the process of application. Like any moral theory discourse ethics cannot evade the difficult problem of whether the application of rules to particular cases necessitates a separate and distinct faculty of *prudence* or judgment. . . . The neo-Aristotelian way out of this dilemma is to argue that practical reason should forswear its universalistic intent in favour of a more contextual faculty of judgment.
>
> (Habermas, 1990, p. 206).

In this passage Habermas both diagnoses a major problem with his position and acknowledges that his communitarian opponents might be better placed to solve it than he. But despite this he continues to take the view that valid inferences can be made from general norms to particular cases, and implies that a solution to his 'difficult problem' will at some point be found. This is to fail to appreciate the profundity of the problem of transitivity and how it strikes at the very core of his rationalist ethics.

Habermas treats social norms as analogous to the propositions which constitute, in his view, truth claims in science. Propositions are statements with determinate meanings, independent of how they are used or who believes in them. If norms are propositions then this must be true of norms. As propositions they simply cannot be used in different ways in different contexts, by people who give them different meanings – these different meanings would actually correspond to different propositions and thus different norms. If norms are propositions, then what particulars a norm correctly applies to may be inferred from the norm itself without the mediation of context, and the sameness relation is transitive. Conversely, if the sameness relation is intransitive, then indeed 'no norm contains within itself the rules for its application', but then no norm is a proposition either and the 'difficult problem' of its application is insoluble without a complete abandonment of Habermas' propositional framework. If sameness is intransitive, then propositions represent illegitimate reifications of verbal activities, and to treat norms as propositions is an illegitimate reification of the procedures through which we co-ordinate our actions. But sameness is indeed intransitive.

Habermas mentions the alternative approach of neo-Aristotelians, who hold that rules and norms are only properly applicable in particular situations, and that their implications are not determinate over all possible domains of application. This might be thought an advance over an unrestricted universalism; the norm of respect for life, for example, is much easier intuitively to apply in familiar everyday circumstances than it is in the machine-rooms of the more technologically advanced hospitals. But how is a sense of what is normative sustained in familiar circumstances? To refer to a 'faculty of judgement' here, or to a 'context-bound reason', does not deal with the problem of transitivity. The point where the wine ceases to be wine cannot be identified by recourse either to the universal or the contextual meaning of 'wine'. We might perhaps say that the precise point is a matter of judgement. But this scarcely implies the existence of an individual 'faculty of judgement' able to discern 'in context' just where the point lies. Nor does it help here to say with Aristotle that possession of the virtue of *phronesis* permits such problems to be solved. For this virtue is an acquired capacity that facilitates the discovery, in context, of 'the right answer', and the intransitivity of sameness implies that there is no such answer. When we say that the precise point is a matter of judgement, we are indicating that people may reasonably disagree on where it lies. They may disagree as rational agents, because there is no decisive indication of how exactly the analogy between what is in the wine bottle and instances of acknowledged sound wine should be extended. It is the same whenever any rule or norm is applied. Indeed, what is interesting about the application of norms to particular cases is how much agreement is evident in practice, given that such agreement is compelled neither by nature nor by reason.

To understand how rules or standards are applied and extended is to understand their very nature. It does not involve individuals independently addressing rules as propositions, or objective standards as externalities. Because of the problem of transitivity, to orient to supposed rules or standards in this way would permit a proliferating incidence of individual disagreement that would evaporate our culture and drain all shared significance from our language, leaving us as so many close-packed Robinson Crusoes. The problem of transitivity is overcome in our practice because we are not independent: it is a soluble problem only because of our mutual accountability and susceptibility. Our sense of there being some correct way of taking a rule on, given by something separate from us, is not derived from communion with some Platonic entity floating in the invisible universe of the individual mind. It derives from specific visible instances of rule use, wherein fellow members, predisposed to act in co-ordination, sustain, through their collective agency in relation to rules, an ongoing agreement in their practice as they apply them.

Habermas and MacIntyre both propound a rationalist ethics. They seek to move away from personal feelings to impersonal criteria, from mere opinion to justified conviction, from subjectivity to objectivity, from people to rules or standards. But a move to rules or standards, however objective, is not a move away from people at all, but *toward* them; for the sense that there is a correct way of taking a rule on in any given case is a collective accomplishment of persons. Moreover, these must be persons inherently inclined to go forward together in concert; since the empirical analogies naturally suggested by existing instances of rule use will by no means suffice so to take them forward. What we recognise as routine rule-following is only intelligible as the activity of profoundly sociable human beings. It has to be carried out by social agents with a mutual accountability and susceptibility that disposes them to move their practice into alignment with that of others. Neither Habermas' social agent engaged in communicative action, nor MacIntyre's social agent embedded in tradition, practice and role structure, is a genuine social agent in this sense. Habermas, than whom no philosopher has been more concerned with reification, preserves what is in the last analysis an independent individual by linking her autonomous reason to propositionally expressed reified rules and norms. MacIntyre, whose work on cultural traditions does appear to invite an analysis of 'objective standards' as 'intersubjectively maintained standards', nonetheless fails wholeheartedly to take up the invitation. When it comes to the crucial issue of the relationship between persons and rules or standards, neither philosopher is willing to take the necessary step beyond the traditional bounds of individualistic rationalism.

Responsible agents and cultural traditions

Both Habermas and MacIntyre acknowledge that human beings are social agents. Yet both go out of their way to retain a residual individualistic rationalism, especially in their understanding of moral rules or standards, even though they are aware of many of the difficulties to which this gives rise. Possibly, they fear that the move to a collectivist account of rule-following and an uncompromising account of social agency would throw moral philosophy into disorder, but it is not clear that this has to be the case. Such a move is bound to have implications concerning the basis of moral authority, but, contrary to what is sometimes asserted, it does not entail the priority of the collective over the individual in moral and ethical matters, or locate moral and ethical authority in culture or tradition. Social agents, as described here, are accountable to *each other*, not to culture, or tradition, or even the collective in an abstract sense; and their mutual accountability neither requires nor disposes them to equate what is good or right with what is collectively held to be so. MacIntyre points out that 'this is good' does not mean 'this is what I feel to be good'. But, equally, it does not mean 'this is what we feel to be good', or even 'this is good by the standards we currently accept'. Moral and ethical discourse is no more a discourse of collective preference than of individual preference. When a member says that something is right or good she need not imply that it is generally accepted by members of her collective, any more than when she says that something is true she need imply that it is generally believed by members. Members do *not* take the ethical standards of their own culture as definitive. Indeed, they indicate the error of doing this by routinely recognising a distinction between what is really moral and ethical and what is currently considered to be so. The fact that no member is a mere microcosm of her culture is actually celebrated in culture, which routinely represents itself and its standards as vulnerable both to the immanent and to the external criticisms of members.

Members do often judge the opinions and actions of each other by reference to shared standards of what is good or right. Yet they also feel free to pronounce on the goodness or rightness of the very shared standards that are used in such judgements. Diverse references to what is good and right at one and the same time sustain whatever sense there is that shared ethical and moral standards exist, and serve as the means to change that sense. 'Good' and 'right' here may be compared with 'true', which is used in scientific communities both to assert the authority of scientific representations as renderings of the world, to take note of their lack of identity with what they represent, and to challenge them as authoritative representations. These different, not to say conflicting, modes of use of 'truth' may be deployed perfectly smoothly and harmoniously in scientific cultures. Indeed, it is their availability that allows the constant modification of the knowledge of a scientific tradition to proceed in harmony with the business of transmitting what it consists in at any given time as correct. Analogously, it is precisely through their being routinely used in different, 'inconsistent' ways that terms like 'good' and 'right' function effectively in moral discourse. 'Good' and 'right' may be thought of as *operators*, used in the work of creating, sustaining, adjusting, reconstructing or dismantling specific shared conceptions of 'the good' and 'the right'. As a contingent fact, most uses of these terms may simply articulate existing standards, and the only shared sense of what is good or right in the membership may be provided by existing standards. But to equate proper use of these terms with use in accord with such standards would be a particularly objectionable reification, even though the standards may be essential to intelligible use of the terms. These are terms put to diverse uses in the elemental discourse through which interacting responsible agents devise, encourage and realise action for their collective good. (In the context of this discourse, of course, references to how agents could 'act otherwise' do real work, and the role of moral and ethical predicates therein will vary according to how those references are evaluated.)

Our ideal vision of a good society will not remain unchanged if we reflect on how societies are constituted of and by responsible agents. It is natural to express such an ideal by referring to accepted rules of right conduct, or shared conceptions of what is good practice or a good way of living. But rules and practices are not self-sustaining in the context of a changing environment, nor are those rules and practices at the centre of moral and ethical life automatically sustained by individual expediency and self-interest. Work is needed to sustain them, and to modify and develop them. On the account given here that work consists in social agents making evident in discourse and practice why this or that instance of goodness or rightness is indeed 'really' good or right, or why after all it is not and some alternative is. But if this work is necessary then it needs to be incorporated into our ideal vision of the good society itself. We need to conceive of the moral and ethical discourse of a good society as having at once a descriptive and a performative dimension. And if we are content, for simplicity to speak of one mode of use of terms like 'good' and 'right' as involving the routine articulation of shared standards of goodness and rightness, then we should acknowledge another mode of use wherein they serve to question those very standards, as the prelude to refashioning them or else reasserting them.

It could well be that both Habermas and MacIntyre would agree in finding a vision of this kind wholly unacceptable. Fundamental to any such vision are social agents causally linked to each other, generating moral order and collective goods in the course of interactions that have to be understood entire as physical processes, materially incarnate in specific settings. For Habermas, this must count as a fundamental constraint on the universalisability even of the highly attenuated moral and ethical relations he attempts to describe. The rationalist imagination is curbed in a fundamental way by irritating empirical contingencies like physical proximity. At the same time, however, the proposed picture is in radical discord with that of MacIntyre, in that it offers a tacit vindication of modern societies and of the specialised state institutions that lie at the core of them. MacIntyre has long figured amongst the most ruthless critics of differentiated societies and the liberal state, and of the ethical life of their members, but he has criticised them above all for embodying a form of individualism that at the same time he knows cannot exist. His magnificent polemics against the characteristic individualistic forms of self-understanding of these societies also, in a sense, connive with them.[13] What surely ought to be remarked of the modern liberal state is how it allows leeway for the exercise of the formidable self-organising powers of social agents, mediates between the groups and collectives arising from their exercise, and remains responsive to a remarkable if imperfect degree to the needs and demands of all of them. A modern differentiated society, organised around a liberal state, could indeed be a nightmare for the independent individuals who are incapable of constituting it, but as a container for social agents it has its merits, merits that both critics and defenders disdain to mention. In truth, the liberal account of how best to order institutions is highly plausible, but only because the liberal account of individual human beings is not.

The picture of things being hinted at here suggests a certain one-sidedness in both of the contrasting moral and ethical ideals for which Habermas and MacIntyre provide paradigms. Habermas recognises the existence both of accepted moral and ethical standards in specific cultural traditions, and of discourse wherein they are critically reflected on and questioned, but his own ethical theory attends exclusively to the latter. It is a theory typical of an Enlightenment thinker, indifferent to the contingent achievements of tradition, attentive to the ethical value of rea-soned critical reflection upon them, inclined quickly to pass over the fact that the latter is parasitic upon the former. Indeed, for Habermas the settled moral and ethical standards of traditions are addressed, not as ingredients and facilitators of a good life, but as particularisms which pose the danger of war. Habermas' concern as a moral philosopher is wholly with what might securely bridge the gaps between such danger-ous particularisms. In the MacIntyre of *After Virtue*, on the other hand, the emphasis is very much the other way. Here the particularisms of tra-ditions are celebrated as the essential context of a good life and the objec-tive standards incarnate in traditions are taken as definitive of what 'good' and similar terms mean. It is the use of such terms as operators that is passed over – or even condemned. Indeed, it is worth suggesting here that much of the allegedly incoherent ethical discourse condemned by MacIntyre as emotivism might be better described as a manifestation of valuable long-term projects of ethical and moral reconstruction in which social agents are using terms like 'good' as operators.[14]

Even so, the effort necessary to sustain, as well as to elaborate and modify, tradition does not go altogether unrecognised in *After Virtue*; it is given implicit recognition as an aspect of tradition itself. The dynamism and creativity intrinsic to all manifestations of tradition – those elements systematically omitted from the caricatures of tradition in Enlightenment thinking – are given their due in MacIntyre, particularly in his wonder-fully insightful discussion of what is involved in participation in a prac-tice (1981, p. 187). And to recognise an inherent creativity and dynamism in the moral and ethical dimension of tradition as he does, it is necessary also to recognise a performative element inherent in all moral and ethical discourse, even though MacIntyre himself does not emphasise the point.

It is but a short way from here to a crucial insight. If it is recognised that traditions exist and persist only through the continuing collective efforts of the social agents who inhabit them, then entirely routine activ-ities within a tradition and non-routine encounters with those outside it stand revealed as having just the same form and demanding just the same skills, powers and susceptibilities. Continuity is established between, at one extreme, those actions wherein members take tradition forward in concert with each other, and, at the other, those actions wherein members seek meaningful engagement with outsiders and aliens. And between the two extremes are many of the kinds of co-operative interaction charac-teristic of differentiated societies, including those with what were earlier described as stranger-members, in all of which moral and ethical predi-cates may be found functioning both as descriptive terms and as perfor-matives. In a nutshell, once tradition is understood for what it is, action extending across and beyond traditions is understood as well. With a correct understanding of the nature of tradition, the contrast between tra-dition and reason dissolves away. Indeed, it becomes possible to recog-nise it as just another variation on the false contrast between individual and society that a proper understanding of the social agency of human beings transcends.

Notes

1 The relevant passage of the *Treatise* (Hume, 1740, p. 469) is often quoted, partly, of course, because he left a great deal more to be said on the matter.

2 A morality based on the secondary virtues clashes not just with MacIntyre's rationalism but with the ideal of Enlightenment rationalism as well. On the face of it, to resolve disagreement by compromise is close to the kind of thing that Habermas might recommend: as the outcome of a dialogue between initially different moral or ethical positions, it looks like something wherein reason has overcome the particularities of tradition. Indeed the affinity here probably contributes significantly to the perceived attractions of Habermas' moral philosophy. But a rationalist philosopher would indubitably want to emphasise that compromise is a substitute for rational agreement not an expression of it. Even for an Enlightenment rationalist the ubiquity of compromise might count as an indication that peace is being preferred to rationality.

3 Parasitic though they are, secondary virtues have now as a matter of contingent fact become primary, whilst uncompromisingly authentic direct action on the basis of primary moral or ethical commitments is condemned as deeply pathological. We have even developed a special vocabulary for those who make serious efforts to act authentically: they are fundamentalists and/or fanatics. And we associate behaviour of this kind with a whole range of reassuringly negative images: the mindless repetition stereotypically imputed to 'traditional' societies, the practices of our political enemies in such societies and their alleged undue propensity to violence, the brandishing of sacred texts evidently well past their sell-by date. For those comfortable with the relevant mode of speech, we have, as it were, learned to condemn what smacks of rationality as irrational, and to celebrate what is irrational as rational.

4 Shapin and Schaffer (1985) have used the political theory of Robert Boyle to symbolise the modern solution, and his controversy with Thomas Hobbes as a symbol of its triumph over earlier alternative solutions. One merit of this treatment is that it directly displays modern natural-scientific knowledge as a part of the modern solution.

5 For communitarianism as social movement see Etzioni (1993), and for its use of a rich and varied range of intellectual resources see Etzioni (1995). For the cited accounts of social agency see Sandel (1996), Taylor (1989), MacIntyre(1981).

6 Habermas is remarkably sensitive to the innumerable contingencies that are relevant here, but he invariably rationalises the way that they operate. He seems to identify the empirical as the irrational, and the irrational as the great source of fear. Thus, the only remedy he will contemplate to the limits of reason is yet more reason, and to those who give warning that this may merely intensify the problem he pays no heed. Presumably even love and compassion are terrible in their naked empirical state, caused who knows how, causing who knows what. The alternative view of David Hume surely merits consideration.

7 It may seem like mere pedantry to question the empirical basis of this account of the modern condition; but the frequency of moral disagreements in a society is not a reliable indicator of the extent and intensity of moral disagreement. There may actually be an inverse relationship here. Certainly, current endless arguments about what is good and/or right are often so trivial as to suggest a level of agreement, not to say quiescence and conformity, without obvious historical parallel. And the arguments themselves often betoken not individual difference but status difference and status competition. It may make little difference to how we evaluate modern societies, but it is as well to be clear why individuals prefer Nike to Reebok.

8 Later books – for example, MacIntyre (1988) – suggest that he is even closer to Habermas on the power of individual reason than is here implied. Certainly, MacIntyre has always rejected cultural relativism, and neither he, nor it would seem any other neo-Aristotelian or communitarian moral philosopher, has been willing to identify the internal objective standards of cultural traditions as the *fundamental* bases of moral and ethical judgements. Presumably, none of these philosophers wishes to exempt from rational critical appraisal, and thus in effect to defend, traditional racist beliefs, or hallowed customs like radical clitoridectomy, or attempts to realise *telos* by transportation to a spacecraft in the lee of the Hale-Bopp comet. But to the extent that they acknowledge the possibility of the external rational criticism of traditions, and compromise their insistence on the embeddedness of standards, so their position moves closer to the Enlightenment view.

9 Looked at from the perspective of macro-sociology, this was part of a process, ongoing through much of the nineteenth century, wherein a combination of bureaucrats and technical professionals won out against priests and clerics and transformed the division of intellectual labour, and the distribution of emoluments across it, very much to their own advantage. Looked at from the perspective of micro-sociology, it was part of a process of transformation of institutionalised cognition which led to logical empiricism, and other less startlingly labelled but substantially similar twentieth-century philosophies.

10 It would be a simple matter to illustrate this point with the work of Habermas and MacIntyre, for example, by looking at their commentaries on Garfinkel or Goffman. Both these rationalist philosophers are singularly maladroit in their handling of empirical materials and lacking in proper appreciation of their value. The point particularly needs to be made in the case of Habermas, since he extensively cites naturalistic studies and empirical findings to support his ideas. He uses an evolutionary approach to human behaviour, both at the phylogenetic and the ontogenetic level, to equate what is most ethically advanced with what is most evolved, and pays particular attention to the 'moral' significance of work in developmental psychology. He moves from the observed ubiquity of forms of behaviour to their conjectured universality and thence to their desirability. He argues that some forms of (communicative) behaviour are in a sense necessary to being human, and then infers their morality from their necessity. Perhaps because of his intense anxiety about the involvement of reason in social life, he grasps at every opportunity to add to its empirical plausibility, and ends up taking as much interest in the nature of the human species as any sociobiologist. What must be said here is that whilst a vast range of studies is cited, a relentless selection, variation and elaboration is practised upon them. And even after this the support they provide

for his ideas is somewhat like that of a plinth on which theory is perched, rather than evidential support as usually understood. Indeed, there is a duty to say that Habermas does not so much use empirical studies as practise Procrustean violence upon them. It is hard to imagine, for example, how anyone with a shred of empirical curiosity could read Habermas (1987, 1990, 1992) on the relationship of his moral philosophy with Lawrence Kohlberg's 'moral psychology' without intense exasperation. What stands revealed, in this instance as in others, is not that proper awareness of the corrigibility of observation and the contingency of empirical knowledge claims which is become commonplace today. Nor is it a recognition that empirical materials need actively to be organised, interpreted and given a degree of coherence that in themselves they do not possess. It is rather a deep lack of *respect* for what is empirical that is evident in his approach. Habermas is a profoundly unscientific thinker, and his work strikingly demonstrates how Enlightenment thought may be radically different from scientific thought.

11 Mary Hesse's *The Structure of Scientific Inference* (1974) offers a remarkably clear and systematic account of the issues here. See also Quine (1960), Goodman (1978) and Hesse (1980).

12 The point is central to sociology as well as to philosophy, and is especially important in the sociological study of knowledge, science and technical expertise (Barnes *et al.*, 1996; Collins, 1985). It is interesting too how those sociological theorists who have dismissed empiricism as nonsense and spoken of a move to a post-empiricist social theory have encountered all the old problems of assimilating the particular to the general that empiricism used to highlight. The result has been an effort to provide functional equivalents to empiricism from within a rationalist framework. But the 'post-modern' and 'nihilist' positions that have thereby emerged embody all the limitations of the rationalism they apparently criticise; for indeed they are just extreme expressions of that doctrine.

13 MacIntyre assails modern, differentiated, societies for their emotivism and ethical atomism, their materialist consumerism, their lack of genuine social relationships and domination by instrumental and exploitative ones, and especially for their bureaucracy and managerialism, including the managerialism gone mad of ubiquitous therapy. It is odd how both defenders of these societies and critics like MacIntyre concur on their individualism, and particularly so, perhaps, that their own favoured individualistic ideologies depict them as vicious and inhuman and imply a disastrous future for them. A properly informed description of them would surely produce a far more favourable picture.

14 We live at the time of a broad and continuing empowerment that has weakened the positions of hitherto overwhelmingly dominant élites and institutions and made it impossible for them any longer to impose a ubiquitous genuflection toward their favoured forms of culture. In these circumstances a great deal of cultural experimentation and reorganisation is ongoing, and diversity, even incoherence, in moral and ethical discourse is very much to be expected, perhaps welcomed, as the sign not of a corrupt condition but of some small movement away from it. None of which is to deny the repulsiveness of some examples of the cultural experimentation in question, or the impoverished conception of the human condition implicit in other examples.

9

ON THE FINE LINE BETWEEN STATUS AND STATE

Empirical study suggests that human beings are 'highly gregarious, inter-dependent social primates'. In the previous discussion this view of human beings was elaborated; they were identified as mutually account-able and mutually susceptible social creatures. At the same time, it is gen-erally accepted that human beings normally operate as free agents acting voluntarily. Hence, it is necessary to acknowledge that human beings freely choose and freely act as mutually accountable and susceptible crea-tures; and indeed that they do so whilst affecting and being affected by each other as creatures of this kind. The strangeness of this image needs to be acknowledged. As we normally see things, a free agent is in a dig-nified individual state, marked by independence. As presented here, she is in a dignified social state, possessed of face and status, and lacking independence precisely by virtue of this. Indeed, if the present argument is correct, the characteristic accomplishments of human beings are pre-cisely the products of their lack of independence as responsible agents. Their cultures, institutions and forms of life; their inventions and inno-vations; their ability to generate and direct awesome concentrations of power; are all the result of their collective agency, which derives in turn from the mutual susceptibility linked to their concern with face and status.

Clearly, there is a tension between what is being claimed here and our normal vision of things, and whilst there is no reason to give any special standing to the latter, it does of course command respect and cannot merely be waved away. The work of Erving Goffman suggests one pos-sible way of reconciling the two accounts. Goffman offers revelatory insights into the operation of the deference-emotion system through which human beings affect each other causally as interacting mutually susceptible social creatures. But he also describes how in the same inter-actions it is necessary to acknowledge the status of the other as a sacred entity. In normal social interaction, on Goffman's account, we affect the state of the other whilst respecting her status. Indeed, the way we affect state is crucially structured and organised by the way we respect status.

Once more we encounter the problem of the relation of status and state that has accompanied the argument from the beginning of this book. In everyday understanding the status relation with the other is primary, whereas a theoretical perspective ought also to extend to state and causal transformations of state.

No properly attuned reader of Goffman will doubt the breadth of his sociological understanding, the sympathy for his fellow human beings incarnate in his writing, or indeed his stature as a moralist. His rationalist critics, who include both Alasdair MacIntyre[1] and Jürgen Habermas, are simply deaf to his methods of communication and hostile to his empiricism and naturalism. Yet there is some slight excuse for the negative reactions that he so frequently evokes. Goffman attends to both the sacred and the profane dimensions of social interaction; he understands that its description lies right upon the boundary between the discourse of status and that of state; and he identifies the taboos and avoidances elicited by proximity to that boundary. Even so, he documents and illustrates the profane far more vividly and effectively than he does the sacred. Indeed, in many of his case studies, he signally fails to convey a proper sense of the dignity inherent in the encounters of mutually susceptible human beings, and for all his insight into the deference-emotion system, his actual examples of its operation only occasionally involve genuinely mutually susceptible persons.

Two distinct kinds of character appear in most of the dramas Goffman presents. One is indeed a susceptible social agent sensitive to withdrawal of deference. But the other is a calculative rational agent who manages and exploits the social agent. These characters are connected in a number of ways. Sometimes they are victim and predator; sometimes the link is less clear-cut and involves interdependence; sometimes the two characters are part of the same individual person. For the most part, however, their relationship is a tragic one and neither party ends up being ennobled by it.[2] There is in Goffman a lack of confidence in human sociability and an acceptance that it is liable to be suborned by artful instrumental manipulation: our susceptibility to others is presented as both the essential basis of social life *per se* and as something that threatens to betray us into a particularly dismal and impoverished way of living it. Like the work of Michel Foucault and Alasdair MacIntyre, Goffman's points to a possible future dominated by a generalised obsession with control and manipulation. But whilst this makes Goffman interesting as a prophet, it means that as a sociologist he is unduly selective with his examples. The normal operation of the deference-emotion system as *mutually* susceptible persons interact must be prior to any artful manipulation of it, which is surely why susceptibility is essential yet unmentionable. Our marvellous abilities to do things together achieve their finest expression where our concern with face and status is activated, but not made the target of conscious manipulation and control. There is too little illustration in Goffman of this normal mode of operation: too little on the micro-sociology of the building of bridges and the fighting of battles, for example, or the climbing of mountains and the making of music.

The general form of Goffman's sociology is close to that of some of the great macro-sociological theorists, and particularly to that of his acknowledged source of inspiration Emile Durkheim. It is a sociology that treats human beings as social creatures and their activities as patterned and orderly in consequence; it sees pattern and order extending beyond the micro-level; and it proposes to understand it in causal terms. The importance of this kind of sociological theory needs to be reasserted within social theory as a whole, wherein the role of sociology has been in decline and even its own former practitioners now sometimes prefer to speak instead as cultural theorists or discourse analysts or something similar. Far from being impossible to sustain, as is often claimed, a causal orientation to human interaction is straightforward to employ; and the institution of causal connection may readily be reconciled with the institution of responsible action as such interaction is described and explained.

What holds back an approach of this kind is that theorists tend to be involved in political projects wherein it matters little what the actual characteristics of individual human beings might be, projects focused wholly on status, as it were, and not on state. It may be that the kinds of project that Michel Foucault famously analysed will come to mind here, but let us pass over these and focus instead on what arguably has been a nobler enterprise. There is no doubt that in the last few decades a major aim of theoretical discourse has been to decouple individuals, whether human beings generally or those in especially disadvantaged and invidiously treated groups, from the constraint of external powers, particularly state powers and the authorities that exercise them.[3] A domain for action devoid of external interference has been sought, and the explicit demand has been for an area of 'free choice', one where the individual has a 'right to choose' created by withdrawal of external constraint. In this discourse choice features as absence, and the problem of the nature of free agency need never arise: that which is done in the space created by withdrawal is rendered as chosen as a matter of etiquette, as it were. A classic illustration of this is, of course, the for the most part successful effort to legalise abortions under a 'pro-choice' slogan.

In the discourse of choice as absence, 'the individual' features as a social status, and what is permitted to the status is conventionally formulated in terms of rights to choose. The discourse is employed in the refashioning of social structure – in shaping and reshaping the rings of action and expectation surrounding statuses or social positions. But the statuses in question here are designated not in terms of occupation, or kinship, or gender, but simply as identifiable individuals. That the point has rarely been put in this way is no doubt because it is normal to contrast statuses with the individuals who move in and out of them, and to regard individuals themselves as defined in terms of their own inner nature, their own intrinsic characteristics and powers. But there are problems with this view of things, which become evident if we consider how individuals are identified in practice. +

All societies distinguish individuals by means of their names, which names confer a status upon them. And this status is one with which the individual has a lifelong association. How do we attribute names and recognise their bearers? To be sure, an important part of this practice involves recognition of the empirical characteristics of named individuals: distinctive facial characteristics are very frequently involved. But it is clear that superficial characteristics of this kind are merely used as *indicators* that we are in the presence of 'the same individual' once more. They are not definitive of who the individual is. We may easily fail to recognise an individual when next we meet her, and the failure may be no lapse on our part. It may be that the face of the individual has itself radically changed – out of all recognition, as is sometimes said. What then constitutes 'the same individual', given that individuals remain the same persons, with the same names, over their entire life-courses, during which time all manner of empirical changes occur to them? No physical changes to an individual, whether developmental/natural or environmental/accidental, entail a revised understanding of who the individual is, however radical such changes may be. Nor does it help to turn to behavioural or dispositional characteristics, or to the elusive 'mental' characteristics associated with 'personality'. All these characteristics may vary radically, together or separately, whilst their individual possessors remain the individuals they always were. We do not change an individual's name, or otherwise count her another person, when we consign her to an asylum or watch her travel the long road to oblivion via Alzheimer's disease. Rather, she continues to be counted the person she always has been – the occupant of the status denoted by her name.

It is easy to ignore how reference to an individual is reference to a status because this particular status is unique in being inalienable from a specific human body and co-extensive with its life-course: there is scarcely ever any practical need to contrast body and status in this case. But the contrast does need to be taken into account to understand why an individual remains who she is regardless of changes in her intrinsic characteristics: she is the individual she is, rather as a banknote is the sum of money it is, because of externalities in the form of the orientations adopted by others toward her. At the same time the indissoluble association of body and status cannot be ignored, since the body serves as an essential marker and focus for the orientations that constitute the status. In *Naming and Necessity* (1980), Saul Kripke argues that it is not the empirical characteristics or describable properties of a human being that make her an individual of a specific name, but nonetheless her physical manifestation is relevant to how she is identified. Human bodies, being material objects, manifest continuity in space and time. They can be monitored from instant to instant as 'the same individual' even though any or all of their properties change from instant to instant. As such they can serve as markers of the continued existence of an individual person, of whom no valid description in terms of nature or properties or powers is possible.

On Kripke's account of naming, individual human beings arrive in the world in a particular way, and whatever arrives in that way is normally assigned a name. From that original 'baptism' of an individual, whatever persists in spatio-temporal continuity with the object of baptism is the individual of that name. No matter that the object in question changes in all manner of ways. It remains the body of the individual, the marker of her presence, the changing material accompaniment of the entity that is the unchanging subject of references to her. In effect, the individual 'herself' is referred to as an essence lying behind the visible, variable physical and social phenomena that document her existence. Indeed, the immemorial conception of a human being as an immortal soul in a mortal body offers a remarkably good model of how the individual is treated in our discourse.

Kripke's account is of great sociological interest. An individual is defined not by her nature or any constancy or distinctiveness therein, but as a continuous line through space/time. To be sure who she is, it is necessary to monitor her movement over time. Of course, no individual ever monitors the movement of another this thoroughly, but a collective may come close to doing so, and make continuing reference to her on this basis. Then the name of the individual, iterated in the speech of the surrounding collective, may become, as it were, a label tied to her, like a name-label is tied around a plant in a nursery. And this virtual label, constituted of ongoing speech-acts, may be put to use just as the name-label on the plant. Members may leave the collective and re-orient to a given individual on their return by reference to the virtual label. Or recognition on the basis of facial features may be checked and updated by reference to the label. In this way naming activity, and indeed the entire institution of the naming of individual persons, may be understood as a collective accomplishment through which a physical body and an associated essence are tracked over a life-course, and kept visible as entities we orient ourselves toward. Addressing this account naturalistically, it implies that what actually allows identification of 'the same' human being in a changing body is not the essence of an individual within but continuing references to that essence from without. It is the ring of speech and action around the body, no particular part or component of the ring but merely the persistence of such a ring over time, that constitutes the human being *qua* individual. If the ring disappears, then the body becomes a mere material object and its status as an individual lapses.

Statuses are amongst the great inventions of humankind. The discourse that makes use of them, like a simple form of algebra, permits concerted efficacious action in the face of the unknown – and of all manner of disagreements concerning that unknown. Institutions are built around statuses. A practice is instituted: at its focus stands a status, the necessary basis of co-ordination and co-operation, the incidental basis of speculation and controversy. So it is with individuals. As to their nature, our capacity for disagreement is limited only by the extent of our ignorance. But as foci for the rings of actions and expectations that define powers and prohibitions, rights and responsibilities, entitlements and obligations, they allow the co-ordination of much of our collective life. And a great part of the discourse of choice, and notably the discourse of choice as absence, is implicated in the constitution and reconstitution of these rings.

Statuses may be attributed to all manner of things and objects. Such attributions classify things not by anything internal to them but by what lies outside them – what is directed toward them, or attached to them, or associated with them. Indeed, what constitutes a status may not merely lie beyond the boundary of the object classified; it may be smeared across the whole of the collective which recognises it. That something counts as having a status is what constitutes its having the status.[4] Status classifications have strange self-referring and self-validating properties that make them hard to understand, a problem which is intensified by their representing a radical departure from the accepted paradigm of classification in general use amongst us. Paradigmatically, we think of the classification of things as being based on their own internal, intrinsic properties, on aspects of their own nature as it were, not on aspects of the context in which they reside. But in truth this paradigm fails to represent not just some but *most* actual acts of naming and classification. It is commonplace to characterise even physical objects by reference to what surrounds them rather than what constitutes them, as with holes and ridges and cavities, valleys, lakes and islands. And it is even more commonplace to classify things by reference to function or utility, and hence by the orientation toward the things of the people who surround them, as with tools and furniture, doors and fences, crops and weeds, and of course social statuses of all kinds. Even in the natural sciences it is commonplace to classify by reference to the externalities of context (planets, parasites) and function (reagents, enzymes, counters, spectrometers). Just like ordinary members, natural scientists classify the things around them, and particularly the things they work with, in a profoundly teleological way, but this kind of classification is even less remarked upon in the context of science than it is in the context of everyday life.

Our dominant form of naming and classification refers to context and confers status. Our dominant paradigm of naming and classification imagines that reference is made to the nature of the thing classified. Why this curious incongruity exists it is hard to be sure. But there is no doubt that it does exist, and that there is a continuing inclination to understand the dominant form in terms of the dominant paradigm. The consequence is that what is due to status is attributed to nature instead. The tendency to ask what in the banknote makes it so much money is ever present. Moreover, since in status-based discourse there is a void at the centre of every ring of references, speculation about the nature of what lies there (that is, about state) may proceed without disturbance to the practice associated with the status itself. Thus it is that individuals with rights to choose are easily rendered as individuals natively imbued with powers of choice. What is treated as autonomous becomes what is of its nature autonomous. And what individuals are allowed and expected to do is made visible as precisely what they are equipped by nature to do.

One of the virtues of traditional styles of sociological thought, with their holistic and structural tendencies, is that they have sustained at least an implicit awareness of what is involved in classification by status. And indeed the way that status is persistently transformed into nature (state) through processes of naturalisation, reification and hypostasisation continues to be pointed out throughout the literature of sociology, wherein the political and ideological significance of processes of this kind is made abundantly clear. Yet sociological theory engages in these very processes when it allows its concern to justify the autonomy associated with status to inspire presumptions of autonomy as an individual state. Theories of the state or nature of human beings – of their capabilities, inclinations, susceptibilities – are indeed worth seeking. But they should represent idealisations and generalisations from empirically observed activity, not naturalisations of moral and ethical aspirations. Unfortunately, in sociological theory just as in moral philosophy and political theory, conceptions of human beings relate less strongly than they should to empirical considerations. As a result, references to an unconditioned reason, to free will and to individual agency, all of which may have a function in discourses concerning statuses and associated rights and responsibilities, continue to be employed as if they describe the intrinsic powers of a person. And the enlightening image of human beings counting each other as, and thereby knowing each other to be, independent individuals, by virtue of being occupants of statuses they have themselves jointly created as social agents, remains somehow elusive.

This image merits a prominent place in our thinking, especially in sociological theory. It can throw light on a number of problems in this context, including what seems currently to be regarded as the most important of all, that of the relationship of agency and structure. Suppose we think of so many responsible agents, acting and interacting together as members on the basis of their shared knowledge. Now concentrate on that part of their shared knowledge which is knowledge of their own social and institutional order, made of statuses and the associated rights, powers, responsibilities, and so forth.[5] This is knowledge of things that are what they are because they are counted as being what they are, that is, because they are known to be what they are. To put it another way, this is knowledge of what is known, knowledge that constitutes its own referents: a status, for example, exists only to the extent that it is known to exist, and by extension we might want to say that institutional order in general exists only to the extent that it is known to exist (Barnes, 1983,

1988; Searle, 1994). Institutional order exists as members' knowledge; it is constituted as that knowledge. But what is thereby constituted is what has prompted theorists to speak of the *objective* existence of social structure, or a social system.[6]

It is important to recognise how very strong our intuitive sense can be that there is something out there pressing upon us, constraining us, forcing us to act as otherwise we should not, and that it is something more than 'just other people'. Of course, few would deny that the something in question is connected with other people. In everyday experience there is ample awareness of how actions are constrained by what people tell us, and what we believe about them. And needless to say, throughout the social sciences there is a recognition that how one person acts may be constrained by what others do, or by what they expect, or by the information they communicate. But the overall 'systematic' coherence in the doing, the expecting and the informing, across great numbers of members, and over periods during which memberships change radically, may nonetheless induce the strong conviction that there is something there, independent of the membership, that has to be taken account of, just as they apparently take account of it. Thus, references to an objective structure or system understandably become, in the eyes of many theorists, unavoidable, even though they recognise how notoriously difficult it is to locate and identify just what is being referred to.

The previous discussion offers insight into the nature of this difficulty. Members' references to elements of social systems or structures seem (indeed are) just like their references to elements of natural systems, which encourages the thought that things external to the collective are being referred to, things analogous to those that constitute physical nature as it were. But the referents in question are not external to the collective at all. Social structure, if one wishes for simplicity so to bundle together the foci of all these references, is constituted as a distribution of self-referring knowledge carried by the relevant collective of responsible agents.[7] As such, it is difficult to identify and study for two reasons. First, not only is it not separate from the members that carry it; it actually consists in those very elements of their awareness that constitute their knowledge of it, which serves as a truly remarkable form of concealment. Secondly, it exists as a delocalised phenomenon, which makes its nature peculiarly difficult for the mind to grasp, rather as the nature of a hologram is hard to grasp compared with that of a photograph. To understand how a social structure is manifest at any point it is necessary to look, not to the point itself, but to the distribution of knowledge across the collective as a whole. That which constitutes structure at a given locale is a property of the entire ensemble of locales it encompasses. The occupant of a status, for example, counts as such only because of the orientation to her of everyone else: the fact that she has that status is a fact about members generally. Given these difficulties, it is small wonder that social structures are so often hypostasised into external objects; but this particular reification affords nothing by way of useful simplification and merely confuses the understanding.

Institutional order does indeed exist, and manifests itself as a persisting macro-pattern in social activity. Indeed, it can be studied from the outside, and characteristics of the pattern unremarked by members themselves can be identified and described using theorists' own categories. It may also, for most practical purposes, be addressed as an independent entity from the inside. Any individual member may make such a very small contribution to the order that she can overlook it and treat the order as pure externality.[8] Then she will know the order as a given, and be disposed by that knowledge to act in ways that sustain it and encourage others so to know it and so to sustain it. On this basis she, and analogously everyone else, will make the very small contributions that together do indeed sustain and reconstitute the institutional order. The order will thereupon persist as the accomplishment of a membership wherein the only 'social' constraints upon members are those that they place on each other through their actions and interactions. It will be an order, that is, wherein no external 'objective' constraint exists at all. However, if the theorist (wrongly) does what the member (usually rightly) does, and overlooks the member's 'insignificant' contribution to the institutional order, then instead of seeing that order as intersubjectively constituted and wholly internal to the membership she will see it as wholly external and objective. A truly minute error in the understanding of individual actions will generate a monumental misconception of the nature and location of institutional order, the order that most theorists have referred to as social structure (Barnes, 1983).

A conception of social structure as consisting in members' knowledge of it is of considerable theoretical importance, but it is a modest conception justifiable only in pragmatic terms. Combined with the similarly modest conceptions of collective and individual agency outlined earlier it could be said, perhaps, to offer a solution to the problem of relating agency and structure. If you wish to understand this relationship, it could be said, ask what is the relationship between what agents know and how they act and you may find your answer.[9] But it is important to recognise the forced character of this way of putting things, and that it involves what, here, is an alien idiom. The problem of agency and structure would not normally arise out of the approach taken in this book. The task of sociology, as it is conceived of here, is to understand human beings as responsible agents engaged with their environment through the mediation of their inheritance of knowledge. That is all. This is simply to hark back once more to the picture sketched at the end of Chapter 5. The two parts of this book end in the same way, with the same vision. There may now be a little more complexity in the vision; and some of the different strands in it may have been unravelled and explicitly distinguished. Nonetheless, it remains uncompromisingly monistic naturalistic. It is a vision, that silently questions the need for the metaphysical convolutions running through the structure/agency debates, in sociology and social theory, and implicitly reproaches the tendency of theorists in these debates to constantly relapse into unsatisfactory dualist modes of thought.[10]

It is extremely difficult to 'find' social structure. And it is very easy to misunderstand and misrepresent what prompts us to make reference to it. However, it is unlikely that the mere existence of these difficulties is a sufficient basis for understanding the problems that have arisen in this context, or that their identification will prove in practice sufficient to solve them. It is important here to take historical contingencies into account, and to recognise the role of the contrast between individual and society, or social structure, in the ancestry of sociology and much of social theory. This contrast has had, and continues to have, political salience. Theorists have always involved themselves in struggles against systems or structures, and when people so struggle their task may only be made more difficult if it is acknowledged as a struggle against part of themselves. And there is as well, of course, a micro-politics of dualisms, wherein theorists seek exclusive territorial rights for themselves and demarcate boundaries with ontological claims: this has been a major preoccupation in the human sciences since Durkheim characterised society as a *sui generis* reality.[11]

Along with these things, however, must be set the ubiquitous tendency of human beings to underestimate the extent and importance of their own sociability. The more this is left out of account, the greater the inclination to dualism. In the extreme case, where the individual is considered as an independent atom, the only available locations in which to place the products of our sociability are those wholly internal to the individual, and those entirely external to the group of immaculate individuals wherein she 'belongs'. Conversely, the more that our sociability is recognised, the easier it becomes to see what is apparently external to individuals (and much that is apparently internal to them as well) as features of networks of interacting social agents. The problem is that because of the way we relate to each other in statuses, through the institution of responsible action, and because of our need to hold each other to account in that framework, we are chronically inhibited from moving in the latter direction.

At the end of Part 1, I suggested that a more explicit recognition of how we are affected by others in the course of social life might perhaps be a great good. By a willingness to think of ourselves in the frame of the institution of causal connection, and to make our susceptibility and vulnerability to others visible by that means, we would become more aware of the necessity of this aspect of our nature in our lives, and more inclined to set value on what otherwise might appear as human weakness. And later chapters have echoed the point, hinting at how in this way we could become more appreciative of some of the gentler elements of social interaction, whilst still recognising the virtues of a robust discourse of individual responsibility. Returning to the suggestion now, with a little more awareness of how an unreflective concern with face and status can trivialise our lives and despoil them with the stress of a gratuitous competitiveness, it may seem still more plausible. But there is another side to the problem. To become more aware at the level of reflection of what we all conspire to ignore at the level of ordinary interaction cannot be without risk. Following Erving Goffman, we could say that our very sociability is just what blinds us to that sociability, and that fear of undermining the whole discourse of status and responsibility, and weakening the relations of mutual respect that link us all together, makes us reluctant to pull at the blindfold. Indeed, this kind of risk confronts all of the social sciences, to the extent that they are seriously pursued; and the dilemma it represents is also a dilemma for any natural science that would turn hard around and apply its methods and theories to the study of human beings. Nor is the dilemma going to disappear. For we shall never achieve, this side of paradise, a sublime discourse of status utterly devoid of all concern with state.

Notes

1 There are many ways of reading Goffman. He has often struck me as being scientific in orientation, although not of course in the false sense of the term that has it imply number-fetishism and other perversions. His own self-presentation is as the humble ethnographer of everyday encounters, but it need not be taken at face value. He can also be read as a powerful sociological theorist, or, at the other extreme, as someone who brings something close to a novelist's imagination to the task of understanding social life. Alasdair MacIntyre, however, reads him as a moral philosopher, and nicely illustrates how description and evaluation are easily confused in that field. In Goffman's picture of modern life, we are told, there are no objective moral and ethical standards, only those produced in interaction. Life is a matter of realising one's will, and others are merely the means to that end. Presentation and performance are all there is to a person; there is no integrated authentic self behind them. The good for man is honour, the regard of others. But this leads MacIntyre to bracket Goffman with Nietzsche and Sartre, and to condemn him for the same flawed ethical vision as theirs. It is odd that MacIntyre should mistake a description of the modern condition very close to his own for an account of how it rightly ought to be. It is tantamount to his misrepresenting himself as an emotivist. (Cf. Macintyre, 1981, pp. 115-17.)

2 It is possible to respond to these vignettes at a number of levels. First, there is the pathos of the susceptible individual responding to communications as if genuine when in truth they are not – as well, of course, although this is often backgrounded in Goffman, as the corruption of the knowing, manipulative source of the communications. Second, there is the tragic state of social life as a whole which these little dramas symbolise – one full of knowing manipulators and their subjects, of personnel managers and public relations officers, advertisers and image consultants, counsellors and therapists, and

countless others, professional and amateur, all with a trained familiarity with the deference-emotion system and other media of mutual susceptibility and all operating upon others on the basis of it. And third there is what may count for many as the greatest tragedy of all, the increasing complicity of the compliant subjects of manipulation. For if these were once unwitting victims, increasingly they are so no longer. Now they willingly offer themselves as the targets of manipulative discourse, even pay for it, in the clear knowledge that the messages received are not 'genuine' but are rather designed to act on their purchasers in a specific way. So it is that people now fill themselves with self-esteem or self-confidence rather as they fill the tanks of their motor-cars with petrol.

3 It may be that, in our culture, the tendency to devalue sociability and deference to others is heightened and intensified due to our enduring concern to secure the independence of persons from the power of hierarchies and bureaucratic institutions. In the context of this project, subjection to external powers has been denounced as demeaning, and this stress on the indignity of deference to external powers may have encouraged us to see indignity in our deference to each other.

4 Searle (1994) gives a particularly lucid account of how statuses are constituted and hence of how social reality is constructed. For an earlier closely analogous account, see Barnes (1983, 1988).

5 The problems associated with the term 'knowledge' discussed in part one need to be borne in mind here: to have taken explicit account of them in the main text would have made for an inordinately laboured discussion. The way that the main text speaks of dividing knowledge into two parts represents another oversimplification; it would have been intolerable in a discussion of undifferentiated societies.

6 Giddens' idiosyncratic terminology demands use of the second term here, but I shall continue to refer to social structure in its traditional sense.

7 This picture is itself a reified one that needs to be elaborated in a number of respects. See Barnes (1983, 1988), and also n.5 above.

8 On occasions, of course, individual members may make very large contributions to the constitution of social structure, and/or possess the power to disrupt it by a single action. For examples, and an account of the nature of the power involved, see Barnes (1998).

9 An explicit theory of knowledge and how it is known would is necessary here, of course. There are many different accounts in the literature, each with very different implications in the present context. My own extended involvement with the problems of the sociology of knowledge has led me to adopt and advocate the finitist account implicit here, that I have set out at length elsewhere. See Barnes (1982a, 1982b), Barnes et al. (1996).

10 Roy Bhaskar is perhaps the best source for the opposed view, since he is an enthusiastic metaphysician. Anthony Giddens writes in a different style; even at its most 'philosophical' his theorising has a certain eclecticism, not to say a touch of the Heath Robinson, about it - a virtue perhaps in this context. Despite his stress on agency and structure as a 'duality', he is sometimes read as a dualist, and not altogether without reason, since he continues to advocate use of both notions independently. Nonetheless, a pragmatic dualism is perhaps as much as he can be accused of. And from the much more aggressively dualist perspective of Margaret Archer (1988, pp. 72–96) he is not a

dualist of any kind but a 'conflationist'. Yet even Archer herself, so it turns out, is 'not asserting dualism but rather the utility of an analytically dualistic approach' (1988, p. xviii). And just as Giddens sought to get beyond dualism with 'duality', so she speaks of 'overcoming dualism by making consistent use of analytic dualism' (1988, p. 307). In a later book (1995), however, this desire to 'overcome' dualism is combined with attempts to entrench it ever more deeply in ontology: see also King (1999). It is hard to say from the outside what is at issue in these esoteric debates amongst realist social theorists.

11 As fields and specialties have subsequently differentiated further, so, sadly, have 'ontologies' proliferated. It has been suggested that the move to a post-empiricist philosophy of social science has accelerated the tendency still more. Here is yet another reason for regretting the turn from empiricism.

BIBLIOGRAPHY

Abell, P. (1991). *Rational Choice Theory*. Aldershot, England: Elgar.

Adams, J. (1995). *Risk*. London: UCL Press.

Antaki, C. (1988). *Analysing Everyday Explanation*. London: Sage.

Antaki, C. (1994). *Explaining and Arguing*. London: Sage.

Archer, M. (1988). *Culture and Agency*. Cambridge: Cambridge University Press.

Archer, M. (1995). *Realist Social Theory: the Morphogenetic Approach*. Cambridge: Cambridge University Press.

Asch, S. (1956). *Studies of Independence and Conformity*. Washington, DC: American Psychological Association.

Banton, M. (1983). *Racial and Ethnic Competition*. Cambridge: Cambridge University Press.

Barnes, B. (1982a). *T.S. Kuhn and Social Science*. London: Macmillan.

Barnes, B. (1982b). On the extensions of concepts and the growth of knowledge, *Sociological Review*, Vol. 30, pp. 23–44.

Barnes, B. (1983). Social life as bootstrapped induction, *Sociology*, Vol. 17, pp. 524–45.

Barnes, B. (1988). *The Nature of Power*. Cambridge: Polity.

Barnes, B. (1992). Status groups and collective action. *Sociology*, Vol. 26, pp. 259–70.

Barnes, B. (1995). *The Elements of Social Theory*. London: UCL Press.

Barnes, B. *et al.* (1996). *Scientific Knowledge: a Sociological Analysis*. Chicago: Chicago University Press.

Basalla, G. (1988). *The Evolution of Technology*. Cambridge: Cambridge University Press.

Bauman, Z. (1989). *Modernity and the Holocaust*. Oxford: Polity.

Baxter, H. (1987). System and life-world in Habermas's theory of communicative action. *Theory and Society*, Vol. 16, pp. 39–86.

Beck, U. (1988). *Risk Society:Towards a New Modernity*. London: Sage.

Beck, U. *et al.* (1994). *Reflexive Modernisation*. Cambridge: Polity.

Becker, H.S. (1970). *Sociological Work: Method and Substance*. London: Allen Lane.

Bhaskar, R. (1979). *The Possibility of Naturalism*. Brighton: Harvester.

Bloor, D. (1997). *Wittgenstein, Rules and Institutions*. London: Routledge.

Bourdieu, P. (1990). *The Logic of Practice*. Cambridge: Polity.

Calhoun, C. (1982). *The Question of Class Struggle*. Chicago: University of Chicago Press.

Coleman, J. (1990). *Foundations of Social Theory*. Cambridge, Mass.: Harvard University Press.

Coleman, J. and T. Fararo, T. (1992). *Rational Choice Theory: Advocacy and Critique*.

Newbury Park, Calif.: Sage.

Collins, H.M. (1985). *Changing Order*. New York: Academic Press.

Collins, R. (1979). *The Credential Society*. New York: Academic Press.

Collins, R. (1986). *Weberian Sociological Theory*. Cambridge: Cambridge University Press.

Coulter, J. (1989). *Mind in Action*. London: Macmillan.

Deaux, K. and Emswiller, T. (1974). Explanations of the successful performance of sex-linked tasks, *Journal of Personality and Social Psychology*, Vol. 29, no. 1, pp. 80–5.

Durkheim, E. (1915, 1976). *The Elementary Forms of Religious Life*, London: Unwin.

Edwards, D. and Potter, J. (1992). *Discursive Psychology*. London: Sage.

Elster, J. (1984). *Ulysses and the Sirens*. Cambridge: Cambridge University Press.

Elster, J. (ed.) (1986). *Rational Choice*. Oxford: Basil Blackwell.

Elster, J. (1989). *The Cement of Society: a Study of Social Order*. Cambridge: Cambridge University Press.

Etzioni, A. (1993). *The Spirit of Community*. New York: Crown Publishers.

Etzioni, A. (1995). *New Communitarian Thinking*. Charlottesville: University Press of Virginia.

Feinberg, J. (1970). *Doing and Deserving: Essays in the Theory of Responsibility*. Princeton: Princeton University Press.

Feinberg, J. and Gross, H. (eds) (1975). *Responsibility*. Ensino, Cal.: Dickenson.

Friedman, J. (ed.) (1996). *The Rational Choice Controversy*. New Haven: Yale University Press.

Gagnier, R. and Dupre, J. (1998). Reply to Amariglio and Ruccio, in M. Osteen and M. Woodmansee op. cit.

Garfinkel, H. (1967). *Studies in Ethnomethodology*. Englewood Cliffs, NJ: Prentice-Hall.

Gergen, K. (1994). *Realities and Relationships*. Cambridge, Mass.: Harvard University Press.

Giddens, A. (1976). *New Rules of Sociological Method*. London: Hutchinson.

Giddens, A. (1979). *Central Problems in Social Theory*. London: Macmillan.

Giddens, A. (1984). *The Constitution of Society*. Cambridge: Polity.

Gilbert, W. (1992). A vision of the grail, in D. Kevles and L. Hood, op. cit.

Gluckman, M. (ed.) (1972). *The Allocation of Responsibility*. Manchester: Manchester University Press.

Goffman, E. (1967). *Interaction Ritual: Essays on Face-to-Face Behavior*. New York: Doubleday.

Goodman, N. (1978). *Ways of Worldmaking*. Brighton: Harvester.

Granovetter, M. (1974). *Getting a Job: a Study of Contacts and Careers*. Cambridge, Mass.: Harvard University Press.

Green, D. and Shapiro, I. (1994). *Pathologies of Rational Choice Theory*. New Haven: Yale University Press.

Habermas, J. (1984). *The Theory of Communicative Action. Vol. I, Reason and the Rationalization of Society*. London: Heinemann.

Habermas, J. (1987). *The Theory of Communicative Action. Vol. 2, Lifeworld and System: a Critique of Functionalist Reason*. Cambridge: Polity.

Habermas, J. (1990). *Moral Consciousness and Communicative Action*. Cambridge: Polity.

Habermas, J. (1992). *Postmetaphysical Thinking*. Cambridge: Polity.

Hardin, R. (1995). *One for All*. Princeton: Princeton University Press.

Harré, R. (1986). *The Social Construction of Emotions*. Oxford: Blackwell.

Harré, R. and Gillett, G. (1994). *The Discursive Mind*. London: Sage.

Harré, R. and Madden, E. (1975). *Casual Powers*. London: Blackwell.

Hart, H.L.A. and Honoré, A.M. (1959). *Causation in the Law*. Oxford: Clarendon Press.

Hart, H. (1968). *Punishment and Responsibility*. Oxford: Oxford University Press.

Heckathorn, D. (1989). Collective action and the second order free-rider problem, *Rationality and Society*, Vol. 1, pp. 78–100.

Heider, F. (1958). *The Psychology of Interpersonal Relations*. New York: Wiley.

Heritage, J. (1984). *Garfinkel and Ethnomethodology*. Oxford: Polity.

Hesse, M.B. 1974. *The Structure of Scientific Inference*. London: Macmillan.

Hesse, M.B. (1980). *Revolutions and Reconstructions in the Philosophy of Science*. Brighton: Harvester.

Hewstone, M. (1989). *Causal Attribution*. Oxford: Blackwell.

Hobbes, T. (1651, 1968). *Leviathan*. C.B. Macpherson (ed.). London: Penguin.

Hogarth, R. and Reder, M. (eds) (1987). *Rational Choice: the Contrast Between Economics and Psychology*. Chicago: Chicago University Press.

Hume, D. (1740). *A Treatise of Human Nature*. (Edited by Selby-Bigge.) Oxford: Clarendon Press.

Jaspars, J. *et al. (eds) (1983). Attribution Theory and Research*. London: Academic Press.

Jeffery, C.R. (1967). *Criminal Responsibility and Mental Disease*. Illinois: Thomas.

Jones, S. (1994). *The Language of the Genes*. London: Flamingo Press.

Jones, S. (1996). *In the Blood: God, Genes and Destiny*. London: HarperCollins.

Kahneman, D. *et al.* (eds) (1982). *Judgement Under Uncertainty: Heuristics and Biases*. Cambridge: Cambridge University Press.

Kant, I. (1781). *Critique of Pure Reason*, translated N. Kemp-Smith (1964). London: Macmillan.

Kelley, H.H. (1967). Attribution theory in social psychology, in D. Levine, op. cit.

Kelley, H.H. 1973. The processes of causal attribution, *American Psychologist*, Vol. 28, pp. 107–28.

Kevles, D. and Hood, L. (eds) (1992). *The Code of Codes*. Cambridge, Mass.: Harvard University Press.

King, A. (1999). Against structure: a critique of morphogenetic social theory, *Sociological Review*, Vol. 47, pp. 199–227.

Kripke, S. (1980). *Naming and Necessity*. Oxford: Blackwell.

Kripke, S. (1982). *Wittgenstein on Rules and Private Language: an Elementary Exposition*. Oxford: Blackwell.

Kuhn, T.S. (1970). *The Structure of Scientific Revolutions*. 2nd edn. Chicago: University of Chicago Press.

Kuhn, T.S. (1977). Second thoughts on paradigms, in *The Essential Tension*. Chicago: University of Chicago Press.

Lane, R. (1991). *The Market Experience*. Cambridge: Cambridge University Press.

Lea, S. *et al.* (1987). *The Individual in the Economy*. Cambridge: Cambridge University Press.

Lerner, M.J. (1980). *The Belief in a Just World*. New York: Plenum Press.

Levine, D. (ed.) (1967). *Nebraska Symposium on Motivation 15*. Lincoln: Nebraska University Press.

Lloyd-Bostock, S. (1983). Attributions of cause and responsibility as social phenomena, in J. Jaspars *et al.*, op. cit.

Loyal, S. (1997). Action, Structure and Contradiction: a Contextual Critique of Giddens' Theory of Structuration. PhD Thesis: Exeter University.

McCloskey, D. (1986). *The Rhetoric of Economics*. Brighton: Wheatsheaf.

McCloskey, D. (1994). *Knowledge and Persuasion in Economics*. Cambridge: Cambridge University Press.

MacIntyre, A. (1967). *Secularisation and Moral Change*. Oxford: Oxford University Press.

MacIntyre, A. (1981). *After Virtue*. London: Duckworth.

MacIntyre, A. (1988). *Whose Justice? Which Rationality?* London: Duckworth.

Mackay, D.(1967). *Freedom of Action in a Mechanistic Universe*. Cambridge: Cambridge University Press.

Marwell, G. and Ames, R.E. (1981). Economists free ride, does anyone else? *Journal of Public Economics*, Vol. 15, pp. 295–310.

Milgram, S. (1974). *Obedience to Authority*. New York: Harper and Row.

Miller, A. (1986). *The Obedience Experiments: A Case Study of Controversy in Social Science*. New York: Praeger.

Mills, C.W. (1940). Situated actions and vocabularies of motive, *American Sociological Review*, Vol. 5, pp. 904–13.

Mixon, D. (1989). *Obedience and Civilisation*. London: Pluto Press.

Moore, S. (1972). Legal liability and evolutionary interpretation, in M. Gluckman, op. cit.

Mullen, B. and Johnson, C. (1990). *The Psychology of Consumer Behaviour*. Hillsdale, New Jersey: Erlbaum.

Nelkin, D. and Tancredi, L. (1989). *Dangerous Diagnostics: the Social Power of Biological Information*. 2nd edn, 1994. Chicago: Chicago University Press.

Osteen, M. and Woodmansee, M. (eds) (1998). *New Economic Criticism*. New York: Routledge.

Parker, I. (1992). *Discourse Dynamics*. London: Routledge.

Parsons, T. (1937, 1968) *The Structure of Social Action*. New York: Free Press.

Pigden, C. and Gillet, G. (1996). Milgram, method and morality, *Journal of Applied Philosophy*, Vol. 13, no. 3, pp. 233–50.

Pleasants, N. (1999). *Wittgenstein and the Idea of a Critical Social Theory*. London: Routledge.

Quine, W.V.O. (1960). *Word and Object*. New York: Wiley.

Rabinow, P. (1996). *Making PCR: a Story of Biotechnology*. Chicago: Chicago University Press.

Sandel, M. (1996). *Liberalism and the Limits of Justice*. 2nd edn. Cambridge: Cambridge University Press.

Scheff, T.J. (1988). Shame and conformity: the deference-emotion system, *American Sociological Review*, Vol. 53, pp. 395–406.

Schelling, T.C. (1960). *The Strategy of Conflict*. Cambridge, Mass.: Harvard University Press.

Scott, J. (1996). *Stratification and Power: Structures of Class, Status and Command*. Cambridge: Polity.

Searle, J. (1994). *The Construction of Social Reality*. New York: Simon and Schuster.

Selden, J. (1689). *Table Talk: Being the Discourses of John Selden, Esq*. London: E. Smith.

Shapin, S. and Schaffer, S. (1985). *Leviathan and the Air Pump*. Princeton: Princeton University Press.

Shaver, K.G. (1985). *The Attribution of Blame: Causality, Responsibility and*

Blameworthiness. New York: Springer-Verlag.

Simon, H. (1957). *Models of Man*. New York: Wiley.

Simon, H. (1982). *Models of Banded Rationality*. Cambridge: MIT Press.

Smith, J.A. *et al.* (eds). (1995). *Rethinking Psychology*. London: Sage.

Smith, M. and Marx, L. (eds) (1994). *Does Technology Drive History?* Cambridge: MIT Press.

Taylor, C. (1989). *The Sources of the Self*. Cambridge: Cambridge University Press.

Thaler, R. (1991). *Quasi-Rational Economics*. Beverly Hills: Sage.

Thibaut, J.W. and Riecken, H.W. (1955). Some determinants and consequences of the perception of social causality, *Journal of Personality*, Vol. 24, pp. 113–33.

Trevarthen, C. (1988). Universal cooperative motives: how infants begin to know the language and culture of their parents, in G. Jahoda and I. Lewis (eds), *Ethnographic Perspectives on Cognitive Development*, Beckenham, Kent: Croom Helm.

Trevarthen, C. (1989). Signs before speech, in T.A. Seebok and J. Uniker-Seebok (eds), *The Semiotic Web*. Berlin: Mouton de Gruyter.

Trevarthen, C. and Logotheti, K. (1987). First symbols and the nature of human knowledge, in J. Montangero (ed.), *Symbolism and Knowledge*. Cahiers de la Foundation Jean Piaget No. 8. Geneva: Archives Piaget.

Turner, J.C. (1991). *Social Influence*. Milton Keynes, England: Open University Press.

Turner, S. (1994). *The Social Theory of Practices*. Cambridge: Polity.

Tversky, A. (1969). Intransitivity of preferences, *Psychological Review*, Vol. 76, pp. 105–10.

Tversky, A. and Kahneman, D. (1981). The framing of decisions and the rationality of choice, *Science*, Vol. 211, pp. 453–8.

Weber, M. (1968). *Economy and Society: an Outline of Interpretive Sociology*. Berkeley: University of California Press.

Wilkie, T. (1993). *Perilous Knowledge*. London: Faber.

Williams, B. (1981). *Moral Luck*. Cambridge: Cambridge University Press.

Williams, B. (1993) *Shame and Necessity*. Berkeley: University of California Press.

Winner, L. (1977). *Autonomous Technology*. Cambridge: MIT Press.

Wittgenstein, L. (1968). *Philosophical Investigations*. 3rd edn. Oxford: Basil Blackwell.

INDEX